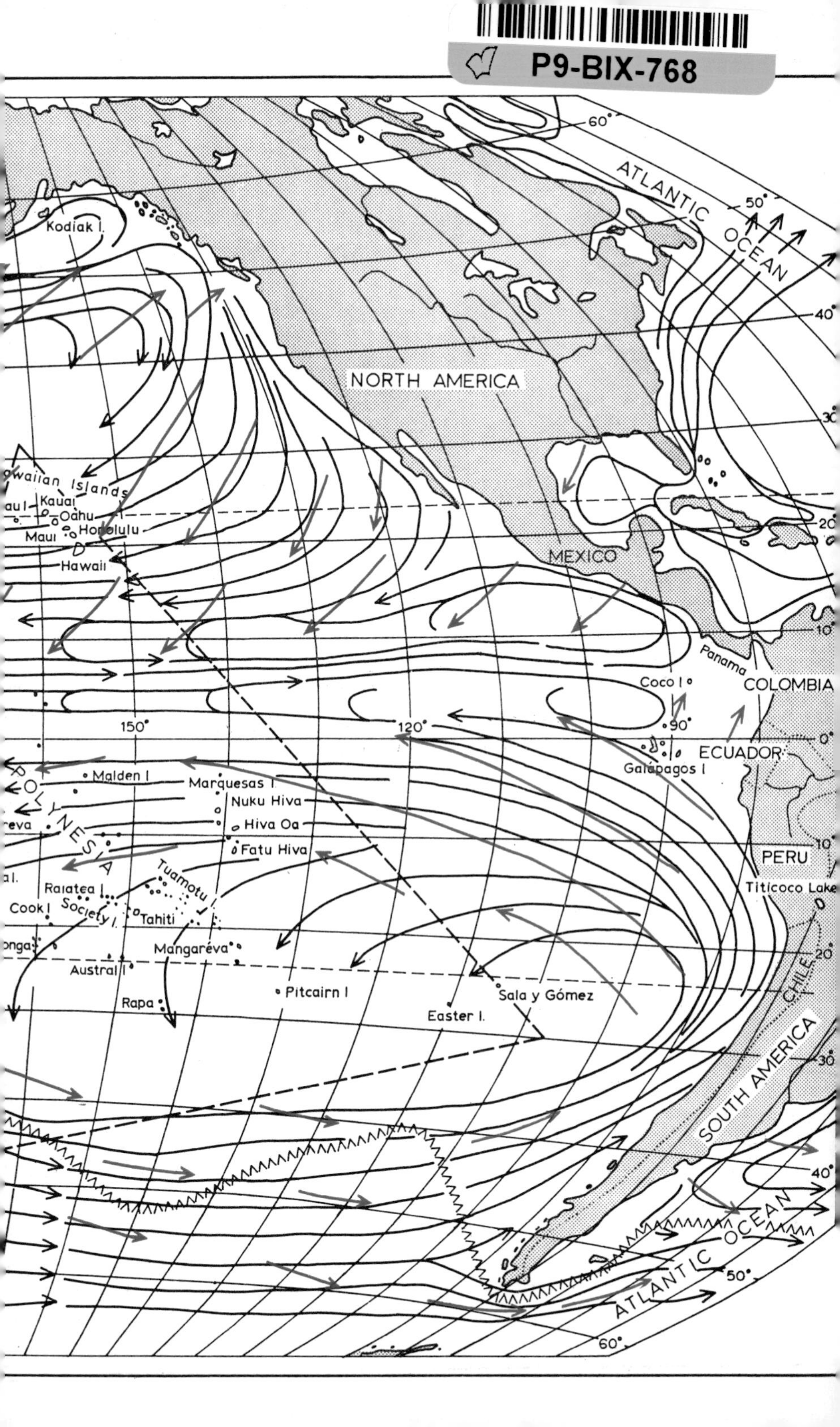

NORTH AMERICA
ATLANTIC OCEAN
Kodiak I.
Hawaiian Islands
Kauai
Oahu
Maui
Honolulu
Hawaii
MEXICO
Panama
COLOMBIA
Coco I
Galápagos I
ECUADOR
PERU
Titicoco Lake
CHILE
SOUTH AMERICA
ATLANTIC OCEAN
POLYNESIA
Malden I
Marquesas I.
Nuku Hiva
Hiva Oa
Fatu Hiva
Tuamotu I.
Raiatea I
Society I.
Tahiti
Cook I
Mangareva
Austral I
Rapa
Pitcairn I
Easter I.
Sala y Gómez
150°
120°
90°
60°
50°
40°
30°
20°
10°
0°

SEA ROUTES TO POLYNESIA

BY THOR HEYERDAHL

The Kon-Tiki Expedition

Aku-Aku

American Indians in the Pacific

WITH EDWIN N. FERDON

The Archaeology of Easter Island

THOR HEYERDAHL

SEA ROUTES TO POLYNESIA

With Editorial Notes by Karl Jettmar, PhD
Professor of Ethnology, University of Heidelberg
and a Foreword by Hans W: son Ahlmann, PhD
former President of the International Geographical Union

RAND McNALLY & COMPANY
Chicago New York San Francisco

FIRST PUBLISHED IN GREAT BRITAIN
IN 1968

Rand McNally & Company edition published in the United States and possessions in 1968

Library of Congress Catalog Card Number 67-13756

PRINTED IN GREAT BRITAIN

FOREWORD

Thor Heyerdahl's two popular books, *Kon-Tiki* and *Aku-Aku*, are world-famous. But few have had the opportunity of attending any of the many lectures at congresses and other scientific gatherings where he has spoken of his researches and their results in a form readily understood even by non-specialists. For this reason it has long been desirable that there should be a representative collection of these papers, most of which have appeared in English. Those reproduced here give, in his own words, a wider and deeper understanding of his contributions towards clarifying the history of the Pacific islands. His theory of the course of events gave rise to a widespread, often heated, international debate. The criticism, however, has gradually died down and has given way to even greater recognition and tokens of confidence. In 1966 he led a symposium at the Thirty-seventh International Americanist Congress in the Argentine and also delivered one of the introductory lectures at the Eleventh Pacific Science Congress in Tokyo.

The selection of the papers in this book was made, in consultation with Thor Heyerdahl, by Karl Jettmar, Professor of Ethnology at the University of Heidelberg, who is also responsible for the brief summaries which introduce each chapter, and which Heyerdahl has checked. They cover the period 1951–64, most of them being from the 1960s. They are fittingly introduced by a lecture recalling and explaining how, from the outset of his work on the settlement of Polynesia, Heyerdahl conceived the idea that a great deal of the immigration took place from South-east Asia, though with the important qualification that this settlement had been preceded by an earlier one from South America. There follows Heyerdahl's basic thesis of the Pacific as a living geographical unit, with the great ocean currents forming the natural routes. Their importance in this respect increases the further we go back in time and the more primitive the resources available to man, making him follow the currents more or less passively. In conception as in execution, the *Kon-Tiki* expedition has much in common with Fridtjof Nansen's drift with the ice current across the Arctic Ocean on board the *Fram*.

To explain the *Kon-Tiki* expedition as a purposeful link in Heyerdahl's study of Polynesian history comes his comprehensive analysis (1964) of the scientific proofs of an early connection between the Pacific archipelago and South America left by cultivated plants. Heyerdahl had arrived at the theory of the westward voyages by the pre-Incas of Peru and their crossing of the ocean by means of balsa rafts several years before the *Kon-Tiki* expedition. When gathering this timber for his own raft, he also followed the ancient Indian practice of choosing raw logs instead of dried ones which soon sink. Scientists and the general public overlooked these preliminaries to the *Kon-Tiki* expedition based on extensive studies, regarding the expedition chiefly as a daring piece of adventure. It was indeed full of excitement. The story of the adventures of these six lonely men on their 101 days at sea, propelled by the South Equatorial Current, has fascinated several million readers in something like fifty languages. The vital point as far as Heyerdahl was concerned was that the expedition proved the possibility of reaching Polynesia on a balsa raft and populating it from South America. This was so contrary to the accepted ideas and dogmas of archaeologists and anthropologists that it took several years to convince them. One should beware, therefore, of unfounded arguments against him that are based on failure to appreciate the weaknesses of the Mercator projection's rendering of areas and distances, giving an incorrect impression of the respective proportions of land and sea areas. In this book we can follow the documentation of his results from both the Galapagos Islands and Easter Island. His big expedition there, with five archaeological experts, he equipped at his own expense. Not only was the popular book *Aku-Aku* a great success, he now received scientific recognition in full measure. Before his arrival on the island, hardly anyone had ever used a spade there to delve into the past. Extensive and systematic excavations now led to significant results concerning the Polynesian and non-Polynesian elements of the island's population. The chapter on the famous giant statues is the text of Heyerdahl's lecture to the Swedish Society for Anthropology and Geography in Stockholm in 1962, when he was presented with the Vega Medal, its most distinguished award. Two years later, he received a similar award from the Royal Geographical Society in London, for his important contributions to the study of cultural connections across the Pacific in the past.

Thor Heyerdahl now lives with his wife and fellow-worker, Yvonne, and their three small girls in their village of Colla Micheri in the mountains of the Italian Riviera. There he has found the peace and isolation which he sought in order, with his unbounding energy, to complete his scientific work.

HANS AHLMANN

PREFACE

An extract from a speech to the Royal Geographical Society, London, June 8, 1964

The greatest urge for scholarly endeavour rises from an interplay of both encouragement and opposition. Encouragement is a satisfaction, but opposition is a challenge. I am sure that I am not the only one who has learnt that mere success is not enough; resistance and opposition, sometimes even assaults and defeat, are necessary in the building up of scientific truth and expansion of human knowledge. In the moment of a shattering gale this fact may not always be so easy to appreciate, but in moments of fair wind, like today, we can well admit it and let the knowledge serve us and others in moments of new tempests and gales.

Each of us will have experienced this interplay in a different way, so I may be excused for resorting to some selected examples among my own observations. When I first had the great pleasure of appearing before the Royal Geographical Society it was to report an expedition which was born from opposition and defeat that took the form of a challenge which again led to an experiment. I had originally launched the premature claim that voyagers from aboriginal Peru had sailed into the Pacific and settled Polynesian islands prior to the arrival of the present Polynesian stock. The argument was rejected and seemingly disproved by citations from authoritative publications which stated that the South American water craft were not sea-worthy and could not stay buoyant even as far as the Galapagos Islands. Opposition, and not recognition, thus gave birth to the *Kon-Tiki* expedition, which disclosed that the balsa raft voyagers of ancient Peru were in possession of a remarkable deep-sea vessel which surpassed any Polynesian canoe, or even the Viking ships, in buoyancy, security, and carrying capacity, although not in elegance or speed.

Further opposition prompted me to bring the first professional archaeologists to the Galapagos Islands. Sceptics had now admitted the sea-going qualities of the balsa raft and the practical possibility of aboriginal voyages from Peru to Polynesia. Yet it was argued that aboriginal South Americans had certainly hugged the coast of the mainland, otherwise the Galapagos Group, nearest of all the oceanic islands, would have been discovered and visited by the Incas or their predecessors prior to the arrival of the Spaniards, who discovered the group by off-shore drift in 1535. The resistance led to the first excavations ever attempted on the arid and uninviting Galapagos Group. Four prehistoric occupation areas on three separate islands were discovered, represented by nearly two thousand ceramic sherds from at least 131 aboriginal pots, Chimu pottery frogs, an Inca clay whistle, flints, obsidian, and other stone artifacts. An analysis by experts at the United States National Museum established that the Galapagos Group had been repeatedly visited by coastal people from pre-Inca Ecuador and North Peru since at least Coastal Tiahuanaco times, and South American archaeology was thus for the first time pushed 600 miles into the open Pacific.

How could these repeated visits to the Galapagos be possible if the balsa rafts, as indicated by the *Kon-Tiki* expedition, were unable to turn and tack against the wind? This problem prompted the construction of a new balsa raft which was launched off the open coast of Ecuador. A renewed experiment with the native *guara*, an ingenious system of movable centre-boards which are alternately lowered and raised fore and aft of the bipod mast, finally resulted in the rediscovery of how the ancient Peruvians were able to tack their sailing-rafts against the wind to reach any point desired at an angle to the wind sharper than any old-fashioned European sail-boat could possibly manage.

At this the Pacific was open for early South American voyagers as much as for peoples out of Asia. The opposition then moved on to challenge: Easter Island is located half-way between South America and the rest of Polynesia, why was it settled last and not first if the immigrants came from South America? Why is there no sign of another culture underlying the present Polynesian on that island? Why was pottery unknown to the discoverers of

Polynesia? More field-work was needed to get the answers. Digging on Easter Island, combined with pollen samples from the bogs, revealed that the first settlers, introducing South American useful plants, had reached the island at least a thousand years earlier than previously assumed by science, and a non-Polynesian culture, with an array of parallels to ancient Peru, underlies the present Polynesian stratum on the island. Simultaneously a number of institutions sent archaeological expeditions to Polynesia for the first time, and it was discovered that pottery had been a cultural element of the earliest population in Polynesia. Thus, our knowledge of the past of Polynesia is steadily changing, together with the arguments of the opposition. Only if and when opposition ends, and Polynesian students all agree, shall we come to the doldrums in local research, and we shall no longer progress in our knowledge of the truth.

T. H.

ACKNOWLEDGMENTS

The author wishes to thank the various publications in which the essays contained in this volume originally appeared. Details of original publication is included in the editorial note introducing each chapter. He also wishes to make acknowledgment to United Press and Associated Press for the photographs which are reproduced as plates 7a and 7b.

CONTENTS

ILLUSTRATIONS

PLATES
after page 208

MAPS

CHAPTER 1

SEA ROUTES TO POLYNESIA

EDITORIAL NOTE. *In the twenty years which have elapsed since the Kon-Tiki expedition Dr Heyerdahl has continued to seek and to correlate additional evidence in support of his theory.*

His adventurous journey on a balsa raft from South America to Polynesia aroused world-wide interest, not only amongst scientists, but also amongst the general public, to whom it was presented both in the form of a popular book and as a film. The press was not slow to see in Dr Heyerdahl a twentieth-century Viking, who had challenged not only the ocean waves but also the leading academicians of the day by his assertion that the Polynesians had come from South America and not from South East Asia. Only a few people had read his first scientific report, which he had published in International Science *(New York) six years before the Kon-Tiki expedition. In that report, which was based on detailed arguments, he advanced the view that the raft sailors from South America were merely the first people to have settled in Polynesia. Later they were overtaken by a second migratory wave consisting of Asiatics who had travelled by a circuitous route via the North Pacific.*

In his 800-page monograph, American Indians in the Pacific. The Theory behind the Kon-Tiki Expedition, *Dr Heyerdahl repeats the view, one to which he has always subscribed, that, whilst the historically significant root of the complex racial and cultural structure of Polynesia lay in Asia, the line of communication between Asia and Polynesia ran across the North Pacific rather than through Melanesia and Micronesia.*

The shortened version of Dr Heyerdahl's theory which now follows was first given as a lecture at the University of Pennsylvania in Philadelphia and was published under the title 'Sea Routes to

Polynesia' *in* Expedition. The Bulletin of the University Museum of the University of Pennsylvania, *Vol. 4, No. 1, pp. 22–9, 1961.*

Two hundred years ago it was a common presumption that the Polynesian tribes on the isolated islands in the East Pacific were American Indians, carried there, like all the early Europeans, by the prevailing easterly winds and currents. From the time of Magellan, through the discovery of Polynesia in 1595, until the time of Captain Cook in the latter half of the 18th century, it had been quite impossible for any European ship to force its way from the European colonies in Indonesia to any part of Polynesia. All voyages in the Polynesian part of the ocean, without exception, followed the Humboldt Current and the trade winds from South America westward to Polynesia. To return from there to America, it was necessary to sail on westward, straight to Indonesian waters, and then to take the long curve northward along the coast of Asia to reach America again in the extreme northern latitudes above Hawaii.

However, at the time of Captain Cook, it was discovered that the Polynesian islanders and the Malay tribes had certain words and linguistic roots in common, and from that moment it was universally accepted that the Polynesian Stone Age tribes had accomplished what no European sailing vessels had managed: an eastward voyage from the Malay domain to Polynesia. This sound linguistic argument was also strongly backed by the observation that the Polynesian islanders possessed pigs, chickens, bread-fruit, banana, sugar cane, yams, taro, as well as outrigger devices on their canoes, all of which were unquestionably Asiatic culture elements, absent and unknown in the Americas.

Ethnographically, the problem of Polynesian origins thus did at first appear to be an easy one. However, as physical anthropologists, archaeologists, and ethnologists began to penetrate deeper into the Polynesian problem in the nineteenth and twentieth centuries, insurmountable obstacles arose. Anthropologists like Wallace, Deniker, and Sullivan pointed out fundamental differences between the Polynesian and the Malay tribes in stature and body build, cranial form, nose form, beard and body hair, and even in hair texture, eyes, and pigmentation. More recently modern blood surveys carried out by the Commonwealth Serum Laboratories in Melbourne have found such fundamental differences in hereditary blood pattern as to exclude the possibility that the Polynesians may be direct descendants of Malay or South-east Asiatic tribes. Simmons, Graydon, Semple, and Fry, in a joint report of their survey published in the *American Journal of Physical Anthropology*, December 1955, concluded 'that there is a close blood genetic relationship between American Indians and Polynesians, and that no similar relationship is evident when Polynesians are compared with Melanesians, Micronesians, and Indonesians, except in adjacent areas of direct contact'.

Independently, archaeologists and ethnologists, in spite of a concentrated search throughout the Malay area for Polynesian physical and cultural vestiges, failed to encounter any such remains, and revealed instead the existence of fundamental cultural obstacles whose discovery argued against a spread of Polynesian culture from the Malay domain. The fact that the very special Polynesian culture pattern was already developed prior to its spread into the East Pacific is revealed by its comparative homogeneity throughout Polynesia, from Hawaii in the north to New Zealand in the south, and from Samoa to Easter Island. This, too, shows a comparatively recent departure and spread of the far-flung Polynesian tribes, and Polynesian experts have proposed that the last main movement into Polynesia occurred as late as about the twelfth century AD. Yet none of the characteristic Polynesian artifacts appear in Indonesia or on the Micronesian-Melanesian islands separating the two areas, the only possible exception being certain types of stone adzes in the northern Philippines, which, however, were abandoned there and replaced by other tools more than two thousand years before the last Polynesian immigration. Iron had spread from the Malay peninsula through Borneo and Java by 200 BC, yet no form of metal was known anywhere in Polynesia.

A corresponding problem was the complete ignorance of both pottery making and weaving among all Polynesian tribes, two highly important indicators of cultural diffusion which we somehow shall have to account for one way or the other, since both ceramic art and the loom were widespread culture elements in nearly all circum-Pacific areas, and firmly established in Indonesia since early pre-Christian times. The wheel, of great antiquity and importance in the Old World, was also unknown in Polynesia in spite of the local presence of paved roads. Betel chewing, a deeply rooted cultural characteristic from Indonesia eastward as far as and including Melanesia, disappears abruptly on the frontiers of Polynesia, where the traditional kava-drinking begins, a custom unknown in Indonesia. Palm wine, so old and widespread in Indonesia, was entirely unknown in Polynesia, as was any kind of alcohol prior to its introduction by Europeans. Stringed musical instruments, which had their world evolutionary centre and greatest type variety in Asia and Indonesia, were unknown among all the music-loving Polynesians; and the bow and arrow, as a fighting weapon, disappeared abruptly on the transit line from Melanesia to Polynesia. A recent study by Anell (1955) in an effort to localize a Polynesian point of departure in the Malay Archipelago on the basis of a study of fishing implements, failed to find a single trait common to the two areas. Anell concludes that the Polynesian fishing culture cannot have had its origins in the Malay domain, but must belong to a distinct northern fishing culture which in the Pacific area is restricted to North-east Asia including Japan, North and South America, and the Oceanic Islands of Polynesia and Micronesia.

It is thus quite understandable that, when existing theories of Polynesian origins were reviewed by Sullivan in 1923, and by Williamson in 1939, they both concluded that no two of the existing theories were alike, and that a student was left completely at a loss as to the centre of origins and migratory route of the Polynesian people. When I carried the same survey up to date in 1952, more than thirty scientists had published more than thirty different and mutually contradictory theories in an effort to bring the young Polynesian tribes out of the Old World. Most of them proposed that two—some said three—different people with different cultures had reached Polynesia independently and at different times. However, the only common guide-post, followed by all, was the Malayo-Polynesian linguistic clue. As a physical relationship between Polynesians and Malays was found inadequate and impossible, and as the linguistic conformity was diffuse and sporadic, with one root appearing here and another there among widely separated Malay tribes, there was room for unlimited speculation; for this, most recent students had turned to the Asiatic mainland. It was quite apparent, for linguistic reasons, that some contact at some time must have existed between Polynesian and Malay parental stocks, but it became increasingly doubtful whether the Polynesian ancestors ever dwelt inside the Malay domain. The Malays, no more than the Polynesians, were autochthonous to their present island habitat. Certainly the Malays had reached their present archipelago through migrations from the nearby mainland coast, and the parental contact between the two may well have antedated this geographic displacement.

On the basis of the remarkable vagueness and contradictory nature of the Malayo-Polynesian theory, I deemed it desirable to re-examine the value of the outrigger and the much cited domesticated animals and plants as evidence of Polynesian voyages from Indonesia. The result was, at the least, surprising. The prominent Polynesianist and defender of the Malayo-Polynesian theory, Sir Peter Buck, had, as early as 1938, clearly demonstrated that the early settlers of Polynesia reached their present habitat in the East Pacific ignorant of any of the Indonesian plants in question. He showed that such important Old World food plants as the breadfruit, banana, yam, and the finer taro had not been brought eastward from Indonesia by Polynesians at all, but had been relayed or carried along by the old intermittent Melanesian migrations from Indonesia and New Guinea as far as their eastern outpost of Fiji. In Fiji these originally Indonesian plants were subsequently picked up by Polynesian visitors from the east, who, according to Buck's thesis, had arrived by way of the atolls

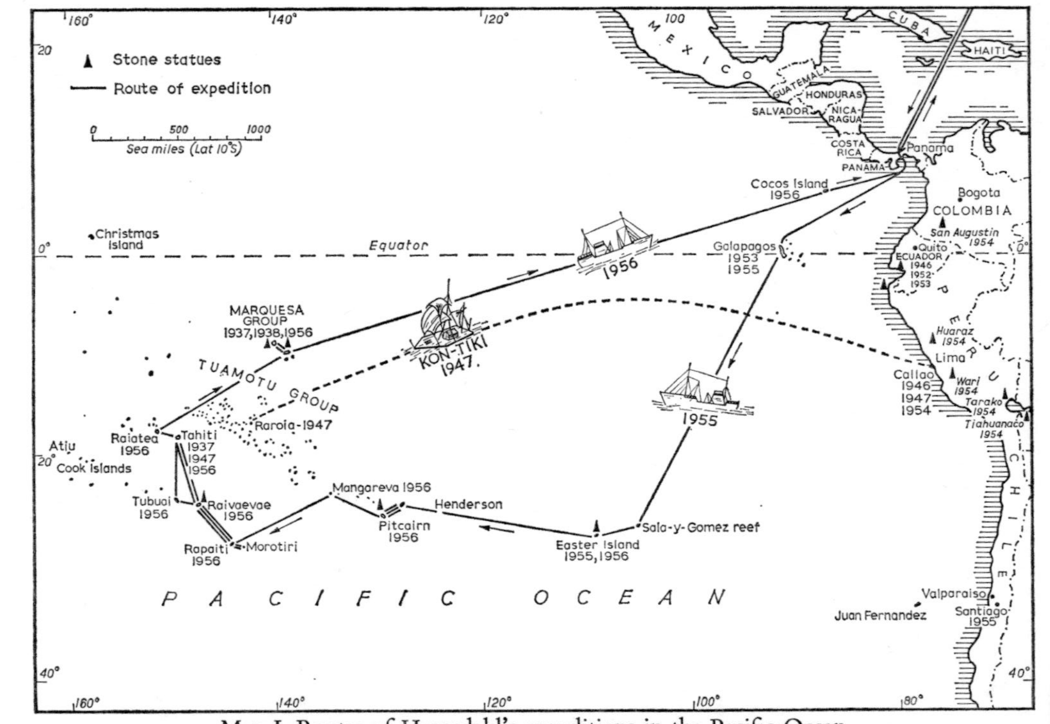

Map I. Routes of Heyerdahl's expeditions in the Pacific Ocean

Only two of Heyerdahl's expeditions have been marked. His voyages to the Marquesas Islands in 1937, to the Galapagos in 1953 and his various voyages along the coast of South and Central America have not been included.

of Micronesia where all these plants were unknown. Precisely the same was the case with the Old World pig and chicken, which admittedly were entirely unknown to the original settlers of Polynesia, until they, according to Buck, were fetched by visitors to Fiji in traditionally recorded times. This will also explain the curious absence of these important animals from all the numerous Maori tribes who had first settled New Zealand at different periods from Polynesia proper, but who had isolated themselves from the rest of the islands in the fourteenth-century before the pig and chicken were known there. The fact that all the Maori tribes, as well as the Morioris on Chatham Island, isolated themselves from their parental stocks in Nuclear Polynesia at an early time, whereas the rest of the Polynesian tribes continued inter-island trade and contact right up to the time of European discovery, leaves the Maori and the Moriori as the only examples of the pure pre-fourteenth-century Polynesian culture. It is also remarkable that the invention of the important outrigger was unknown to all the Maori and Moriori tribes at the arrival of the Europeans. The rest of Polynesia, when acquiring the pig, chicken, and Melanesian cultivated plants from adjacent Fiji, universally adopted also the genial device of outrigger attachment to stabilize their plank canoes. It is noteworthy that it was the Melanesian type of single outrigger which they adopted and that the two-sided, or double outrigger, in use throughout Indonesia, never reached Polynesia.

Thus, upon critical examination, the few arguments from the material culture which had been used to bolster the linguistic evidence of Polynesian origins in Indonesia prove to be unfounded and deceptive, and they may instead be turned around and added to the rest of the negative evidence when we ask: How could the original immigrants to Polynesia have come from Indonesia, or even crossed the Melanesian buffer territory, and still remained ignorant of the single and double outrigger, the pig and the chicken?

Another remarkable fact now established by linguists and archaeologists is that all traces of Polynesian settlements inside

Melanesia and Micronesia are of late Polynesian arrivals westward from Polynesia proper, rather than eastward from Indonesia. It is pertinent to ask: How could open neolithic boats from Indonesia outdo European ships until the eighteenth century by forcing their way against all prevailing winds and currents through four thousand miles of enemy occupied territory of Micronesia or Australo-Melanesia, and even without leaving any traces *en route*? The late prominent navigator, de Bisschop, tried in vain for three years to press an Asiatic junk eastward to duplicate an early Indonesian migration to Polynesia, but he was constantly pushed back short of Micronesia and finally gave up, arguing with good reason that such a primary migration was not feasible.

What does actually happen to a primitive craft if it enters the uncharted ocean of the Philippine Sea to search for unknown land? It is immediately trapped by the Japan Current and carried toward North-west America by a route north of Hawaii; from the Canada-Alaska coast the natural drift bears directly down upon Hawaii. This we know well from the great many drift voyagers brought by the Japan Current to North-west America in modern times, and by the fact that the natives of Hawaii at the time of European discoveries made some of their largest canoes of drift timber from the North-west American coast.

A primitive voyage of primary discovery from Indonesia to Polynesia is only possible with the natural curve of the elements across the extreme North Pacific and thence down upon Hawaii. If we accept this undeniable practical fact, our problems immediately begin to disappear. The navigational obstacle is ruled out. The four thousand mile deep, hostile areas of Micronesia and Melanesia are circumnavigated, and only secondarily entered at a later date and from the opposite side. With the North-west Coast archipelago as a stepping-stone, the absence of pottery among the Polynesian tribes becomes quite logical, as the entire North-west Coast remained ignorant of pottery until the time of European arrivals, in contrast to nearly all other circum-Pacific lands. The coastal tribes in this extreme North Pacific island area, instead of pottery, used the stone-lined earth oven, precisely as it reappears among all Polynesian tribes. The absence of the loom in Polynesia also becomes quite logical, for the same North-west Coast island area was one of the rare circum-Pacific localities where the loom was unknown until historic times. Lacking the loom, the local coast dwellers carved grooved bark beaters of wood and whale-bone, identical to those used throughout Polynesia, and made their garments by beating the soaked inner bark of certain trees. The cloaks made by the New Zealand Maori, who never obtained the tropic tapa-yielding tree, were so much like the bark cloaks of the North-west Coast Indians that trained observers have found it necessary to make a close inspection to distinguish them. The vast chronological gap between the Neolithic Age in Indonesia and Polynesia, is easily spanned with a stepping-stone on the North-west Coast where the culture remained neolithic until European times; and where the basic tool, as in all Polynesia, was an adze rather than an axe, hafted upon the identical type of elbow-handle in both areas. One of the most specialized adze blades in Polynesia reappears archaeologically on the North-west American coast. Here too we find, deeply rooted in archaeology, the other specialized Polynesian artifacts which were entirely missing in South-east Asia, the peculiar bell-shaped, D-shaped, and T-shaped stone pounders, which had started their local evolution as pestles, and all the equally specialized polished stone and whale-bone clubs of the *patu* and *mere* type. The bow and arrow was disregarded as a fighting weapon, as in Polynesia. In both areas drums, rattles, and wind instruments made up for the conspicuous absence of stringed instruments, while some of the carved anthropomorphic flageolets among the Maori and North-west Coast tribes are like enough to appear as imitations. The large wooden canoes upon which the North-west Coast tribes based their purely maritime culture could carry upwards of a hundred men, and early voyagers commented upon their remarkable similarity to the Maori war canoe. As in Polynesia, the North-west Coast canoe was occasionally converted to a double canoe by tying two together and covering them with a plank deck, when deep sea voyaging was undertaken. The similarity of these craft goes beyond details of construction—form and dimensions, mutual sewing of side planks, and separate bow and stern pieces with heads raised on swans' necks; it includes the attitude towards them—such details as the habit among some Maori and North-west Coast tribes of turning their war canoes round shortly before landing, as only the gods were supposed to land bow first.

All these seemingly unwarranted but compelling parallels and identities between the coastal archipelago of North-west America and outlying Polynesia have with regular intervals been pointed out by early voyagers and modern anthropologists, together with many other striking analogies, ranging from the unique type of composite wooden fish hook to the carved wooden posts and gabled plank houses with entrance through the straddled legs of a totem pole. Dixon pointed out that Cook, Vancouver, and other early voyagers familiar with both areas were much struck by the cultural similarities between these two Pacific regions. It is worthy of note that the same voyagers who detected the linguistic affinity between Polynesia and Indonesia found all the correspondences in material culture centred on the North-west American coast. The correspondences in social systems, customs, and beliefs are at least equally striking, and have repeatedly been pointed out in the literature.

In calling attention to this North Pacific archipelago above Hawaii as a perfectly logical stepping-stone from East Asia to Polynesia, I do not at all propose a new origin for the last arriving Polynesian immigrants, only a new route, and the linguistic origins remain unchallenged. There has never been presented any linguistic evidence tying Polynesian migrants to either the Melanesian or Micronesian route. Linguistically, one geographic stepping-stone is as feasible as the other. There appears to be no direct evidence for a passage of proto-Malay speech through the North-west Coast archipelago. But this may be due to the fact that, as opposed to the isolated Polynesian tribes in Oceania, the tribes of the continental North-west American archipelago have drastically developed and altered their own speech since their settling of the local coast upon their arrival from Asia. This can be proved by the fact that the Kwakiutl, Haida, Salish, Tsimshian, Tlingit, and Nootka all speak exclusively different languages, in spite of a close unity in both race and culture. Probably because of this deceptive discrepancy, no serious effort has been made by modern scholars to search for a root relationship between the North-west Coast languages and that of either Malay or Polynesian tribes. An effort was actually made by Campbell in the late nineties, and his conclusion was that the Haida language of the Queen Charlotte Islands, as much as the Polynesian, should be included in the Oceanic family, and he postulated that the Haida speech must have derived from early immigrants from the South Seas. About the turn of the century, Hill-Tout presented a linguistic study entitled 'Oceanic Origin of the Kwakiutl-Nootka and Salish Stocks of British Columbia . . .' He argued that the now different languages of these North-west Coast tribes seemed to be distorted remains of an early common language that had been directly related to the present Polynesian tongue. His study deserves attention, and the whole problem ought to be seriously investigated.

The next, and perhaps the principal, question is whether there is genetic evidence for the North-west Coast tribes being a feasible missing link between the physically diverging Indonesian and Polynesian tribes. This can again be answered in the affirmative. In stature, body build, head form, nose form, hair texture, beard and body hair, and pigmentation, where the Polynesians differed drastically from the Indonesian people, they concur remarkably with the distinguishing characteristics of the Haida and Kwakiutl of the south-central archipelago of the North-west Coast. Of quite recent years, the blood factors have added the strongest argument in favour of genetic relationship between Polynesia and North-west America, both of which areas concur, in contrast to Indonesia, with an almost complete absence of the dominant Indonesian B factor, a high O, and a surprisingly high A. The lack of the B factor would indicate that the mutual Malay–North-west

Coast Indian–Polynesian spreading centre was in a somewhat northerly area of coastal East Asia, and that the Malays inherited the dominant B gene after reaching their present domain. In his paper on 'Blood Groups and the Polynesians', the prominent Australian authority, Dr J. J. Graydon (1952) put the Polynesian–North-west Coast Indian relationship which I have proposed to a further test by including other blood factors in the survey. He reported discovering that also in other respects the blood patterns of these two adjacent peoples were 'strikingly similar', and that 'both are remarkably unlike' the blood pattern of Indonesia and Micronesia. He concluded: 'It is submitted that the serological evidence presented in this paper supports a Polynesian-Amerind relationship, making it probable that the islands of Polynesia have been settled largely by migrations from continental America.' Later the noted British serologist, Mourant (1954) in his monograph on 'The Distribution of Human Blood Groups', took up the same problem, and concluded: 'Observations on the ABO, MNS and Rh blood group systems are therefore all consistent with the theory of Heyerdahl.' I may add as a curiosity that, having spent several months among Bella Coola-Salish and Kwakiutl Indians, after a year in south-east Polynesia, I was struck by the physical similarity which in the Bella Coola area frequently took the form of resemblance to individual persons I had known on the islands.

To summarize, I propose that the East Asiatic element in the Polynesian race and culture entered Polynesia at Hawaii, and with the North-west Coast area as a logical, feasible, and necessary stepping-stone.[1]

However, neither Indonesia nor North-west America alone or combined will satisfy to explain the complete picture of Polynesia island culture. Most anthropologists agree that the Polynesian race and culture is composite of two—some claim three—elements. There is ample evidence of a racial and cultural substratum throughout most of Polynesia, and most notably on Easter Island, the lonely outpost nearest Peru. My second postulation is that the ancestors of the present Polynesian stock, upon reaching Polynesia in the beginning of our millennium, were not the true discoverers of these islands, but were preceded by islanders of Andean origin. These former inhabitants were responsible for the fitted megalithic masonry and for the anthropomorphic stone statues raised on the marginal islands nearest America, for the original introduction of the Maori Polynesian dog, for the spread to Polynesia of the 26-chromosome cultivated American cotton, together with the sweet potato, the gourd, and several other American elements in the Polynesian flora, including the important sweet-water totora of the Easter Islanders, and the chili pepper found locally by the arriving Europeans. Numerous elements in the Polynesian culture are borrowed from the proto-Polynesian stratum, which even affected marginal Melanesia. The art and custom of trepanning, unknown throughout South and East Asia, is one valid example, the ceremonial drinking of *Kawa*, a salivary ferment, is another, with a continuous distribution from Central and South America through Polynesia, until it ends abruptly in the marginal area to the west where the custom of betel chewing comes in from Asia. The sling as a fighting weapon is unknown in Indonesia, and yet the three specialized South Sea types, the band sling, the pocket sling, and the slit sling, are direct repetitions of the three Peruvian types. Mummification was unknown in Indonesia, but in spite of the unfavourable climatic conditions it was practised in Polynesia with a method corresponding to that used in Peru. Feather cloaks and mantles for distinguished persons, characteristic of far-flung Polynesian culture, were unknown throughout the Old World, but characteristic of New World cultures, including archaeological Peru. The special single and composite fish hooks of Polynesia, none of which are known in Indonesia, appear sporadically in archaeological middens from Ecuador down to northern Chile. The complicated Polynesian *kipona*, or elaborate mnemonic system of knotted strings, cannot be compared to the single string with knots for recording a number as occasionally found throughout the world, but is a direct repetition of the Peruvian *quipu*.

Many more examples from the material and social culture as well as the mythology of the two areas could be included. It will suffice here to add that, although the final immigrants to Polynesia came from an area where the earth oven and the bark beater took the place of pottery and loom, their predecessors on the islands cannot have been ignorant of these arts. It is known today that a pottery-making culture actually did exist at one time in Polynesia. Small fragments of different red wares have been encountered archaeologically in both the eastern and western extremities of Polynesia, with the earliest date so far from the Marquesas group. In the same group, and also elsewhere in Polynesia as far west as Fiji, the American 26-chromosome cultivated cotton grows wild, unused and superfluous to the present Polynesian islanders, but certainly brought to the islands for some purpose by the people who undertook the original migration.

CHAPTER 2

POSSIBLE AMERICAN ROUTES BEFORE COLUMBUS

EDITORIAL NOTE. *From the full version of his theory as formulated in 1941 (since when he has concentrated principally on individual issues) it is evident that Heyerdahl did not assume the feasibility of migration without due regard for the problems involved. On the contrary, he took full account of the extraordinary difficulties facing ancient man.*

In view of the change which has taken place in the general attitude to the question of migration across the endless expanse of the oceans such reticence is necessary. For a while it was believed, especially in the USA, that the settlement of the New World had been effected during a limited period of time in the remote past and that the only route used had been that by way of the Bering Strait. Consequently any similarities between the cultural phenomena of the New World and the more highly organized Old World were always interpreted in terms of parallel development. To-day this Monroe doctrine of cultural history is outmoded and there is a growing tendency to assume a whole series of voyages of discovery on the part of Asiatic peoples. Similarly it is assumed that the Vikings were not the first men to cross the Atlantic.

In this boom of migration theories it is positively salutary to read Dr Heyerdahl's account, which is based not only on the mariner's chart, which in itself is often misleading, but also on the winds and currents. The following text first appeared in the Actas y Memorias del XXXV Congreso Internacional de Americanistas, *Mexico 1962 under the title 'Feasible Ocean Routes to and from the Americas in Pre-Columbian Times', Mexico 1964.*

This paper is a brief survey of feasible ocean routes which, from a purely practical point of view, could have brought aboriginal man to or from the Americas in pre-European times. It is by no means inferred that the routes discussed have all been followed by pre-Columbian voyagers, although it seems quite apparent that there would have been no effective barriers for early man along the routes suggested. The purpose of the survey is thus not to argue diffusion, but to analyse the practical problems involved for those who propose trans-oceanic connections between any given areas in the Old and the New Worlds.

During the last decades it has been an accepted premise among leading New World anthropologists that North and South America have been successfully isolated from the rest of the world but for an admitted leakage across the Bering Strait area and/or the Aleutians. At the formation of modern American anthropology a cautious and mathematically rigid approach to the problems replaced the former freedom of speculation. Existing theories of diffusion were found to be premature, and a strong demand arose for facts and further research. A deluge of confusing theories were swept away by one emerging fact: Although man was certainly not autocthonous to the New World, yet there seemed to be no evidence of secondary cultural contact with any outside area prior to the arrival of Europeans in historically recorded times. There was nothing to prove that the cultures of aboriginal America were not evolved entirely independent of those of the Old World. To modify this picture of effective isolation the burden of proof was passed in its entirety to those who believed in trans-oceanic diffusion.

No conclusive argument could be mustered by the diffusionists by pointing to cultural parallels in art or implements, since independent evolution along parallel lines was always an obvious alternative to trans-oceanic diffusion. Naturally then, from an early time, unbiased observers attached the greatest importance to available genetic evidence, and the best arguments for independent evolution were provided by ethno-botany. The pioneering work of de Candolle (1884) had concluded that agriculture was based on entirely different botanical species in the Old and the New World, and his follower Merrill (1930, 1931, etc.) became a foundation pillar for those who spread the teachings that botany provided a conclusive proof against any contact in any direction between the Old and the New World outside the Arctic area. However, as a more cautious study of plant geography, taxonomy, and historic evidence proceeded, the botanists, including Merrill himself, started to yield ground. In 1946[1] Merrill admitted that aboriginal voyagers 'did introduce into Polynesia one important food plant of American origin, the sweet potato, . . . well before the advent of the Europeans in the Pacific Basin'. In 1950[2] he added that also the cultivated gourd was common to the Old and the New World prior to Columbus, and he started for the first time to suspect that it might have been carried by aboriginal man across the open ocean separating Polynesia and America. In 1954[3] he went even further and wrote: 'It would be foolish to assert that there were no communications across the Pacific in pre-Magellan times . . .' He states[4] that we now have 'incontrovertible evidence' that the cultivated gourd was present both in the Old and the New World in pre-Columbian times, and[5] that man was obviously responsible for its distribution. He now furthermore admits[6]: '. . . and, to add another statement which may seem shocking, it is most certain that the Polynesians introduced the coconut on the west coast of America . . .' In addition he also writes[7] of another plant: 'We may reasonably admit that one, or a few, of the numerous Polynesian plantain varieties may have been carried by the Polynesians themselves to South America, . . . It might be that a form introduced on the coast of Peru was transported over the Andes, thus reaching the upper waters of the Amazon.' He finally comments[8] on the 26-chromosome American cotton hybrid which appears in aboriginal Polynesia: 'This hybrid may well have reached Tahiti, through the agency of man, before the voyages of the Polynesians had ceased.'

Other Pacific ethno-botanists have added the pineapple, the papaya, the totora, the yam bean, the *Heliconia*, the *Argemone*, the

Polygonum, and other cultivated plants and weeds to those which argue aboriginal voyages from South America to Polynesia. We shall not go beyond the admissions of the late Merrill, however, to abide by the judgement of one of the founders of the isolationist view. In his final publication Merrill[9] renounced the opinions he had formerly so forcefully impelled on the field of anthropology, saying that he now admitted pre-historical diffusion of agriculture and of civilization based on the cultivation of plants. He took the reservation that there were limits to diffusion in ancient times, but allowed that, in addition to the Viking arrival across the North Atlantic, on rare occasions castaways from Africa may have reached the east coast of America, that some Polynesians similarly reached the west coast, and finally, that natives of South America may have left the New World and 'reached some of the Pacific Islands on balsa rafts'.

We need no further concessions to require a revision of the former arguments for necessary isolation. It is useless, when ethno-botany proves the opposite, to argue that the absence of the wheel, the true arch, or stringed instruments reveal that New World cultures had no contact with the Old World. At any rate, these same culture elements were lacking in Polynesia also, and yet no one has considered this to be a proof against contact between *Polynesia* and the Old World.

It would indeed be very foolish to rush to the opposite conclusion and assume that the oceans provide no barrier to aboriginal man, or to believe that we may now entirely abolish the concept of New World isolation. There is no reason to go much further that what Merrill has actually done: to admit that on rare occasions castaways from Africa may have driven to America, whereas a two-way contact appears to have taken place between South America and the adjacent Polynesian islands. The main issue is that the science of botany, which originally bred and nursed the theory of isolation on presumed negative evidence, now comes back with positive facts to demonstrate oversea leakages in the agricultural areas of the New World.

Without question, an ocean is normally more effective than a desert, a swamp, a jungle, or a tundra when it comes to stop the geographical progress of aboriginal man. But an ocean has pathways as alive as a river, as opposed to man's other geographical hindrances. The claim by Merrill in 1954 that man's chances of survival were slight on long oversea voyages is thus a very sweeping statement, and needs marked regional modifications. There are, in fact, two basic observations which are normally overlooked by modern anthropologists. One is the fact that the distance between two antipodal points is never shorter along the equator than along the great circles curving by way of the northern or the southern hemispheres. The second is that the voyaging distance of a surface craft travelling straight from one geographical point to another is not equal to the measurable distance between these two points, nor is it equally long in both directions.

The first case may be illustrated by the following characteristic example. Dealing with the interesting discovery of certain ceramic parallels between Japan and Ecuador, a recent editorial comment in a leading periodical[10] states that the Equatorial Counter Current 'flows straight toward Ecuador', whereas 'the Japan Current loops through the North Pacific'. This common and widely used phrasing is deceptive, since in reality the seemingly looping Japan Current is both the straighter and the shorter of the two routes. This will appear instantly if we turn our attention from the conceptive Mercator's projection and consult a realistic globe.

Few anthropologists appear to realize than an itinerary even from the Malay peninsula *by way of the Aleutian Islands* to Ecuador forms a perfectly straight line, as straight as it is possible to travel between these two points. It is entirely deceptive to look for a short-cut by way of the equator, which loops as much as any other great circle across the Pacific although it is not discernible on a map.

Thus, too, China and Peru form antipodes. The distance as the crow flies between the Pacific coast of South China and the Pacific coast of Peru is just as short by way of the North or the South Pole as by way of the equator. No line between these two opposing Pacific coasts is straighter nor shorter than the one which, on a Mercator's map, wrongly appears to loop through the extreme North Pacific. If we bend a wire along a globe from coastal South China to Peru following the equator, we may hold both ends firm and twist the same wire upwards to pass through the Bering sea as well without any adjustments.

Once we bear in mind that the vast Pacific is not a level plain but a complete hemisphere with equal curves in all directions, we get entirely different premises for voyages by aboriginal craft in an unmapped ocean. A primitive deep-sea voyager finds himself in the centre of what seems to him an unchangeable horizontal disk of water wherever he proceeds to move.

The second point where more caution is definitely wanted in studies of early ocean voyaging pertains to the quotations of erroneous voyaging distances between fixed points at sea. The dead distance between two points may be quoted in miles, but commonly has little bearing on the actual water span to be traversed between them. Indeed, we know nothing about the voyaging distance confronting an aboriginal ocean voyager until we know the ratio between the speed of the local current and the technically produced speed of the craft in question. The slower the artificial propulsion of the craft the greater discrepancy between the measured distance and the one to be actually travelled. There may thus be an overwhelming difference between the actual voyaging distance of a modern ocean liner and that of a primitive craft moving in an equally straight line above the same stretch of firm ocean bottom. The remarkable extent of this difference may be illustrated by an ocean crossing in aboriginal craft familiar to the writer.

The dead distance separating Peru from the Tuamotu Islands is approximately 4,000 miles. Yet, after crossing only about 1,000 miles of surface water, the *Kon-Tiki* craft actually reached the Tuamotu Islands from Peru. If another primitive craft had been able to travel with the same speed and in an equally straight line, but in the opposite direction, it would have had to traverse about 7,000 miles of surface water to reach Peru from the Tuamotus.

The reason is that the ocean surface itself was displaced about 3,000 miles, or about 50 degrees of the earth's circumference, during the time needed for the crossing. This means that, in travelling distance, the Tuamotu Islands are located only about 1,000 miles from Peru, whereas Peru is located 7,000 miles from the Tuamotu Islands once a voyager proceeds into the ocean with a travelling speed equal to that of *Kon-Tiki.*

Similarly, the dead distance between Peru and the Marquesas Group is approximately 4,000 miles, and the average set of the local current is about 40 miles a day. This means that, if an aboriginal craft is propelled westwards with a surface speed of 60 miles a day, it will actually make 60 plus 40 equals 100 miles a day, and complete the voyage from Peru to the Marquesas in 40 days. Travelling the opposite way in a straight line and with the same speed it will advance 60 minus 40 equals 20 miles a day, and thus need 200 days to get from the Marquesas to Peru.

If, however, the craft can only make 40 miles a day, it will move west with a speed of 40 plus 40 equals 80 miles a day, and still reach the Marquesas after only 50 days, but if it aims in the opposite direction it will make 40 minus 40 equals 0 miles a day, and never even get away from the Marquesas Islands.

These data do not only refer to the local ocean, but to a greater or lesser degree to any oceanic crossing in primitive craft, and, combined with the curvatures of the great oceans, are decisive factors in the considerations to follow. Today they represent the basic principles in modern deep-sea navigation, and once they were even directly decisive in forming the itineraries of all pioneering voyages to and from the Americas in historically recorded times prior to the existence of local maps. There is no reason to assume that they were of less importance in forming itineraries through the same unmapped oceans prior to written record, if ever man steered into the same mobile and hemispheric water-wastes at that early period.

There are three main oceanic entrance routes to the New World, two on the Atlantic side and one on the Pacific; and two main routes of departure, both on the Pacific side. The routes are so well defined that each of them may well be named after its historically recorded discoverer.

The *Leiv Eiriksson route* is favoured by very short distances, and a fast sweeping current running along the east and south coasts of Greenland across to Labrador and Newfoundland. In the period from 986 to about 1500 AD the Norsemen founded settlements with 280 farms, an episcopal residence, and 17 churches on the south-west coast of Greenland, and although maintaining regular contact by open boat with Iceland and Norway, these early European colonists lived for five centuries only 200 miles away from the American coast, prior to the arrival of Columbus. Written records from the eleventh to the fourteenth century show that at least five visits were undertaken to the New World. Records from 1516 listing hides of black bear and sable among trade items brought from Greenland, if correct, evince trade activity across the Davis Strait. Greenman,[11] suggests that upper palaeolithic man had still easier access to north-eastern North America along the edge of the glacial front which, at the time, spanned the local ocean at the latitude of Ireland. Certainly, a crossing from North Europe by Arctic hunters at that early period would seem to be feasible. Whether it actually occurred remains to be proved.

The *Columbus route* is considerably longer, but offers gentle climatic conditions and extremely favourable ocean currents and prevailing winds. Properly, it is born along the north-west African coast and runs with the Canary Current straight to the West Indies and the Mexican Gulf. It receives a strong southern feeder from Madagascar and South Africa, which also enters the West Indies but by way of the Brazilian coast. Although born as two separate African units these two ocean pathways may well be considered as subdivisions of one sea-route pulling tropic America close to Africa, and yet setting Africa far apart from the New World. The travelling distance is quite considerably shorter than the one undertaken by the *Kon-Tiki* raft, and the travelling conditions quite similar. Whether the local ocean was crossed prior to Columbus is not yet known; the route is highly feasible for African castaways, and certain botanists, including Merrill, have proposed that some African cultivated plants may originally have reached the agricultural areas of America this way.

There is no favourable departure route for aboriginal man on the American east coast. The cold southbound Labrador Current dominates the temperate areas of North America, and the warm Gulf Stream is born among tropically accustomed aborigines who would be little prepared to survive the long northbound drift into the cold North Atlantic.

Turning next to the Pacific side, the conditions are reversed. Although the European explorers first reached the Pacific coasts of Asia, no crossing to America was effectuated from that side, nor any attempt to penetrate into the Pacific Ocean. Not until Columbus had brought Europeans to the New World was the Pacific Ocean entered, but by Magellan and subsequent voyagers all of whom entered the Pacific from the American side.

The principal South Pacific sea route may be termed the *Mendaña route* in reference to the first European who embarked in the New World on a voyage of discovery to Melanesia and subsequently Polynesia. But since the first Mendaña expedition was expressly organized in search of inhabited Pacific islands reported by Inca merchants, and, according to contemporary written Spanish records, allegedly visited by Inca Tupac Yupanqui himself, it might equally well be termed the *Inca route*. The potentiality of this ocean pathway for aboriginal craft was first demonstrated with the *Kon-Tiki* raft, and subsequently by three (now five)[12] more raft expeditions from Peru, two of which landed with its crew in central Polynesia, and one being on the way to Melanesia in good shape when local authorities intercepted its drift in Samoa. The Inca route will aid aboriginal voyagers from most of Chile, any part of Peru, and southern Ecuador to various parts of Polynesia and beyond. Botanical evidence shows that the voyage has been effected prior to Mendaña's crossing. A return voyage across the same stretch of ocean was found impossible by the early Spaniards, who were forced to return to Peru in the high latitudes north of Hawaii. Although we shall later return to the two possibilities of getting back, there is no natural sea route leading to the New World in the southern hemisphere.

Prior to Mendaña's discovery of Melanesia and Polynesia, Saavedra had left the Pacific coast of Mexico in 1527, and crossed the enormous empty Mid-Pacific ocean north of the equator and south of Hawaii, without finding a single island until reaching the Philippines. In the Philippines he waited for a change in the wind to try to return to Mexico. He made his first attempt on a south-west wind the following year, but the wind failed and he had to return to the Philippines. After still another year he tried once more by following the coast of New Guinea, and then steered north until he died at 27° N. His successors followed his orders to sail to 31° N. latitude, but encountered contrary winds, and returned to Indonesia. Thus, the first attempt to return to the New World across the Pacific failed.

This *Saavedra route* from Mexico to Indonesia seems extremely long, but is in reality quite considerably reduced by the quickly sweeping, powerful North Equatorial current, and aided all the way along by a strong following trade wind and favourable climatic conditions. The early Spaniards regularly followed the Saavedra route from Mexico to their colonies in the Philippines in the generations that followed, but it was not until 1565 that they discovered the only natural passage from Indonesia back to Mexico in the high latitudes north of Hawaii.

This important route to America, the only natural access to the New World on the Pacific side, may well be referred to as the *Urdaneta route*, after the pioneer who showed this way to subsequent voyagers through his written records. Actually, Arellano completed the same crossing three months before him in 1565, but provided no record of this course. Urdaneta, however, kept a journal of the voyage and made scientific observations which were followed for a long time on the subsequent voyages from the Philippines to Mexico. This Urdaneta route is drastically reduced in length by the eastbound Kuroshiwo Current which brings warm water and mild climate directly from the Philippine

Sea to North-west America, and thence follows the coast to Mexico. The contrary winds of the trade-wind belt are avoided, and, as stated, the loop in going north of Hawaii is entirely illusive even in dead miles.

The eastbound Urdaneta and the westbound Saavedra route form a continuous unit revolving between the Old and the New World north of the equator. Such theories of trans-Pacific contact as proposed by Ekholm, Heine-Geldern, and others become meaningless if we ignore their geographic and historic implications, but feasible, from a navigational viewpoint, if we take them into account. There are no other natural escape-routes across the Pacific. The Equatorial Counter Current figures prominently on many maps as running east between the large westbound North and South Equatorial Currents. This so-called counter current is nothing but an interrupted series of upwellings, and is of scant use to trans-Pacific voyagers. Saavedra and subsequent voyagers until modern times were unable to detect or make use of this equatorial route, and two experiments with aboriginal craft in modern times will further illustrate its limited value. De Bisschop, prior to the last World War, spent three years in a Chinese junk, making nautical surveys of the Equatorial Counter Current to study its serviceableness for aboriginal migrations from Indonesia to Polynesia. He was constantly opposed by the trade wind and the everpresent Equatorial Currents which overran the supposed counter-stream and made his progress impossible. He concluded:[13] 'As a seaman, I have primarily strived to study and throw light on the maritime difficulties of such a migration; they are . . . too numerous!' And[13] '. . . very little can be said as well about the speed as about the direction of this current, indeed even concerning its existence'.

In recent years Ingris made two attempts to reach Polynesia from South America by balsa raft. On his second attempt he succeeded, but on his first attempt he started too far north and got into the doldrums where his raft got becalmed and drifted helplessly about. He struggled for weeks to return with the Equatorial Counter Current, but in vain, and he finally had to be towed back to Panama with a tug.[14] Undoubtedly, due to the local upwellings and frequent dead winds the narrow area termed the Equatorial Counter Current offers, in certain places, less resistance and set-back to a premeditated eastbound voyage than do the quick flowing currents on each side, and a forced Polynesian voyage to South America in this latitude is undoubtedly feasible. But there is no local sea-route aided or enforced by geographical factors, and a trans-Pacific journey between antipodal points along this line is directly meaningless and uncalled for.

Another possible way for locally acquainted mariners to force a premeditated voyage back to America is in the eastbound current of the South Pacific below what mariners term the 'Roaring Forties'. The intimate vicinity of the drifting ice and the high frequency of gales make this severe region unfavourable for small craft, however, and scarcely attractive for aboriginal crew departing from a temperate Polynesian area. De Bisschop tested this route, too, but after nearly 7 months of suffering, the bamboo raft dissolved nearly a thousand miles from Chile where it was just entering the area where the eastward drift turns north and flows back to Polynesia. Through radio a rescue ship was summoned and the raft abandoned. The local route was found exceedingly difficult and definitely requires the advance knowledge that South America lies ahead. It is probably feasible, although this remains to be proved.

After his rescue De Bisschop went to Callao to terminate his efforts by sailing another raft along the Mendaña or Inca route from Peru to Polynesia. His raft was flimsily built of cypress logs and started severe saturation. Yet it passed the Marquesas Islands after 75 days and drifted a thousand miles farther west before it sank at sea. The crew continued with the current on a float of mere scrap, and got safely ashore on their own accord in Manihiki of the Cook Islands, except De Bisschop himself who was tragically killed during the actual landing. On his four Pacific voyages in primitive craft this outstanding navigator has clearly demonstrated that it is difficult to find any natural sea routes in this ocean other than what we have termed the Inca, the Saavedra,

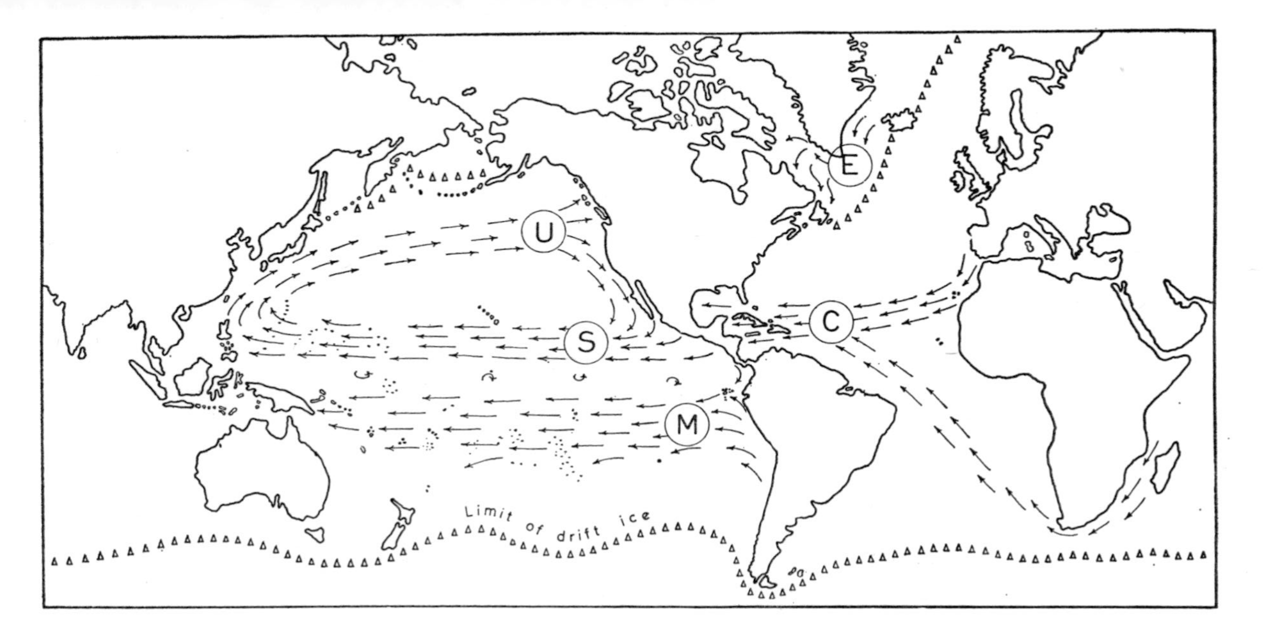

Map II. Feasible sea-routes to and from the Americas in early times

C: The 'Columbus Route' from Africa to the Gulf of Mexico; E: the 'Leif Ericsson Route' from North-west Europe to the North-eastern part of North America; U: the 'Urdaneta Route' from Indonesia to North-west America and Mexico; S: the 'Saavedra Route' from Mexico to Micronesia and Indonesia; M: the 'Mendana Route from the Andes Coast to Polynesia and Papua-Melanesia.'

and the Urdaneta routes and, furthermore, that America is well isolated from Asiatic influences across the South Pacific.

To summarize: The possibility of trans-oceanic contact with aboriginal America is very limited, but not absent. There is no natural departure route on the Atlantic side, but one possible route of access in the extreme north-east, which might have been more prominent in glacial times; and another possible route of casual arrivals from Africa in the Mexican Gulf area. From the Pacific side, a natural departure route leads from Mexico and Central America to Indonesia, and still another leads from Peru to Polynesia and the islands beyond. A major natural entrance route leads from Indonesia and Japan to North-west America and Mexico, and the latter is flanked in the Arctic by the almost terrestrian stepping-stones of the Aleutians and the Bering Strait. Forced crossings outside these natural ocean routes require supreme navigational skill and, almost certainly, the knowledge that land lies ahead.

CHAPTER 3

PLANT EVIDENCE FOR AMERICAN CONTACTS

EDITORIAL NOTE. *Heyerdahl has now afforded a systematic review of the sea-routes leading to and from the New World. Whether these feasible routes were actually used, by whom they were used and when, are questions to which we are now able to attempt an answer by comparing the findings of different scientific disciplines.*

Comparative philology is an obvious but not always a productive source of proof; and then there is the popular method of citing particular instances in which individual cultural elements reveal a marked degree of similarity. But the uncertainty of this method is so great, since such elements might well have undergone a parallel development, that, in order to reduce the risk of error, such instances are admitted in evidence only when they appear concentrated in arrays. Thus genetic findings are more reliable. In this particular case, however, zoology is not very helpful, which has meant that the investigations carried out by botanists during recent decades have become more and more important.

Dr Heyerdahl has familiarized himself with all the relevant material and provides us here with a clear synopsis, which incorporates the findings of recent research; it also shows that natural scientists are by no means infallible and are quite capable of succumbing to the prejudices of scholars in other fields.

The account given in this chapter was first published under the title: 'Plant Evidence for Contacts with America before Columbus' in Antiquity, *volume XXXVIII, pp. 120–33, Cambridge, 1964.*

From the time of European discoveries until the latter part of the last century many theories were current concerning aboriginal voyages to and from the New World in pre-Columbian times. From the turn of the century until most recent decades they were all abandoned by competent scholars in the field, with the express exception of the documented Norse landings in the north-eastern parts of North America during the opening of the present millennium. What was the main cause of this marked change from extreme diffusion to extreme isolationism among students of American prehistory?

There may be several reasons for this trend among Americanists. One is the increased demand for scientific evidence and fact rather than speculation, another is the discovery that ethnographic parallels in art and utensils within two separated areas may be due to independent evolution along parallel lines. Undoubtedly, however, a major bias in the general movement towards the isolationists' view was the evidence brought forth with the birth of American ethno-botany. Two prominent botanists have already been mentioned in this connexion, Alphonse de Candolle and his follower E. D. Merrill.

In his pioneering work, *Origin of Cultivated Plants* (published in 1884), de Candolle accumulated the botanical evidence available at that time, and drew the interesting and highly significant conclusion that: 'In the history of cultivated plants, I have noticed no trace of communication between the peoples of the old and new worlds before the discovery of America by Columbus.'[1] This was a genetic argument of paramount importance in the discussion that went on among contemporary ethnologists and prehistorians. Why, if there were regular lines of contact between pre-Columbian America and the Old World, had not any of the Old World cereals been introduced to early Mexico or Peru, or American corn to the rest of the world?

As a close follower of de Candolle on whose teachings he based his view, Merrill adopted and developed the view that there had been no contact between the Old and the New Worlds prior to he arrival of the Vikings and Columbus. By the strength of his opinions and the vigour of his arguments, Merrill became one of the foremost propounders of the now growing hypothesis that the great oceans surrounding the tropic and temperate zones of the New World had provided a complete and successful barrier to any form of prehistoric navigation. Merrill, however, went further than de Candolle. Whereas the latter had only concluded that plant evidence available to him failed to indicate Old World contacts with aboriginal America, Merrill insisted that the negative plant evidence *did prove* that there could have been no such contacts. As late as 1937 Merrill wrote: 'As agriculture in America was autochthonous, we may assume that so were the cultures based upon it.'[2] This rather categoric and constantly reappearing statement from a leading botanist—one of the few to enter early into the field of ethno-botany with authoritative conclusions that had a direct bearing on the question of ethnic movements—could not fail to impress contemporary anthropologists who had indeppendently observed the lack of certain important Old World inventions in the New World culture pattern, such as the wheel for pottery and transportation. In the early decades of the present century, ethno-botany had established itself as a science giving sound genetic support for current thought in New World anthropology.

However, Merrill's conclusions were challenged by botanists and plant geographers holding a conflicting view. Among the most notable were O. F. Cook, C. O. Sauer, G. F. Carter, J. B. Hutchinson, R. A. Silow, S. G. Stephens, C. R. Stonor, and E. Anderson, all of whom produced historic or genetic evidence arguing that cultivated plants had been carried by aboriginal man across the tropic oceans surrounding the New World. The progress of modern archaeology yielded important botanical information not available at the time of de Candolle, and it became increasingly difficult for Merrill to sustain his categoric view which he defended with tenacity in the 1920s and 1930s.

The validity and strength in Merrill's negative reasoning depended on the absolute and unconditional absence of cultivated plants of common origin in the two hemispheres. Such negative evidence, although not conclusive, weighed heavy as an argument against trans-oceanic voyages. However, a single plant that made exception to his rule would make his argument invalid. Merrill had, so to say, to keep his barrel water-tight. The loss of a single stave would render it unserviceable and turn his negative reasoning against him with the multiple force of positive testimony.

In 1946 Merrill tore off the first stave from his seemingly water-tight barrel. His personal studies of plant geography and taxonomy combined with historical evidence presented by R. B. Dixon and others forced him to admit that aboriginal navigators at least had crossed the ocean from the New World to the islands of Polynesia. He wrote: 'they did introduce into Polynesia one important food plant of American origin, the sweet potato, and spread it from Hawaii to New Zealand . . . well before the advent of the Europeans in the Pacific'.[3]

Further studies of the origin and spread of the American sweet potato, combined with the practical demonstration in 1947 of the seaworthiness of a South American balsa raft, finally made Merrill turn around to say, in 1954: 'It would be foolish to assert that there were no communications across the Pacific in pre-Magellan times . . .', and he now states that the very cultivation of the American sweet potato all over Polynesia before Cook's first voyage offers positive evidence of pre-European contact.[4] He also emphasizes the great care needed for such a successful transmission, stating that the navigators must have carried it across from America as a living plant, in soil, otherwise no sweet-potato tuber could possibly retain its viability in a humid atmosphere, at sea level, for longer than a month, or at the most six weeks. He points to the fact that the *Kon-Tiki* raft took in excess of three months to make the passage.

In the meantime the pre-European distribution of the coconut, too, had taken on a new aspect. De Candolle had been in personal doubt as to its origin and movements. The numerous species of the sub-family (*Cocoinae*) to which the coconut belongs are characteristic of tropical America, none occurs in Asia, and only the cultivated and highly useful species (*Cocos nucifera*), is found from Meso-America in aboriginal settlements all the way down across the Pacific to Indonesia and coastal Asia. Botanical evidence thus made de Candolle favour tropic America as its only natural home. Later he modified his view: 'The inhabitants of the islands of Asia were far bolder navigators than the American Indians. It is very possible that canoes from the Asiatic Islands, containing a provision of coconuts, were thrown by tempests or false manœuvres on to the islands or the west coast of America. The converse is highly improbable.'[5] Others pointed to the fact that, apart from the lack of related genera in the Old World, it would be quite surprising if the coconut palm had spread with voyagers from Indonesia into Polynesia and America without the knowledge of alcohol reaching the two latter areas. Since early aboriginal times a main use of the coconut palm in Indonesia was the bleeding of sap for making alcohol, a beverage entirely unknown in Polynesia and America until the arrival of Europeans.

At the turn of the century a natural trans-Pacific dispersal of the coconut was considered as an adequate solution among many botanists. Guppy wrote in 1906: 'It is . . . to be inferred that it came originally from the home of the genus in America, perhaps as a gift brought by the Equatorial Current from the New World to Asia.'[6]

By 1941 experiments with floating coconuts had been conducted in Hawaii. The results disproved the old belief that a coconut could float across almost any ocean gaps and germinate when washed ashore at the other end. It was discovered that the eyes of a floating coconut will be attacked by fouling organisms and lose their viability on an extensive drift like the one between the New World and Polynesia. By then tedious research by many scholars had disclosed documented evidence proving that the coconut grew in Meso-America on the arrival of Columbus and the early Spaniards. Wiener, André, and Harms also found the coconut to be one of eleven aboriginal plants reproduced in ancient Peruvian effigy jars. Merrill was then gradually forced to yield his second stave: '. . . to add another statement which may seem shocking, it is most certain that the Polynesians introduced the coconut on the west coast of America between Panama and

Ecuador, not too long before the Spaniards arrived'. And: 'The last word has not been yet said as to where the species originated. . . . One thing is certain: the coconut palm was thoroughly established along the wet Pacific coast of Panama and adjacent Colombia before the arrival of the Spaniards.'[7]

Merrill had no sooner stated that he needed to change his earlier published views concerning human transport of the sweet potato and the coconut between pre-Columbian America and Polynesia, when still one more important culture plant fell out of the same barrel: the gourd.

Contrary to Linnaeus, de Candolle, and with him Merrill, had assumed that the gourd was entirely unknown to the aboriginal population of America prior to the arrival of Columbus. Now archaeologists began to find seeds and artifacts made from gourd in early pre-European graves of Peru and Chile. In 1931 Nordenskiöld pointed to the great similarity of artifacts made from dried gourds in pre-Spanish South America and Oceania, and referred to the plant as 'the principal proof of pre-Columbian communication between Oceania and America'.[8]

Buck, in 1938, next used the gourd to argue that Polynesian voyagers must necessarily have reached South America during their long canoe trips in the early part of the present millennium.[9] Repeating his claim in 1945, two years before the *Kon-Tiki* crossing, he argued: 'Since the South American Indians had neither the vessels nor the navigating ability to cross the ocean space between their shores and the nearest Polynesian islands, they may be disregarded as the agents of supply.'[10] This current thought among anthropologists again influenced contemporary botanists, and Eames and St John wrote in 1943: 'It is now believed that before the thirteenth century Polynesian voyagers starting from Mangareva or the Marquesas sailed eastwards, reaching Peru, and then returned. Such a voyage would provide a possible explanation of the introduction of the sweet potato . . . to Polynesia, and the gourd . . . to South America.'[11]

In 1950 even Merrill admitted that the gourd no longer supported his earlier views, 'for it is clear that this cultivated plant did occur in both hemispheres before Magellan's time'. And: 'It may owe its presence in pre-Columbian America to the Polynesian voyagers . . .'[12]

Even this supposition did not hold up in the light of the now gradually accumulating evidence. Contemporary with the *Kon-Tiki* expedition which showed the feasibility of a raft voyage from Peru, Junius Bird excavated the Huaca Prieta refuse midden on the coast of Peru and revealed that the gourd was cultivated and used for artifact manufacture by a fishing culture in South America more than 3,000 years ago, at a period long before any Polynesians had settled their present abode or been able to navigate towards the New World. Chronological evidence accordingly shows that the gourd was older in Peru than in Polynesia, and thus must have been carried from the former area to the latter rather than vice versa. In 1954 Merrill suggested Africa as the original homeland of the gourd while proposing that it reached aboriginal America across the Atlantic. He claims that man was obviously responsible for its distribution also within America and Polynesia.[13]

It now becomes meaningless to argue isolation by merely holding back other loose staves in the remainder of the barrel. Merrill therefore abandons his opposition to the growing evidence that the Pacific island plantain was cultivated in pre-Columbian Peru and Brazil, and not introduced by the Portuguese as he had formerly theorized. Stevenson, Wittmack, and Harms had pointed out that plantain leaves had been frequently identified in aboriginal Peruvian graves, and Rochebrune had found a fruit of cultivated *Musa paradisiaca* in a prehistoric tomb at Ancon on the Pacific coast of central Peru. The early chroniclers Garcilasso de la Vega, Father Acosta, Father Montesinos, and Guaman Poma, all of whom were attempting to distinguish aboriginal from introduced crops, stated unanimously that the plantain was of pre-Conquest cultivation in Peru. Merrill, unaware of this, or ignoring their information, confronted still other documented evidence in the reporting of extensive plantain plantations by the first Europeans to penetrate into the interior of South America.

This species does not spread easily without human intervention; this is a much slower process than the spread of a seed-bearing plant. The rootstock, when mature, must be dug up, divided, and then replanted. With this slow multiplication in mind, it is significant to note that Orellana found plantains growing all along the reaches of the upper Amazon when he, as the first European, descended into the Andean jungle to cross South America in 1540–1. According to Merrill's own theory, the plantain, at the best, could only have reached the island of Santo Domingo in the West Indies twenty-four years earlier. The rapidity of this vast geographical spread, among natives who had not formerly known the plantain and who did not interchange other and more fast-spread elements, seemed little short of miraculous even to the most rigid isolationist, to whom this theoretical diffusion would seem a self-contradiction anyhow. When the other concessions concerning aboriginal South American-Polynesian contacts had been made, Merrill therefore abandoned the theory of a Portuguese introduction of the early Peru-Brazilian plantain, writing in 1954: 'We may reasonably admit that one, or a few of the numerous Polynesian plantain varieties may have been carried by the Polynesians themselves to South America, for the "eyes" (buds) can very easily be transported, over long distances, with a minimum of care and still retain their viability. It might be that a form introduced on the coast of Peru was transported over the Andes, thus reaching the upper waters of the Amazon.'[14]

By this time still another Polynesian plant, overlooked by all, entered into the same discussion. A linted cotton grew wild in the Marquesas Group, the Society Islands, Hawaii, and Polynesian-affected Fiji on the arrival of the first Europeans. The plant was for many years not an ethno-botanical suspect, since the historic Polynesians, like so many other tribes on each side of the Pacific, were ignorant of weaving and produced their scant clothing through the simpler bark-beating method. The possibility of a culturally distinct substratum with pottery and loom had not yet been suspected. Although the arriving Europeans found the Society and Marquesas island cotton to be spinnable, the contemporary islanders were uninterested in European attempts to encourage organized cultivation for laborious spinning and weaving. For years the only noteworthy peculiarity about the linted Polynesian cotton was therefore the fact that cotton of any sort was absent throughout the rest of the Pacific in the direction of Asia, including Australia, whereas it grew in the Galapagos Islands, bridging the gap to the wild and cultivated cottons of the New World.

In 1947, Hutchinson, Silow, and Stephens published a genetic analysis of wild and cultivated cottons throughout the world. They found, much to their surprise, that the Polynesian cottons were of the 26-chromosomed cultivated American species produced through interbreeding by the aboriginal cotton domesticators of Mexico and Peru. All wild cottons throughout the world have 13 chromosomes, and so do all cultivated species in Asia and Africa. But the early cotton domesticators of America had managed to hybridize species respectively with large and small chromosomes, and thus they had artificially produced linted cotton which were all tetraploids, i.e. 26-chromosomed. Including the Polynesian species and varieties, they are the only tetraploids in the entire cotton genus. On purely botanical grounds the three botanists were therefore forced to suggest that the linted cotton had necessarily reached Polynesia 'since the establishment of civilization in tropical America'.[15]

Sauer showed in 1950 that this late and yet pre-European spread of cultivated cotton from America to Polynesia could not be assigned to birds, which do not eat *Gossypium* seeds, or to ocean currents, with cotton being most unsuited to such long-range dispersal by floating. He showed that, although the wild 13-chromosomed cotton might have reached America through natural means in remote geological periods when American geography was different from today, this explanation could not apply to 'the much later time when the tetraploid group originated. Nor does such a hypothesis help to explain the occurrence of cottons with strong American parentage, ranging from the

Galapagos to Fiji. Perforce then we must consider human agencies in the geographic distribution of the *Gossypium* genus. The problem relates entirely to the lint-bearing forms useful to man.'[16]

Carter in 1950 asks: 'Was cotton originally carried as a source of oil seeds, as suggested by Hutchinson, Silow, and Stephens? Or was weaving later given up in the Pacific area for bark cloth?'[17]

At this the spinnable Polynesian cotton had entered into the field of ethno-botany. Even Merrill in 1954, speaking of the identification of the Polynesian cotton as a 26-chromosomed American hybrid, says: 'This hybrid may well have reached Tahiti, through the agency of man, before the voyages of the Polynesians had ceased.'[18]

Confronted with the steadily increasing evidence of direct American-Polynesian contacts in pre-Columbian times, Merrill now gives up his former standpoint, and admits: 'That there were occasional and accidental associations between the peoples of Polynesia and America, and even occasional ones between the American Indians and the eastern Polynesian islands, actually must be accepted; . . .'[19] He no longer considers the Polynesians to be the only Pacific navigators, but even adds: 'We may admit . . . that natives of South America may have reached some of the Pacific islands on balsa rafts.'[20]

By making these concessions in his last publication before his death Merrill has turned a page and marked a mile-post in American and Polynesian ethno-botany. No one had fought for the doctrine of complete American isolation in pre-Columbian times with more passionate conviction than he. To Merrill and his followers any ocean, regardless of its currents, was regarded as a barrier to human movements rather than a mobile sponsor of voyages and drifts. Their critical attitude has undoubtedly served as a most valuable barrier to the surge of diffusionist theories that would otherwise have marred American anthropology today. It should be duly stressed that the concessions of oversea contacts, in line with the gradually accumulating evidence, are confined to aboriginal voyages across the comparatively short ocean stretch between South America and Polynesia, whereas botanical evidence for direct contact with distant Asia or Africa lacks a corresponding array of support.

A coherent geographical area, which may be termed the *kumara* area, comprises southern Panama, Colombia, Ecuador, Peru, Polynesia and Polynesian-affected Melanesia. Throughout this area the sweet potato was not only cultivated but known as *kumara* or variations of this term. The documented evidence of inter-communication within this restricted area is still accumulating, rapidly bringing into the picture more American species useful to the aboriginal Polynesian communities where they were found by early European visitors.

One of the islands at present being re-examined for its context of American plants is Easter Island, a key post in the open ocean separating the rest of Polynesia from the New World. A number of American plants grew on this lonely island on the arrival of the first Europeans. Vast fields with numerous varieties of sweet potatoes were observed, and sweet potatoes were unanimously described by all early visitors as the main food of the natives on the island. Gourds were the only water receptacles, and Chili peppers (*Capsicum*), were brought as gifts to the arriving visitors, an American plant unrecorded from the islands further west.

On the arrival of the Europeans the wild, or presumably wild, flora of Easter Island was exceedingly poor. In 1934 Skottsberg examined the wild local flora and found it to comprise 31 flowering plants, of which 11 were pan-tropical or widespread, capable of having reached the island from either direction and, like its ferns and mosses, through purely natural means. The remaining 20 species, however, had a restricted geographic distribution either to the eastwards or to the westwards of the island and, in part, were species dependent upon human aid for their spread to an oceanic island. Only seven of these were of direct importance to the economy of the Easter Islanders, and of these seven useful, but seemingly wild, plants five had arrived from South America and two from Polynesia. The five South American species include the important *totora*-reed (the principal building and plaiting material of the Easter Islanders), the *toro-miro* tree (only wild local tree, material for wood carving), the *Lycium carolinianum* (only wild local shrub, edible berries), *Cyperus vegetus* (edible roots), and *Polygonum acuminatum* (fresh-water plant of medical use in Peru and Easter Island).

The presence of the two Polynesian species (*Chenopodium ambiquum* and *Solanum insulaepaschalis*) could readily be explained through the pre-European arrival from Polynesia of the ancestors of the present-day Easter Islanders. Skottsberg therefore wrote: 'From a botanical point of view the plants, with the exception of the American species, offer no great difficulties, provided we can rely upon the actuality of the transoceanic migration . . . but the presence of an American element is, in any case, surprising.'[21] The most conspicuous botanical problem was the fact that, apart from an endemic peat-forming moss, each of the two aquatic plants covering the Easter Island crater lakes was a purely American fresh-water plant incapable of such long-range propagation by sea or air. In 1934 Skottsberg left this difficult botanical problem open. Confronted with the new evidence that Polynesia was actually within the reach of aboriginal Peruvian watercraft, Skottsberg subsequently returned (in 1956 and 1957) to the same question.[22] He re-examined the Easter Island *totora*-reed and found it identical, even as to the variety, with the *Scirpus riparius* growing in Andean lakes and cultivated on the Pacific coast of aboriginal Peru for the same purposes as on Easter Island. He dismissed the possibility of direct transport of *totora* reeds across the ocean without man's assistance, and he found it futile to speculate in land connexions. Its only companion in the Easter Island crater lakes, the American *Polygonum*, created independently precisely the same botanical problem. Skottsberg now altered his former view and admitted that an aboriginal human introduction of at least these two South American aquatic species into Easter Island is likely, and will greatly ease the difficult botanical problem of transplantation in pre-European times. The pre-European introduction of the *totora*-reed to Easter Island has subsequently been verified through archaeological dating of tomb material, and pollen borings analysed by Dr. O. H. Selling reveal that

Polygonum pollen suddenly began to deposit in the crater lakes during the earliest human settlement period when land-clearing through deliberate forest fires put an end to the indigenous growth of several subsequently extinct trees and shrubs, including a locally common palm. These fires, started by man, created the barren nature of the present Easter Island landscape, but did not obliterate the simultaneously introduced aquatic species which spread to cover most of the three large, and formerly open, crater lakes.

With the gradually documented evidence of a pre-European growth on Easter Island of such indigenous or early American economic plants as sweet potato, gourd, Chili peppers, *totora*-reed, *Polygonum*, *Cyperus vegetus*, *Lycium carolinianum*, and *toromiro*, one may well suspect a contemporary introduction of certain other American plants that were already present, particularly in deserted areas of Easter Island, when first recorded by Europeans: a small husk-tomato, a semi-wild pineapple, arrowroot, manioc, and tobacco. According to native traditions collected by Thomson in 1889 the latter was brought to the island by the first ancestral settlers, and its local name, *avaava*, indicates that it was originally masticated as in the pre-European Andes, and not smoked (*odmoodmo*) as in historic times.[23] So far the latter plants can be no more than reasonable suspects, and their period of introduction is as yet unknown. It is noteworthy, however, that some of these American plants have been reported as pre-European by botanists in other sections of Polynesia as well.

In his monograph on the genus *Ananas*, Bertoni suggested in 1919 that the American pineapple seems to have spread into the Pacific in pre-Columbian times.[24] Brown showed in 1931 that there is a very strong case for its pre-European growth in the Marquesas.[25] and Degener in 1930 stated that the Hawaiians had been growing a poorer variety of the plant in a semi-wild state long before the first recorded introduction by Europeans.[26] Five years later Bryan wrote: 'The presence of the pineapple and certain other food plants in Polynesia may mean that they even voyaged to the coast of South and Central America.'[27]

The husk-tomato, *Physalis peruviana*, was formerly widespread in eastern Polynesia. In Easter Island and the Marquesas it is nearly extinct, although it is occasionally found growing wild in old abandoned habitation sites, as on the east coast of Fatuhiva. Its occurrence in aboriginal Hawaii was pointed out by Hillebrand in 1888, as part of 'the important American element of the Andean regions which is apparent in the Hawaiian flora',[28] a peculiarity parallel to Easter Island that later also occupied Skottsberg. In 1950 Carter extracts nine Andean plants from Hillebrand's Hawaiian flora and says that the entire list 'deserves to be studied from an ethno-botanical point of view'. He says of the Peruvian-Hawaiian husk-tomato: '*Physalis* is an edible plant related to the American tomato. Jenkins has recently published *The Origin of the Cultivated Tomato.* He considers Physalis to be an older plant food than the cultivated tomato and the tomato to have been domesticated because of its general similarity to Physalis. Like cotton, sweet potato, and Hibiscus, Physalis points again toward Peru.'[29]

In their independent studies of the purely American genus *Argemone*, Prain in 1895[30] and subsequently Fedde in 1909[31] both emphasize that its recorded growth in Hawaii at the time of Captain Cook's discovery of the group is really difficult to explain. In 1932 Stokes states that it is not surprising that the American *Argemone* had reached Hawaii before any Europeans; it may well have arrived with the same water-craft that introduced the equally American sweet potato.[32] Three years later, Yacovleff and Herrera show that the *Argemone* was used in aboriginal Peru for its narcotic and anaesthetic properties.[33] Carter in 1950 correspondingly writes: '*Argemone* suggests that the exchange of knowledge went beyond food plants into medicine and its associated magic and ritual.' Further: 'These items suggest that we are dealing with no weed, but a plant with culturally determined usages. That the plant and its specific usages travelled together suggests purposeful rather than accidental transport. The question of *Argemone alba*, var. *glauca* in Hawaii then assumes new light. ... Such evidence certainly suggests that man carried it to Hawaii.'

And: 'It would be strange indeed if it should prove that only the "cosmopolitan weeds" used by man in America were transported by nature to Hawaii and that the same uses found in America travelled with them as in the case for *Argemone*.'[34]

The papaya is a native of the New World with a larger form that grew from Mexico to Peru and a smaller poorly known lot of indigenous South American species cultivated through the Andean area down to northern Chile. In his study of the Marquesas flora, Brown in 1935 states: '*Carica papaya*. . . . At least two varieties are present in the Marquesas: *vi inana* (*vi inata*), recognized by the Marquesans as one of their ancient food plants, is doubtless of aboriginal introduction. Its fruit is smaller and less palatable than the *vi Oahu* which is claimed by the natives to have been introduced from Hawaii by the early missionaries. . . . The sap of the papaya, preferably that from the male tree (*mamee*), is used as a poultice. A native of tropical America; of aboriginal introduction in Polynesia.'[35]

In the same survey Brown was led, by various botanical evidence, to conclude that 'undoubtedly some intercourse may have occurred between the natives of the American continent and those of the Marquesas'.[36] One such element was the *pavahina* grass (*Aristida subspicata*), named after an important traditional head ornament, and formerly often worn by natives as a tuft tied on to the forehead. Brown noted: 'The presence of this American grass as a dominant element in the prairie of Nukuhiva is of interest. It is not unlikely that it was unintentionally brought in by the early inhabitants, possibly at the same time that the wild pineapple was introduced.'[37]

Of the Marquesan *mei roro* (*Ageratum conyzoides*) Brown similarly writes: '. . . in the Marquesas the fragrant flowers and foliage were prized for the construction of garlands, for scenting coconut oil, and for medicine. Robert T. Aitken also records its use in Tubuai for scenting coconut oil. Pantropic; of American origin, probably unintentionally introduced by early man in south-eastern Polynesia.'[38]

Heliconia bihai is another purely American plant of former economic value which had been carried deep into the island area. Among aboriginal peoples from the West Indies to South America the starchy rootstocks were eaten, and the leaves were used for roof and wall thatching as well as for the manufacture of hats, mats, and baskets. Baker first showed in 1893 that this plant was a native to tropical America, and that the Pacific Island *Heliconia* appeared to him to be only a cultivated form closely related to the Mexican and Peruvian species.[39] Ten years later Cook supports Schumann who inferred a prehistoric introduction of this useful American plant to the Pacific Islands, and says: 'Though no longer cultivated by the Polynesians, it has become established in the mountains of Samoa and in many of the more western archipelagoes. In New Caledonia the tough leaves are still woven into hats, but the Pandanus, native in the Malay region, affords a better material for general purposes and has displaced Heliconia in cultivation among the Polynesians.'[40]

A somewhat parallel case has been suggested for the American yam bean, *Pachyrrhizus*. In 1944 Clausen showed that *Pachyrrhizus tuberosus* 'seems to be native in the headwaters of the Amazon River and its tributaries in Brazil, Peru, Ecuador, and Bolivia'.[41] He states that in part of the West Indies and in South America this appears to be the common yam bean in cultivation, and that it possesses insecticidal properties, which aid in the yam cultivation. *Pachyrrhizus*, known among Quechua Indians as *ajpia*, has almost disappeared from modern Peruvian agriculture, although it was described locally by early chroniclers, and Yacovleff and Herrera in 1934 demonstrated the presence of its roots in pre-Inca graves at the early maritime centre of Paracas, and showed that the plant was also used as a decorative motif in Nazca art on the Pacific coast.[42] Cook, the first botanist to suspect that 'in time and labour of travel' the Pacific Islands are nearer to the high-cultures of Peru than many of the inland jungle areas conquered from Cuzco, suggested that aboriginal human voyages could only explain how the edible tuber of this leguminous vine actually had reached the island area.[43] He says: 'The natives of the Tonga Islands no longer cultivate *Pachyrrhizus* for food, but they nevertheless encourage its growth in their fallow clearings in the belief that it renders them the sooner capable of yielding larger crops of yams . . . the people of Fiji use the fibre for fish lines, and . . . the plant sometimes figures in an unexplained manner in their religious ceremonies, an indication of greater importance in ancient times.'[44] Guppy in 1906 is also puzzled by the unexpected occurrence of this cultigen in the island agriculture: '. . . the home of *Pachyrrhizus* is in America. One may indeed wonder how a plant with such a history ever reached the Western Pacific. It seems to be generally distributed in this part of the ocean, having been recorded from New Caledonia, the New Hebrides, Fiji, Tonga and Samoa. Although its edible roots are only used in times of scarcity, the plant grows wild all over Fiji. . . . In Tonga, according to Graeffe the plant is much employed in preparing the land for yam-cultivation. . . .'[45] Steward in 1949,[46] and Sauer a year later[47] have more recently pointed to the same early American cultigen as an indicator of early trans-Pacific voyages.

The yam itself, *Dioscorea* sp., had acquired a truly trans-Pacific distribution in pre-Columbian times, with edible forms being cultivated from ancient America to Indonesia. A spread of the yam from Melanesia to Polynesia has been generally assumed, but if the use of the *Pachyrrizus* in yam cultivation spread with the yam itself, an introduction of an American species may also be suspected. The New World Tropics hold a number of wild species of *Dioscorea*, some with edible tubers, as reported by Sauer in 1950, but it is not known whether the domesticated American forms have been developed out of these wild American parents. Carter, in 1950, with Gray and Trumbull, show that at least three cultivated root crops, the sweet potato, the yam, and the manioc, were described from the time of earliest Spanish contact with the Caribbean. Oviedo's account of 1535 contains a passage describing the shape, venation, stem, and the hanging habit of the leaf of the yam, differentiating this plant from the sweet potato, and giving the native name as *ajes*. *Ajes* are described also in Navarette's account of Columbus's voyage. Carter concludes: 'Here then is another plant which, like the sweet potato, is propagated vegetatively and hence most unlikely to cross wide seas by wind, drifts, birds, or other non-human agencies, but which crossed the ocean in pre-Columbian times.'[48] Brown collected aboriginal yam in the Marquesas, where its native name is *pu-ahi*, and wrote in 1931: 'The material is not sufficient for accurate determination, but it appears to be near to, if not identical with, *Dioscorea cayenensis* Lamack, a native of Africa, widely cultivated at an early date in tropical America. . . . The subterranean tubers are highly esteemed by the natives for food. . . . Very rare in the Marquesas. Only a single specimen was found in Fatuhiva, the southernmost island of the archipelago. Doubtless of early aboriginal introduction, and, if *D. cayenensis*, which it closely resembles, it would further indicate contact with America'.[49] Jakeman in 1950 includes the yam with a group of selected plants that were probably carried from aboriginal America to Polynesia and adds: 'That most of these plants were not merely carried to the islands accidentally by the currents but were transported purposely by one or more migrating groups of ancient Americans is proved by the fact that few of them . . . could have crossed the ocean without man's aid. . . .'[50]

In contrast, a trans-Pacific plant with ability to propagate to an oceanic area without human aid, is the *Hibiscus tiliaceus*. The hibiscus, as opposed to the hitherto mentioned plants, has seeds adapted for natural dissemination by sea, and might therefore well have preceded any human voyages to Polynesia. Yet, the plant has entered into the ethno-botanical discussion, due to its deliberate cultivation in Polynesia, combined with associated linguistic observations. Brown (in 1935) justly refers to the hibiscus, as 'One of the most useful of all trees cultivated by the early Polynesians'.[51] O. F. and R. C. Cook first brought the hibiscus, or *maho*, into the ethno-botanic discussion by arguing in 1918: 'Though many botanists have written of the *maho* as a cosmopolitan seashore plant, its wide dissemination may be due largely to human agency, as with the coconut palm.'[52] They show that the tree in a wild state is an abundant or even a dominant species in many localities of Middle America, down to the banks of the

Guayaquil River on the Pacific coast of South America, where it was used by the aboriginal population for bark cloth manufacture, for the production of water-resistant cordage and strings, and for kindling fire. They demonstrate that both the special uses and the names of this plant were much the same among the Polynesians. Thus, in tropical America the tree was known as *maho* or *mahagua*, or some variant of this name, and in Polynesian dialects it was known as *mao*, *mau*, *vau*, *fau*, *hau*, and *au*. The two authors concluded:

'The *maho*, *mahagua*, or linden hibiscus is one of the economic plants to be taken into account in studying the problem of contacts between the inhabitants of tropical America and the Pacific islands, in prehistoric times. Though considered a native of America, the *maho* appears to have been distributed over the islands and shores of the Pacific and Indian oceans before the arrival of Europeans. Readiness of propagation and of transportation by cuttings renders this plant well adapted for cultivation and dissemination by primitive peoples. Although human assistance in transportation does not appear to be so definitely required with the *maho* as with the sweet potato and other plants that are grown from only cuttings, the names of the *maho* afford almost as definite indications of human contacts as in the case of *kumara*, a name for sweet potato already known to have been shared with the Indians of Peru. The name *maho* or *mahagua*, with numerous local variants, is widely distributed in tropical America and is closely approximated in many of the Pacific islands in relation either to the plant itself or to its principal uses for fibre, bark, cloth, and firemaking. . . . That the primitive Polynesians were in possession of the *maho* before they became acquainted with the similar Asiatic plants may be inferred in view of the indications that Polynesian names of other important cultivated plants—the paper-mulberry (*Papyrius* or *Broussonetia*), the rose of China (*Hibiscus rosa sinensis*), and the screwpine (*Pandanus*)—were derived from names of the *maho*. The making of fire by friction of wood, and of cloth by beating the bark of trees with grooved mallets, are specialized arts which may have been carried with the *maho* from America, across the tropical regions of the Old World.'[53]

Merrill at the time (1920) opposed this view, arguing that the species was never *cultivated* outside of Polynesia:

'The reasons for its cultivation on some Polynesian islands were undoubtedly that it was the best, or one of the best, of the few fibre plants available to the primitive Polynesians. . . . I maintain on purely botanical evidence that *Hibiscus tiliaceus* is a species of natural pantropic distribution . . . and that it has been disseminated in ages past by ocean currents. [He goes on to say:] That a limited inter-communication between Polynesia and tropical America did exist in prehistoric times is entirely probable, but to argue that the present distribution of *Hibiscus tiliaceus* supports this theory certainly does not strengthen the probability. The generally accepted theory among ethnologists supports an *eastward* culture movement across the Pacific rather than a *westward* one. If the Cook *maho* series is related to the Polynesian *mao* series it would be much more reasonable to view it as coming from the Pacific to America rather than as evincing a migration from America into the Pacific.'[54]

The conflicting theories of the two botanists were subsequently reviewed by Carter in 1950:

'These arguments seem to me to be excellent specimens of the result of fixed ideas. Cook was so intent on proving the American origin of agriculture that he was incautious, if not unwise, in using a halophytic plant with a seed well adapted to water transportation as *proof* of man's carrying plants across the ocean. Merrill on the other hand was either so incensed by Cook's special pleading or so allergic to trans-Pacific contacts (or both) that the violence of his reaction blinded him to the virtues of Cook's arguments. . . . Winds and currents suggest that if the plant was carried across the Pacific by natural means it must have been from America to Polynesia. But natural carriage would leave the problem of usages and name to be solved. . . . The identity of names and uses in Polynesia and America, when coupled with the positive evidence from the sweet potato, makes it certain that whether or not the plant crossed the sea by natural means, man carried the name for the plant and quite possibly the usages across the same seas. It even seems probable that he carried the plant also.[55] [And:] Clearer proof for contact between peoples from the Pacific with the peoples of Middle America could hardly be asked than that supplied by the sweet potato and by the hibiscus known as maho.'[56]

Preconceived opinions on the lack of maritime activity in pre-Spanish America have also affected the botanical discussions of the origin of the common garden bean, *Phaseolus vulgaris*. Last century Könicke, in a paper on the home of the garden bean, pointed out that this crop plant was formerly generally accepted as having been cultivated in Europe by the ancient Greeks and Romans, under the name of Dolickos, Phaseolos, etc. The cultivation of the same bean among the aborigines of America was therefore explained as the result of its post-Columbian introduction from the Old World by the early Spaniards.[57] This was the theory until Wittmack discovered in 1880 the common garden bean among the archaeological excavations of Reiss and Stübel at the prehistoric cemetery of Ancon, Peru.[58] It was there found interred as food with mummy burials long antedating the European discovery of America. Here was suddenly ample proof of the pre-European cultivation of *Phaseolus* in America, and beans were subsequently recovered from pre-Inca sites along the entire coast of Peru. At this time, however, pre-Columbian specimens of the *European* bean were no longer accessible. The view was taken, therefore, that the Old World *Phaseolus* must after all have originated in aboriginal *America*, and been carried back thence to Europe by the early Spaniards.[59] More recently Hutchison, Silow and Stephens pointed out, with corroborative botanical evidence, that the *Phaseolus* beans represent but one more indication of contact between the Old and the New World before Columbus.[60] The same problem concerns varieties of the lima bean, *Phaseolus lunatus*, growing wild in Guatemala and common in the earliest Chimu and Nazca graves of coastal Peru. In 1950 Sauer points to certain very early genetic peculiarities of a race of lima beans of primitive characteristics long under cultivation in parts of Indonesia and Indo-China, and says: 'If, then, south-eastern Asia should prove to be a reservoir of the more primitive lima beans, long since extinct in Peru and Mexico, a further problem of the time and manner of trans-Pacific connection is raised by which the American bean was communicated to the native population across the Pacific.'[61] The same problem is also raised by a related bean, the jackbean, or swordbean, *Canavalia* sp.. Stonor and Anderson have called attention to the following: 'The sword bean (*Canavalia*), widely cultivated throughout the Pacific and always considered to be of Old World origin, is now known from prehistoric sites along the coasts of both South America and Mexico.'[62] *Canavalia* beans excavated from the stratified deposits at Huaca Prieta on the Pacific coast of Peru, dated from between 3000 and 1000 BC.[63] Sauer states that its archaeological distribution and relation to wild species now indicate the jackbean as a New World domesticate.[64]

The above brief survey will show that, not only has anthropological thought for nearly a century been biased by ethnobotanical evidence, but to a quite considerable extent anthropological presuppositions have similarly affected American botany. The literature on the origin and spread of certain American and Pacific island cultigens demonstrates that many botanical assumptions have been based on the conviction that the New World was isolated from the rest of the world prior to the voyage of Columbus. Similarly, it has been taken for granted that only Indonesian craft could move eastwards into the open Pacific, whereas the culture of the South American people was presumably confined to their own coastal waters due to the lack of seaworthy watercraft. The material reviewed above shows that there is adequate evidence of aboriginal export of American plants into the adjacent part of the Pacific island area, with the main burden of botanical evidence confined to the marginal islands of eastern Polynesia, but with strong evidence of contact comprising the entire *kumara*-growing area as far as to marginal Melanesia. The great bulk of the useful plants common to America and Polynesia appears to have spread from South America to the islands, with notably the plantain as a possible exception, representing a transfer in opposite direction. As a marked contrast to the multiple evidence of South American voyages to Polynesia, the botanical support for aboriginal American contact with Asia or Africa is very vague and as yet quite vulnerable. Merrill favours Africa as the original homeland of the gourd, and proposes that it reached America across the Atlantic.[65] If the 13-chromosomed cultivated Old World cotton, together with wild American species, were actually employed in the hybridization of the 26-chromosomed New World cotton species—a question which is still under dispute—then an oversea introduction from the Old World is by far shorter and easier with the westward drifts across the open Atlantic than against the elements across the six times wider Pacific, where no 13-chromosomed cottons exist. The coconut was relayed straight across the Pacific. If it originated in tropic America where all related genera occur, it must have spread with the earliest Pacific voyagers, since it was present in Indonesia at the beginning of the Christian era. The yam has a similar complete trans-Pacific distribution. From a practical point of view, the Mexican beans might well have reached the Asiatic islands with voyagers in the North Equatorial drifts, bypassing Polynesia in the wide open gap between the Marquesas and Hawaii. If the present heated discussions on the early cultivation of American maize in south-eastern Asia end in favour of those who argue pre-Columbian rather than Portuguese introduction, then the same strong ocean river, sweeping from Mexico straight to the Philippines should be taken into account.

To summarize: Since the commencement of cotton, gourd,

and sweet-potato cultivation in the New World, these and several other useful plants have been carried by pre-European voyagers from South America to Polynesia. The possibility of other aboriginal voyages from Africa to Middle America, and/or between Middle America and South-east Asia, is now suspected by various plant geographers, but not yet adequately substantiated. In the future, however, it would be wrong to ignore, as in the past, the conspicuous absence of any effective geographical obstacle preventing voyages by primitive craft from North or South Africa to Middle America, from Peru to Polynesia, from Mexico to Indonesia, or even from Indonesia to Mexico by way of the old galleon return route north of Hawaii. A transoceanic drift by small but buoyant craft following each of these itineraries would call for little efforts from the crew but a desire for survival, yet so far botany can clearly demonstrate only the accomplishment of South American voyages to Polynesia with additional inter-island diffusion of plants in both directions.

In the opening of the ethno-botanical symposium at the Tenth Pacific Science Congress in Honolulu 1961, the chairman, J. Barrau, recommended that the entire evidence pertaining to relationship and spread of Pacific island plants ought to be re-examined in the light of the new evidence that aboriginal craft had been demonstrated capable of carrying New World species to Oceania.[66] In view of the rapidly altered botanical picture created in recent decades by the revolutionizing data provided through archaeological excavations and pollen borings, it may not be too rash to predict that continued collaboration between anthropology and botany will disclose further evidence of man's ability to navigate prior to our own technical era.[67]

CHAPTER 4

INCAS LEAD THE SPANIARDS TO POLYNESIA

EDITORIAL NOTE. *By studying the dissemination of plant life Dr Heyerdahl was able to determine which of the feasible ocean routes were actually used.*

There was evidently a protracted sequel to one of these early routes, that between South America and East Polynesia, for the Incas still knew how to use the same drift current and the reports of their journeys later induced the Spanish to press forward into the Pacific. What transpires from this development is the amazing accuracy of these old reports, from which it is quite evident that they were prompted by something more than vague notions and fabulous exaggerations.

The lecture, on which this chapter is based, was given in 1964 before the XXXVIth International Congress of Americanists in Barcelona under the Title, The Inca Inspiration behind the Spanish discoveries of Polynesia and Melanesia. *A few short passages, which are treated in greater detail in the following chapter, have been omitted here.*

On November 19, 1567, two Spanish caravels left Callao harbour in Peru with an expedition of one hundred and fifty men, ordered by King Philip II of Spain, to visit and convert to Christianity certain islanders in the Pacific Ocean not yet known to Europeans. The Viceroy's nephew, Avaro de Mendaña, was appointed commander of the two ships, and the party included the famous navigator and Inca chronicler Sarmiento de Gamboa, on whose direct initiative the enterprise was begun. After two years in Mexico and Guatemala, Sarmiento de Gamboa had come to Peru in 1559. Here he devoted his first seven years to a study of the aboriginal culture, which finally resulted in his important memorial to Philip II on the history of the Incas. Although it was Sarmiento personally who literally put an end to the Inca history when he pursued and captured with his own hand the last Inca, Tupac Amaru, he was so interested in their oral literature that the Viceroy of Peru called him 'the most able man on this subject that I have found in the country'.[1] It was Sarmiento who first announced the consistent Inca claims that there were inhabited islands far out in the Pacific Ocean, and he was so insistent upon verifying the truth of these Peruvian reports that he finally persuaded the governor to dispatch an expedition to follow the old native sailing directions.

The favourable results of the two Mendaña expeditions are well known, but little attention has subsequently been paid to the Inca stimuli behind the Spanish enterprise. After all, the Solomon Islands encountered by the Spaniards were not in the area defined by the Inca informants. Furthermore, modern observers have assumed that aboriginal Inca craft were incapable of ocean voyaging anyhow. Nevertheless, in 1722, a century and a half after Sarmiento's attempt to follow the Inca sailing directions, the Dutch admiral Roggeveen accidentally stumbled across an inhabited island just where the Spaniards had been told that it should be. However, when Roggeveen discovered Easter Island the contemporary world had long since forgotten the Inca instructions which have survived for posterity only through the manuscripts of Sarmiento and his companions. This fact, combined with the present knowledge that balsa rafts equipped with *guaras* in Inca fashion are capable of return voyages to any section of the Pacific area, warrants a new background study of the Mendaña expeditions, that is, a re-examination of the original Inca reports and an analysis of Sarmiento's motives for believing the Peruvian accounts of extended voyages into the open Pacific.

The Spaniards had associated with aboriginal Peruvians for forty years when Sarmiento convinced his government of the reality behind the Inca claims. In those early decades before the great decline of the local culture the arriving conquistadores were unanimously impressed by the extent of aboriginal deep-sea navigation off Peru. Naturally, the main attention of all the chroniclers was focussed on the important Inca headquarters in the interior highlands, where the tremendous wealth of the ruling classes was accumulated. Yet history supports archaeology in describing a numerous and intrepid population of fishermen and merchants dwelling in large centra all along the unsheltered coast, basing its economy almost entirely on the riches of the off-shore current.

Sarmiento and his contemporaries knew well that long-range watercraft with Inca seafarers had been encountered by his countrymen nearly a year before they first reached the coast of Peru. The log-rafts approaching the advancing Spaniards off Colombia came from local ports, but off northern Ecuador the first advancing forty-ton caravel with ten Spaniards on board encountered a northbound balsa raft of thirty tons burden, with about twenty native men and women from Peru on board. The Spaniards were amazed at the fine rigging and the cotton sails used in the same manner as on their own caravel, and two men and three women among the crew were captured and trained to serve as interpreters on the later advance southwards to Peru.[2]

The navigable and heavily-laden Inca vessel had come from the port of Tumbez three hundred miles to the south, and was possibly bound for Panama where the local natives in 1512 had informed the Spaniards about a southern empire where a numerous population used large rafts which they navigated with sails and paddles.[3] Five more merchant rafts navigating, like the first, with sails, were overhauled by Pizarro's advancing caravel before he reached Peru, and when finally approaching Tumbez the Spaniards were met by a whole flotilla of balsa rafts standing out off the port and carrying Inca troops bound for Puna island 40 miles beyond the horizon.

At the time of Sarmiento's own arrival in 1559, balsa rafts were still used for trade and transportation as far down as to central and south Peru, nearly two thousand miles from the actual balsa forests. His contemporary Lizarraga[4] wrote of the natives of the Chicama Valley: 'These Indians are great mariners; they have large rafts of light timber with which they navigate the ocean. . . .' He states that they communicate with Guayaquil, 500 miles to the north, with balsa rafts heavily laden with provisions and other cargo. Balsa rafts had also been employed by the Inca mariners for conveying guano from the Chincha Islands near Pisco and Paracas to the various provinces of the entire coast. The advancing Spaniards had even found large quantities of balsa logs in the highland near Tiahuanaco, transported there from the coast by Inca Huayana Capac, who had built luxurious pleasure rafts on Lake Titicaca.[5] Sarmiento's generation marvelled at the aboriginal Peruvian seamanship and the buoyancy of their peculiar rafts. They speak highly of the fine masts and yards, and of the aboriginal Peruvian sails which they found equal to their own.[6] The native cotton canvas is praised as 'excellent' and the native rope as 'stronger than that of Spain'.[7] The Spaniards until the time of Sarmiento had themselves made frequent use of the Inca mariners and their balsa raft, which were able to enter surf and shallows where no European boat could venture. Oviedo[8] describes how Francisco Pizarro, with all his people and horses, were transported by sea to Puna island on native sailing rafts navigated by local Indians. Zarate[9] also recorded how his contemporaries would embark with as many as fifty soldiers and three horses on individual balsa rafts, which they let the Indians navigate with their sails and paddles, 'because the Indians are themselves great mariners'. Pedro Pizarro[10] reports how he personally, like Alonso de Mesa, Captain Soto, and many other prominent conquistadores, had been pushed off the rafts by the Peruvians in a terrific surf and were washed ashore half drowned, while the skilled Inca mariners climbed back on the rafts in the tumultuous sea and sailed away from land. Cieza de Leon wrote that the coastal Indians live so much at sea that they have become like fishes, and he recounts how they frequently detached the logs of their rafts at sea so that their less sea-minded enemies on board fell through and drowned. Inca Garcilasso,[11] reported that this treacherous trick was formerly also repeatedly employed by the coastal dwellers when forced to transport highland Incas by sea. They cut the ropes and pushed their passengers into the ocean, saluting each other joyfully from balsa to balsa, 'for those of the coast, being so used to the sea, had the same advantage over the inland Indians as marine animals have over those which live on the land.' These seaboard dwellers were daily on their large rafts and commonly spent weeks at sea with all their family and possessions. From the abundancy of sea-food harvested by them and the still more numerous owners of small reed-boats in the treacherous current twenty to fifty miles off shore, even the inland Inca received fresh supplies of fish carried to the highland in two days by organized *caski*.[12]

Deep-sea fishing and long-range maritime trade and transport formed an integral part of the Inca economic system when Peru was conquered by the Spaniards,[13] and references to this effect are made at least in passing by all contemporary chroniclers in spite of their reports being otherwise entirely focused on the riches and might of the highland rulers. In the judgment of Sarmiento and his contemporaries, Inca mariners with balsa rafts were able to venture as far into the unknown as any European vessel, and this explains why they so rapidly believed in the Inca maritime reports.

Turning next to a selection of some of these rumours, traditions, and historic accounts that circulated throughout sixteenth-century Peru, we may well appreciate that they stirred the imagination of a navigator like Sarmiento and prompted him into action. As a leading Inca historian he became intrigued by the observation that the oral literature of the country contained repeated records of large-scale migrations at sea by balsa rafts, some departing, some arriving, and some representing enduring return voyages with large numbers of rafts.

The region around the Ecuadorian harbour of Manta in the most northerly extremity of the Inca Empire plays an important part in the seafaring accounts of the Inca. That was the area from which the supreme culture hero Viracocha was claimed to have departed into the Pacific Ocean, and where subsequently Inca Tupac Yupanqui, or Tupac Inca, left with his fleet in search of Pacific islands. It is therefore noteworthy that Sarmiento and his companions did not select this northern area for their own departure, but started on the central Peruvian coast and headed for still more southern latitudes.

Tupac Inca was the grandfather of the Inca brothers met by the Spaniards, and Sarmiento had forty-two of the leading Inca historians assembled at one time to get his history correct. Therefore Sarmiento was well aware of Tupac Inca's northern starting point. He wrote[14] about Tupac's conquest of the north coast that he was 'fighting on land and at sea in *balsas*, from Tumbez to Huañapi, Huamo, Manta, Turuca and Quisin. Marching and conquering on the coast of Manta, and the island of Puna, and Tumbez, there arrived at Tumbez some merchants who had come by sea from the west, navigating in *balsas* with sails.' Sarmiento goes on to record the well-known story of how they gave information of some populated islands they had visited, accounts which tempted the highland Inca to challenge his fortune at sea.

'Yet he did not lightly believe the navigating merchants, for such men, being great talkers, ought not to be credited too readily.' However, Tupac's own necromancer gave him certain additional information through clairvoyance, and the Inca decided to visit the far islands. 'He caused an immense number of *balsas* to be constructed, in which he embarked more than 20,000 chosen men; taking with him as captains Huaman Achachi, Cunti Yupanqui, Quihual Tupac (all Hanancuzcos), Yancan Mayta, Quisu Mayta, Cachimapaca Macus Yupanqui, Llimpita Usca Mayta (Hurin-cuzcos); his brother Tilca Yupanqui being general of the whole fleet. Apu Yupanqui was left in command of the army which remained on land. Tupac Inca navigated and sailed on until he discovered the islands of Avachumbi and Ninachumbi . . .'

The duration of his ocean voyage was recorded as nine months, whereas others among Sarmiento's informants said one year. When Tupac came back he had with him 'black people' and other booty that was preserved in the Cuzco fortress until the Spaniards arrived. Sarmiento even interrogated the custodian who guarded these particular treasures.

The northern starting point of the Inca is also reported by Father Miguel Cabello de Balboa,[15] who came to Peru a year before Sarmiento embarked in search of the Inca Islands. Balboa writes about Tupac Inca, referring to him as King Topa:

'. . . and having discussed his ideas and plans with his officers, he set out with his squadrons—now almost innumerable—and took lodgings in Manta, and in Charapoco, and in Piquara, because it would have been impossible in less space to lodge and sustain such a multitude of people as he had brought with him. It was in this place the King Topa Inga saw the ocean for the first time, upon which discovery he caused it to be profoundly worshipped, naming it Mamacocha, which means mother of the lakes. He got ready a large number of the barges used by the natives, which were of hundreds of logs of notably light timber, fastened together one by one abreast, placing on top of the same a hundred floorings of reed-canes plaited together, making very secure and convenient vessels of the sort we have called Balsas. Then, having got together the abundance of these which would be needed for the number of troops who were to accompany him, and having chosen the most experienced pilots that could be found among the natives of these coasts, he went out on the ocean with the same courage and spirit that had governed his success since he was born. Of this voyage I say no more than can be readily believed, but those who have related the exploits of this valient Inga, assure that on this voyage he remained at sea for the duration and extent of one year, some say more, and that he discovered certain islands which were named Hagua Chumbi and Nina Chumbi, and that these islands were situated in the South Seas, on the coast of which the Inga embarked.'

Balboa, too, reports that 'a great number of prisoners whose skin was black' were brought back to South America on board the Inca rafts.

Before Sarmiento reached Peru, Betanzos,[16] who arrived with the discoverers, had recorded the much older legend, about the Viracocha-people's departure from the same Manta coast, a tradition which filled the minds of the population throughout the Inca Empire far more than the recent return voyage of Tupac Inca. The legendary culture-hero Viracocha was firmly believed to have walked with all his pre-Inca people northwards from Tiahuanaco through Cuzco until he reached the Ecuadorian coast, where they assembled at Puerto Viejo near Manta and left into the Pacific. Sarmiento[17] combined these universal Inca reports with the historic fact stressed by him and known to all the conquistadores, that the arriving Spaniards were mistaken for white and bearded Viracocha-people returning from the Pacific, a confusion which permitted Pizarro and his little band of seafarers to conquer, without battle, the vast Inca Empire with its powerful armies and fortresses.

Inca Tupac's choice of starting at the northern ports selected also by his legendary predecessor was probably no coincidence. Manta is almost precisely where the equatorial line runs into the Pacific, and Tupac Inca, precisely like Viracocha before him, worshipped the sun as his own ancestor and protector. Furthermore, Ecuador was the source of all balsa timber used for raft construction down the entire coast of the Inca Empire, and only by bringing his people to the local jungle was it possible for the Inca to obtain the large quantity of balsa logs and bamboo required for building a whole fleet of sea-going rafts. That the expedition subsequently steered towards the southern part of the ocean, however, appears from the Inca information to be considered shortly, which led Sarmiento to search in a direction west-south-west from the harbour of Callao.

Seven hundred miles south of Manta, on the desert coast of north Peru, the Spaniards were met with equally vivid stories about old Mochica migrations by balsa rafts. Father Miguel

Cabello de Balboa[18] thus writes: 'The people of Lambayeque say—and all the folk living with them—that in times so very ancient that they do not know how to express them, there came from the northerly part of this Piru, with a great fleet of *Balsas*, a father of families, a man of much valour and quality named Naymlap; and with him he brought many concubines, but the chief wife is said to have been Ceterni. He brought in his company many people who followed him as their Captain and leader.' The arrival of these balsa raft voyagers marked the establishment of the Chimu dynasty and culture, according to the natives of the north coast.

Corresponding stories with reference to the establishment of the Inca dynasty survived among the natives on the central coast of Peru until the last century.[19] According to the tribes around Lima, the first royal Incas came to power through fraud by deceiving the mountain people about their solar descent. This accusation was first recorded by the Jesuit Anello Oliva,[20] who was one of the sixteenth-century settlers who chose to live among the lowland population. He was told that the first royal Incas descended from ordinary mariners that sailed down from Ecuador:

'Many made voyages along the coast and some were shipwrecked. At last one branch took up its abode on an island called Guayau, near the shores of Ecuador. On that island Manco Capac was born, and after the death of his father Atau he resolved to leave his native place for a more favourable clime. So he set out, in such craft as he had, with two hundred of his people, dividing them into three bands. Two of these were never heard of again, but he and his followers landed near Ica, on the Peruvian coast, and thence struggled up the mountains reaching at last the shore of Lake Titicaca.'

Of course, Ica may never have seen the landing of the first Inca, but the rumours were there, and Ica could, since early pre-Inca times, compete with the forest area in the north as a centre of raft navigation. Father Joseph de Acosta[21] recorded that the

Indians at Ica, and also those of Arica 750 miles farther south, told the Spaniards that in ancient times they used to sail into the South Seas where they visited some islands very far away towards the west. Acosta assumed that these pre-Spanish expeditions had taken place on rafts of inflated seal-skin, but the numerous archaeological hard-wood centre-boards and model log-rafts excavated respectively at Ica and Arica show that precisely these two areas were very early pre-Inca centra for log-raft navigation.[22]

Arica and also Ilo, the two main ports in the coast directly below Tiahuanaco, were likewise specified as favourable starting points to the inhabited Pacific islands, in Captain de Cadres' recorded interrogation of an old sage Indian named Chepo, said to be 115 or 120 years old. Chepo said that the Indians used to embark at the ports of Arica and Ilo, and after two months' journey westwards into the Pacific they would reach first a desert island called Coatu, in which there were three high mountains and many birds. On proceeding to the inhabited islands beyond they should keep this uninhabited bird island on their left side, and thus they would reach next an isolated island called Qüen which was thickly populated and had a chief called Qüentique, and two others named Uquenique and Camanique. Ten days farther west was still another and larger populated island, Acabana. Threatened by death if he concealed the truth, old Chepo thereafter answered the eager Captain with tales of great riches on these far islands. At last he volunteered on his own accord to add that they used rafts of wood for navigation. Although the contemporary Spaniards thought Chepo referred to the Solomon islands, a name they used for all the rumoured islands off Peru, Amherst and Thomson who published an English version of the old handwritten manuscript in 1901[23] thought he may have been relating a garbled version of an actual voyage of the Indians. They point out in a footnote that Easter Island, with barren Sala-y-Gomez in front of it, matches in a remarkable way the description recorded by Captain de Cadres.

In fact, generations before Roggeveen, old Chepo had given the Spaniards a precise sailing direction to Easter Island, from the most convenient ports on the south Peruvian coast. Today we know it to be a fact that, to reach the nearest inhabited island, raft voyagers from Ilo or Arica would first have to head for the barren bird island of Sala-y-Gomez, which to them is in a straight line in front of Easter Island. This raft voyage, aided by the trade-wind and the southern curve of the outer Peru Current, would require roughly two months, just as stated by the old Indian. Chepo's description of Sala-y-Gomez is also to the point characteristic. The barren island is filled with birds that can be seen from great distances, and when first approached from the east it does specifically look like three hills standing out against the sky. These three hills were recorded as the distinguishing mark by the first European discoverers, and are so characteristic that modern maps frequently have Sala-y-Gomez marked erroneously as three separate islands. This impression is highly illusive, however, since the unimpressive islet is almost awash in stormy weather, with only the three high points giving security to the numerous birds. Next, Sala-y-Gomez must, quite correctly, be bypassed on the left side to keep the straight course from Ilo and Arica to Easter Island, the first of the inhabited islands. Mangareva is the next.

Chepo's reference to the Supreme chief of Qüen as Qüen-tique is also interesting when we note that the Easter Island name for chief was recorded as *teque-teque* by the first Spaniards who arrived in 1770.[24]

Thus, in south Peru the aborigines knew both the correct direction and the correct distance to Easter Island, and even pointed out the characteristics of the only landmark to be found en route. Exactly a thousand miles higher up the coast, at Callao, Sarmiento received equally precise sailing directions which shows that the ancient Peruvians were able to pinpoint Easter Island's position through direct cross-bearings. As is well known, internal trouble on the Mendaña expedition disrupted the course set by Sarmiento on advice from the Indians, and it is here necessary to analyse briefly what happened.

In their excellent volumes on the expedition Amherst and

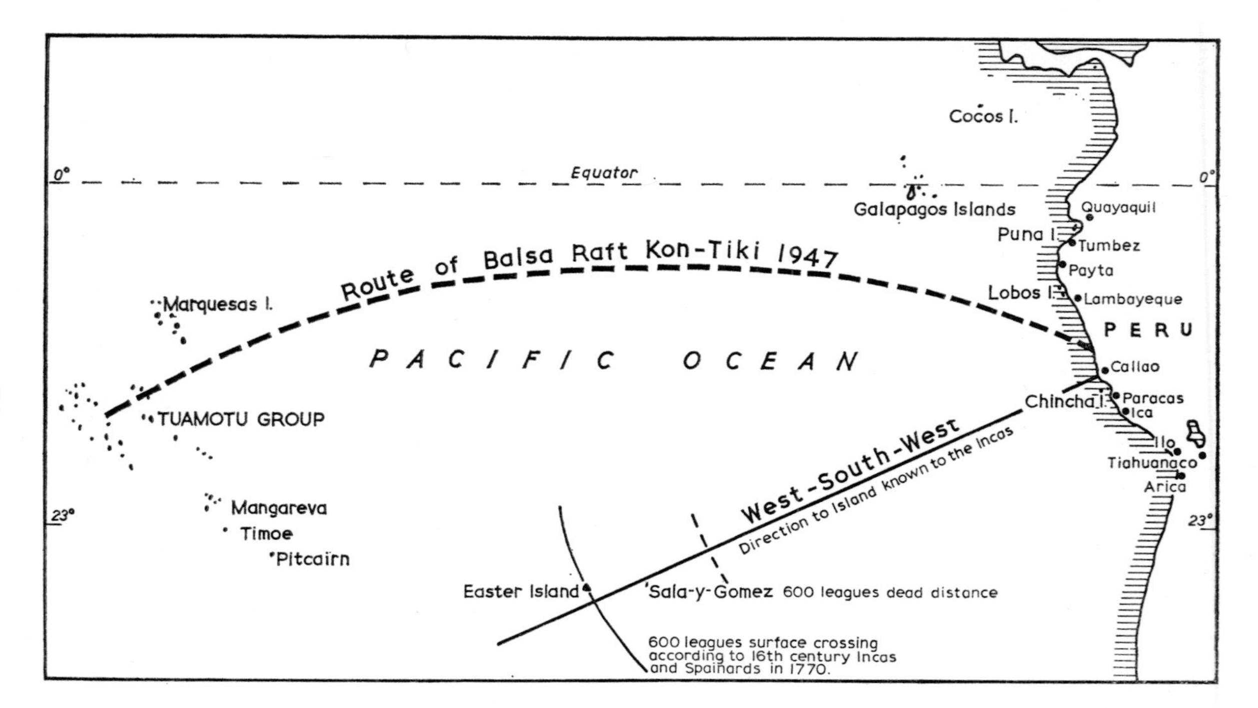

Map III. Route used by the Incas to the nearest island in the Pacific.

Thomson[25] state that, with the dawn of settled government in Peru, the adventurers from Spain drank in greedily the tales of undiscovered islands and a continent in the west which were current among the Indians and seafaring population of Callao. The babble of the taverns became in time debated questions of the Palace, and Pedro Sarmiento de Gamboa 'professed to be able to fix the bearings of these islands; and the learned men in the colony were agreed that they were the outposts of a southern continent which stretched northward from Tierra del Fuego till it reached lat. 15 deg. 5, about 600 leagues from Peru'.

The latter is a truth with modifications. It is correct that there was general consent on the distance of about 600 leagues from Peru. In fact, as shown by the authors,[26] the provisions of the Mendaña expedition were calculated on the supposition that the land was 600 leagues distant from Callao harbour. This is noteworthy, for, when Easter Island was first reached by Spaniards from Peru two centuries later, they gave the position as 'about 600 leagues distant from Callao, and about the same from the mainland of Chile'.[27] Actually, 600 leagues is slightly more than 2,000 nautical miles, and almost exactly the distance to Easter Island. Apart from the distance of 600 leagues there was one more point on which the members of the Mendaña expedition were in full agreement: the nearest island was supposed to be in a direction due west-south-west from Callao harbour. This is evident by comparing the narrative of the voyage written in the interest of Sarmiento with those written by his adversaries, the official expedition chronicler, Catoira, the expedition leader, Mendaña, the chief pilot, Gallego, and an anonymous manuscript by another educated member of the party. They must all have agreed that the reported island was due west-south-west from Callao, for all their logs show that for ten days (Gallego says twelve), they navigated tenaciously in that specific direction.[28] This is the very precise bearing from Callao to Easter Island. At the end of November, still keeping this correct course, they had reached latitude 15°45′ S., and here quarrel began. Sarmiento, although known as an uncongenial person, justly felt that he was the authority on the whereabouts of the islands. Writing in the third person[29] he stresses that it was he who had given to the Governor of Peru 'information concerning many islands and continents which he said existed in the Southern Ocean, and offered personally to discover them in the name of his Majesty, and with that intention he had collected proofs and made charts. . . . It was intended that they should follow the course west-south-west up to 23 degrees, which was the latitude that Pedro Sarmiento had fixed upon. . . .'

Sarmiento's intention of searching in the ocean 2,000 miles west-south-west of Callao would have brought him to the direct vicinity of Easter Island. His advance attempt of calculating also the island's latitude was 4 degrees off, however, yet a fair error when we note that the chief pilot placed their own familiar port of Callao at 12°30′ S., whereas it actually is 11°56′. At 15¾° S. it was this same chief pilot who suddenly disrupted the straight course for Easter Island, and began instead to sail due west. Sarmiento got furious at the interruption, and states in his report: 'Pedro Sarmiento spoke to the General [Mendaña] about this change of course with much persistency, and told him publicly by word of mouth that he ought not to consent to it, and that he ought to have it altered, since he would miss the discovery and be lost. . . .'

But young Mendaña supported the chief pilot, and the expedition now sailed west roughly along the 15th degree for twenty days. It was obvious to the entire expedition that the chief pilot broke the predetermined course far short of the 600 league mark stipulated by Sarmiento, but none objected. The reason was that Gallego, a long-time pilot along the coast of Peru and Chile, had personally received conflicting information from the *Cancilleria* at Lima. Gallego[30] wrote as his own explanation 'I sailed in this latitude because the Señor Presidente had said that in 15 degrees of latitude there were many rich islands, 600 leagues from Peru'. Correctly enough, the chief pilot was now steering straight for the very heart of Polynesia since the bulk of the Tuamotus, the Society Islands, Samoa, Fiji, and numerous other inhabited islands are grouped in a belt between 10 and 20 degrees S. Instead of steering straight down upon isolated Easter Island, the expedition was now heading for the densest section of the Tuamotu archipelago. But at the very last moment before reaching the islands near Pupapuka and Raroia, the fitful pilot suddenly altered course to north-west, and in the latter part of December the two expedition ships passed midway in the open gap between the Marquesas and the Tuamotus. Three weeks later they sighted Nukufetau in the Ellice group, and finally they landed in the Solomon Islands of Melanesia after a total journey of 80 days from Peru. They later needed almost 400 days to fight their way back to Peru, being forced into the high latitudes above Hawaii to overcome the westward winds and currents of Polynesia. Twenty-six years later the second Mendaña expedition set out once more from Callao and ended up in the Marquesas group, marking the first European discovery in Polynesia.

If the pilot had continued to follow Sarmiento's instructions, the Mendaña expedition would have had a maximum chance of discovering Easter Island, and if he had been slightly more persistent in his own alternative they would have run into the Tuamotus. Through his vacillations they missed these nearest islands and ended up in distant Melanesia.

It would have been fully possible for Tupac Inca to have ended up in Melanesia as well, and this would have explained the numerous black prisoners he brought back as curiosities to Peru. Yet there is reason to believe he had found the nearest islands by spreading out his larger fleet. As we have seen, the subsequent population of Tupac's empire knew both the bearing and distance to Easter Island from Ilo and Arica as well as from Callao, and there can be little doubt that this knowledge was shared by Tupac's pilots a few generations before the Spaniards came. The nearest inhabited island beyond Easter Island is Mangareva at the south-eastern extension of the Tuamotu archipelago. That this island was visited by Tupac and his fleet is corroborated by the local population, whose main traditions are centred round the visit of a foreign king named Tupa. The memory of this visitor was first published by Christian,[31] who was unfamiliar with Inca history: 'And the Mangarevans have a tradition of a chief called Tupa, a red man, who came from the east with a fleet of canoes of non-Polynesian model, more like rafts—surely a memory of some Peruvian *balsas*, or raftships.' Rivet,[32] quoting Christian, was the first to suspect that the Mangarevans recalled a visit by Tupac Inca. Buck[33] next published additional details from the old Tiripone manuscript, written a few decades after the European arrival by the son of a Mangarevan chief: 'An important visitor to Mangareva was Tupa. The native history states that he came in the period of the brother kings Tavere and Taroi. . . . Tupa sailed to Mangareva through the south-east passage subsequently named Te-Ava-nui-o-Tupa (great-channel-of-Tupa).' And[34] '. . . the voyager Tupa . . . sailed right down to Mangareva and lay afloat in the Great-pass-of-Tupa. He went ashore at the islet of Te Kava.'

The same native manuscript states that, before Tupa returned to his own country 'he told the Mangarevans about a vast land . . . which contained a large population ruled by powerful kings'.

The *Kava* islet on the east reef where Tupa disembarked, and the Great *Ava* of Tupa which was the mooring place of his fleet of rafts, directly recall the Inca reference to *Ava*-island, or Ava-chumbi, one of the two islands visited by Tupac's fleet. The other island was referred to as Nina-chumbi, or Fire-island, a perfect name for Easter Island where the early visitors from Roggeveen and Gonzalez to Beechey describe how the natives lit numerous fires and sent up columns of smoke around the coast when they approached. Several observers have suggested that Fire-island may refer to the Galapagos group with its usually dead volcanoes, but the Galapagos group was well known to the Incas,[35] and they were not inhabited. The 'black' people could well have been selected among the aboriginals of Mangareva, where Beechey,[36] the European discoverer, found one element in the extremely mixed population that were as dark as Melanesians. Dark-skinned captives would be the only curiosity for the powerful Inca to bring home from any Pacific island. He must have returned to Peru as disappointed as the gold-greedy Mendaña expedition and possibly along a similar northern route, where the dark-skinned prisoners could be supplemented with the metal throne and other souvenirs seen by the Spaniards at the time of Tupac's grandchildren.

The lack of gold and other treasures on the islands discovered, combined with the extremely difficult return voyage to Peru, will explain why all the Mendaña discoveries were lost again for about two centuries, until rediscovered by other Europeans in the latter half of the eighteenth century. Even in this respect the Spanish rulers of Peru followed the pattern set by their Inca predecessors.

CHAPTER 5

BALSA RAFT NAVIGATION

EDITORIAL NOTE. *The chief argument against the sea-routes to Polynesia described by Heyerdahl in the preceding chapter in which South America was the point of departure (this being the crucial point) was the total absence on those waters of sailing vessels of the kind found in other parts of the ancient world. Dr Heyerdahl had to undertake the* Kon-Tiki *expedition in order to prove that a balsa raft was equally capable of covering large distances on the open sea.*

Meanwhile, however, although this daring experiment made a tremendous impression on the general public, it had little effect on the experts. They adopted an entrenched position, asserting that the balsa wood logs would float only for a short time and drawing from the actual events of the Kon-Tiki *expedition the apparently justified conclusion that every landing on a South Sea Island in such a vessel must endanger the lives of its occupants. In the chapter which now follows, apart from presenting a summary of the various extant accounts of balsa rafts, Dr Heyerdahl seeks above all to demonstrate that freshly cut balsa wood retains its buoyancy over a long period. He then closes the chapter by describing an experiment, which proved that with the aid of sails and the guara boards invented and used by the ancient Peruvians the balsa raft was completely manoeuvrable. The dangerous landing made by the* Kon-Tiki *was due solely to the fact that at that time the secret of the Inca and pre-Inca guara technique had not yet been discovered.*

This chapter is based on a combination of one of Dr Heyerdahl's articles, 'The balsa raft in aboriginal navigation off Peru and Ecuador' (Southwestern Journal of Anthropology, *vol. 11, no. 3, pp. 251–64, University of New Mexico, Albuquerque 1955) and his lecture on 'Guara sailing technique indigenous to South America', which appeared in* Actas del Congreso de Amerikanistas *in Costa Rica in 1958.*

THE BALSA RAFT IN ABORIGINAL NAVIGATION OFF PERU AND ECUADOR

Aboriginal navigation in Peru and adjoining sections of northwestern South America is a subject that has been little known and still less understood by modern boat-builders and anthropologists. The apparent reason is that the local boat-building was based on principles entirely different from those of our own ancestry. To the European mind the only seaworthy vessel is one made buoyant by a watertight, air-filled hull, so big and high that it cannot be filled by the waves. To the ancient Peruvians the size was of less importance; the only seaworthy craft was one which could never be filled by water because its open construction formed no receptacle to retain the invading seas, which washed through. Their object was thus achieved by building exceedingly buoyant, raft-like vessels of balsa or other very light wood, or of bundles of reeds or canes lashed together in boat fashion, or by making pontoons of inflated seal-skins carrying a sort of deck.

Such craft tend to appear primitive, incommodious and unsafe to anyone who is unfamiliar with their qualities at sea, and this may be the reason for the widespread and erroneous assumption that the peoples of ancient Peru were without seagoing craft or capable sailors, in spite of their 2,000-mile coastline and their outstanding cultural level in nearly all other respects.

When I first attempted in 1941,[1] to call attention to the possibilities of early Peruvian navigation, the balsa raft was accorded little attention among the few anthropologists who were familiar with its existence as a pre-European culture element, and many did even overlook the fact that it went under sail in pre-European time. The use of sail was not recorded from other parts of aboriginal America. The general impression appeared to concur with the judgment of Hutchinson[2] in his *Anthropology of Prehistoric Peru* of 1875, where the balsa raft was merely described as 'a floating bundle of corkwood'. Three modern writers, Lothrop,[3] Means,[4] and Hornell[5] had presented interesting papers on aboriginal Peruvian craft and navigation, with excellent descriptions of the building principles of the balsa raft, but, on purely theoretical grounds, as we shall see later, they all judged the balsa raft to be water absorbent and useless for navigation in the open sea.

It was on the background of such prejudice that I was stimulated to a further study and reappraisal of Peruvian navigation, since I was led by other observations to suspect that Peruvian balsa rafts had travelled as far as to the islands at Polynesia, 4,000 miles away.

The first record of a Peruvian balsa raft antedates the actual discovery of the Inca Empire. When Francisco Pizarro left the Panama Isthmus in 1526 on his second and more progressive voyage of discovery down the Pacific coast of South America, his expedition encountered Peruvian merchant sailors at sea long before he discovered their country. His pilot, Bartolomeo Ruiz, was sailing ahead to explore the coast southwards near the equator, when off northern Equador his ship suddenly met another sailing vessel of almost equal size, coming in the opposite direction. The north-bound vessel proved to be a large raft, and its crew were the first Peruvians ever seen by Europeans. Immediately afterwards a report was sent to Charles V by Juan de Sáamanos,[6] and the episode was recorded even before Peru itself had been visited. The event was also narrated in 1534 by Pizarro's own secretary, Francisco de Xeres. From both sources we learn that the large balsa raft was captured by the Spaniards, who found a crew of twenty Indian men and women aboard. Eleven were thrown overboard, four were left with the raft, and two men and three women were retained aboard the caravel to be trained as interpreters for the later voyages.

The balsa raft was a merchant vessel heavily laden with cargo. The Spaniards estimated its capacity at thirty toneles, or about thirty-six tons, as compared with the forty tons of their own caravel, which carried only half as many persons as did the balsa raft. The cargo was carefully listed by the Spaniards, and included some items which could only have come from Peru proper.

The craft was described by Sáamanos as a flat raft, composed of an underbody of logs covered by a deck of slender canes raised so that crew and cargo remained dry while the main logs were awash. The logs as well as the canes were lashed securely together with henequen rope. Sáamanos says of the sail and rigging of the raft:

'It carried masts and yards of very fine wood, and cotton sails in the same shape and manner as on our own ships. It had very good rigging of the said henequen, which is like hemp, and some mooring stones for anchors formed like grindstones.'[7]

Ruiz now returned to Pizarro with his prisoners and booty, and a few months later a new expedition, led by Pizarro, pushed southward to the northern coasts of the Inca Empire. On the way to Santa Clara Island in the open Gulf of Guayaquil, Pizarro overhauled five sailing balsas in two days, and opened favourable negotiations with their crews. Then he crossed the Gulf to the Peruvian port of Tumbez, the home of some of his raft captives. When approaching the coast the Spaniards saw a whole flotilla of balsa rafts standing towards them, carrying armed Inca troops. Running alongside the fleet Pizarro invited some of the Inca captains aboard his vessel, and by establishing friendly relations through his interpreters—those captured from the first raft encountered—he learned that the whole flotilla was bound for Puna Island which was then under Peruvian rule.

Other balsa rafts came out of the bay with gifts and provisions for the Spaniards, and we learn from Francisco Pizarro's cousin, Pedro, that a little farther down the Peruvian coast the Spaniards overtook some balsa rafts, aboard which they found precious metals and some of the clothes of the country, all of which they kept, so that they might take them to Spain to show the King.[8]

But even before Ruiz captured the first merchant balsa off Ecuador, the Spaniards had already heard rumours about Peruvian navigation from the natives of Panama. The chronicler Las Casas,[9] son of Columbus's companion, stated that the aborigines in Peru possessed balsa rafts in which they navigated with sails and paddles, and that this fact was also known in pre-Conquest times to the oldest son of Comogre, a great chief in Panama, who spoke to Balboa of a rich coastal empire to the south where people navigated the Pacific Ocean with ships a little smaller than those of the Spaniards, propelled by sails and paddles.

Several of Pizarro's contemporaries recorded details of the craft navigated by the coastal natives of Ecuador and northern Peru: Oviedo (1535),[10] Andagoya (1541)[11] and Zárate (1555),[12] who came to Peru as Royal Treasurer in 1543. Their similar accounts describe rafts made of 'long and light logs', an odd number —five, seven, nine or eleven—tied together with cross-beams covered by a deck; the navigation with sails and paddles; the ability of the large ones to carry up to fifty men and three horses; and the construction of a special cooking place on board. Andagoya, who took part in the earliest expeditions of discovery northward and southward along the Pacific coast, was particularly impressed by the quality of the native henequen rope ('stronger than that of Spain') and the excellent cotton canvas. In describing the ability of the local natives to navigate with regular sails, Zárate stated that the raftsmen of Tumbez in north Peru were great mariners (*grandes marineros*) who played fatal tricks on many of the Spaniards who had voyaged as passengers on their balsa rafts. The natives had simply detached the ropes holding the log raft together, and the Spaniards fell through and drowned while the cunning Indians survived because they were outstanding swimmers. Pedro Pizzaro, who accompanied his cousin during the actual discovery of the Peruvian coast, speaks of similar perils experienced by him, Alonso de Mesa, Captain Soto, and many of his other contemporaries among the conquistadores who had forced the local natives to convey them by sea by means of sail-carrying balsa rafts. Other early chroniclers, among them Cieza de Leon (1553), state that even before the arrival of the Spaniards the coastal Peruvians, who 'swam as well as fishes', lured the highland Incas into the open ocean on board balsa rafts only to undo the lashings of the logs and thereby drown their less sea-minded passengers.

The Italian traveller Girolamo Benzoni,[13] who came to Peru about 1540, published a very primitive drawing of a small-sized Peruvian balsa raft of seven logs, carrying eight Indians. In his text he states that there were rafts for navigating which were much greater made up of nine or eleven logs, carrying sails which varied according to the size of the raft.

Garcilasso de la Vega,[14] who was of Inca descent and left Peru for Spain in 1560, devotes most of his attention to the wash-through fishing craft of reeds or rushes which were numerous and by far the dominant vessel along the Peruvian coast; he says they usually went from four to six leagues off the coast (fifteen to

Vessel from the Chimu culture. Mythical fish and cultural heroes on reed boats with double decks. Note the crew and the cargo between decks. The feet beneath the boats symbolize their forward movement.

twenty-four English miles), and more if necessary. He adds that when the natives wanted to convey large cargoes they used the rafts of wood on which they hoisted sails when they navigated the open sea.

Father Reginaldo de Lizarraga,[15] who came to Peru the same year Inca Garcilasso left, says of the natives of the Chicama Valley: 'These Indians are great mariners; they have large rafts of light timber with which they navigate the ocean, and while fishing they remain many leagues out at sea.' He also narrated how the native merchants of the Chicama Valley communicated with Guayaquil, 500 miles to the north, by means of their balsa rafts heavily laden with sea-food and other cargo.

Father Cabello de Balboa,[16] who came to Peru in 1566,

learned from the Inca historians that some two or three generations before the arrival of Pizarro, Inca Tupac Yupanqui had descended to the coast, and, selecting some of the best local pilots, had embarked with a whole army upon a vast number of rafts and sailed away from the coast. He was absent for about a year. On the return of the flotilla to Peru, the Inca and his captains claimed to have visited two inhabited islands far out in the ocean. Also the chronicler Sarmiento de Gamboa[17] in 1572 recorded these Inca accounts of pre-Spanish voyages by balsa rafts to distant Pacific islands, and this famous navigator admits himself that it was the rumours of Peruvian merchant sailors with balsa rafts and the account of Inca Tupac Yupanqui's voyage of discovery which prompted him to urge the Peruvian viceroy to organize the Mendaña expedition in search of these islands, an enterprise which directly resulted in the European discovery of Melanesia and Polynesia.

The prominent early historian of Peru, Bernabé Cobo, went into considerable detail in describing the remarkable qualities of the balsa timber used for the ocean-going rafts, and also the native ability to navigate and swim. He added:

'The largest rafts used by the Peruvian Indians living near the forests, like those of the harbours of Payta, Manta, and Guayaquil, are composed of seven, nine, or more logs of balsa timber, in the following manner: The logs are lashed one to the other lengthwise by means of lianas or ropes tied over other logs which lie as cross-beams; the log in the middle is longer than the others at the bow, and one by one they are shorter the closer they are placed to the sides, in such a way that, at the bow, they get the same form and proportions as seen on the fingers of an extended hand, although the stern is even. On the top of this they place a platform so that the people and the clothing on board shall not get wet from the water which comes up in the cracks between the large timbers. These rafts navigate on the ocean by means of sail and paddles, and some are so large that they are easily able to carry fifty men.'[18]

The next crude illustration of a balsa raft under sail was drawn by Spilbergen[19] on his voyage around the world in 1614 to 1617. Spilbergen states that when this balsa raft entered Paita harbour, 120 miles south of the Peruvian port of Tumbez, its crew of five natives had been away fishing for two months, and came back with enough provisions on their raft to distribute to the whole Dutch fleet anchored in the bay. The interesting feature in Spilbergen's otherwise crude drawing of the event, is that it shows the crew in action on board the raft, two of them attending the sail, while the other three are navigating the raft without paddles or steering-oar, simply by raising and lowering centre-boards inserted in cracks between the logs. The use of centre-boards was an art which was completely unknown to boat-builders in Europe until about 1870, more than two hundred and fifty years later.

The first unsuccessful attempt to introduce centre-board navigation to Europe was in 1736, after the Spanish naval officers Juan and Ulloa[20] had made an interesting survey of the ingenious art of aboriginal balsa raft navigation in Guayaquil Bay. They published an excellent drawing of a balsa raft at sea, showing such details as the arrangement of the bipod mast with its sail and rigging, the thatched hut amidship, the cooking-place with open fire and the storage of water-jars astern, and the position of the centre-boards inserted near the bow and stern. They claim emphatically that a native crew with sufficient skill in manipulating the centre-boards could sail a balsa raft in any wind as well as a regular ship.

Five years later Lescallier[21] published another drawing of a large nine-log balsa raft with a spacious dwelling amidship and a crew navigating at sea simply by means of centre-boards and a huge square sail on a bipod mast. Lescallier's work published under order of the King of France to serve as instruction for the naval cadets, included a good description of the aboriginal balsa raft and its remarkable steering principles still employed only among its native inventors on the north-west coast of South America. With Juan and Ulloa as his main source, Lescallier emphasized that if the principles of this native centre-board navigation had been known in Europe, many shipwrecked would have saved their lives by sailing their rafts to the nearest port.

In 1801 Charnock,[22] in his great history of marine architecture, made another fruitless effort to introduce the ingenious art of centre-board navigation to the outside world, stating that this method of steering was an art peculiar to the coastal Indians of Peru and Ecuador and hitherto unknown in Europe.

Alexander Humboldt,[23] in 1810, presents a beautiful illustration in water-colour of a large sail-carrying balsa raft with centre-board; and in 1825 Stevenson[24] gave an excellent description of the larger balsa rafts that still covered the coast of the former Chimu habitat as far down as to Huanchaco south of Chicama. Some of these larger rafts had thatched bamboo huts with four or five rooms, and they were 'beating up against the wind and current a distance of four degrees of latitude, having onboard five or six quintals [25 or 30 tons] of goods as a cargo, besides a crew of Indians and their provisions'. Stevenson, too, describes the centre-boards and says: 'By raising or lowering these boards in different parts of the balsa, the natives can perform on their raft all the manœuvres of a regularly built and well-rigged vessel. . . .'

In an unpublished manuscript of 1840, written by George Blaxland[25] and preserved in the Mitchell Library of Sydney, the author reproduces a drawing of a nine-log balsa raft, with sail and centre-boards as the only means of navigation. The manuscript also contains a report from an officer of one of Her Majesty's ships, who had encountered a native Peruvian family on a balsa raft at the island of Lobos de Afuera about sixty miles off the Peruvian coast. The natives were just preparing a raft voyage to the invisible mainland against a contrary wind: '. . . they had been absent from their Native Village three weeks, and were about to return with a Cargo of Dried Fish, the family consisted of Nine persons, with a Number of Dogs and all their goods and chattels. . . . The Vessel I was in, a schooner of 40 tons sailed for the same place in company, and it was surprising to see the manner

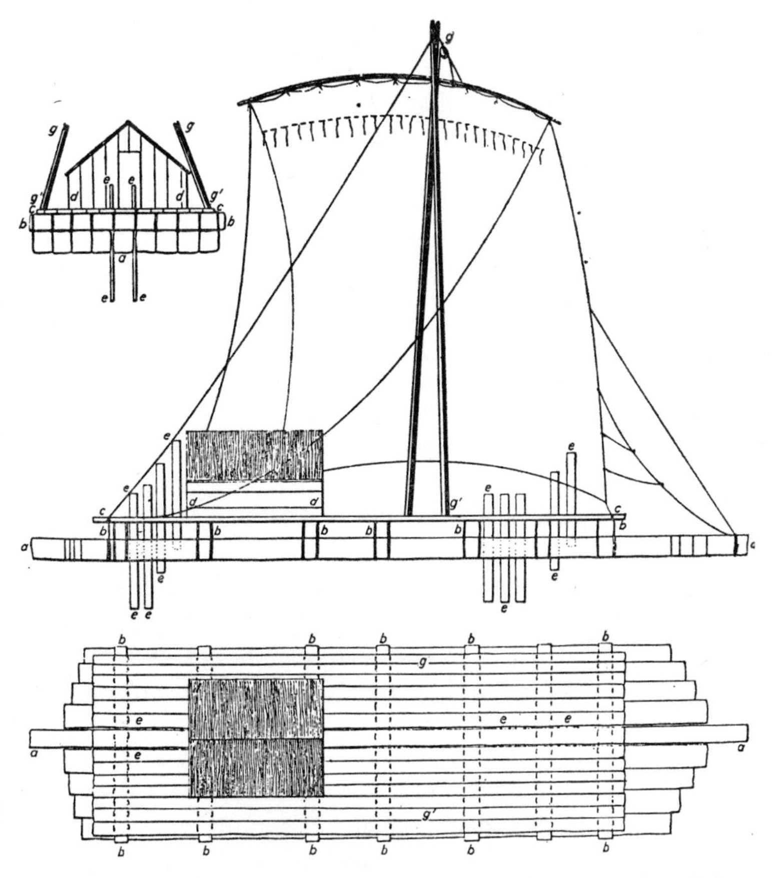

Sketch by F. E. Paris (1841) showing construction of a native balsa raft from the North-west coast of South America.

a: 9 main balsa logs; b: 7 tranverse balsa logs; c: raised deck; d; bamboo cabin with reed roof; e: 9 centreboards; gg': twin mast of mangrove wood, bearing a yard with rectangular cotton sail. Maximum length of raft 80-90 feet; maximum width of raft 25-30 feet; freight capacity 20-25 tons.

the raft held the Wind, going at the rate of four or five knots an hour; we kept together for some time and arrived the next day within a few hours of each other; . . . The whole of the lading of vessels on some parts of the Coast is made entirely by these balsas and at Lambeyeque in consequence of the heavy surf rolling on the shore, a landing cannot be effected but by them; they also carry salt from one port to another two or three hundred miles apart, another proof they are trustworthy.' In 1841 we get a detailed technical draft by Paris[26] in his essay on naval construction among non-European peoples. Paris was in South America in time to see the aboriginal Peruvian balsa rafts before they were displaced by European boat-types at the turn of the century, but he studied them only while moored in the bay. Although he carefully drew and described the centre-boards, or *guaras* as they were termed by the natives, he did not fully understand their technique or function, stating merely that: 'These are driven in to a greater or lesser degree, fore or aft, in order to luff or go about. The rafts have no other methods for steering on the ocean. . . .'

It is quite obvious that a *guara*, or centre-board, as opposed to a paddle or steering-oar, can only be used in connection with a sail. Without a sail a centre-board had no function and no effect. This has already been pointed out by Lothrop[27] and others, and is an important fact in view of the many centre-boards which are found archaeologically in the desert graves on the north and south coast of Peru. The beautifully ornamented hardwood centre-boards from the numerous graves of Paracas and Ica in southern Peru show that sail-carrying rafts were important culture elements even in these southern latitudes, and at periods which not only antedate written history, but even take us right back into pre-Inca time. Bennett,[28] for instance, illustrates one of these beautifully carved and painted centre-boards from the south coast of Peru. Archaeology also furnishes us with some minor but rather important details which remained unrecorded by the early chroniclers and historic observers, namely, how the lashings were secured to the slippery logs, and how the individual logs were shaped in the bow and stern to diminish the water resistance. Such information may be gained from the tiny model rafts—more properly intended as spirit-rafts—which have been found in great numbers in the Arica desert graves still farther south on the coast. These prehistoric rafts were left there more than a thousand years before the arrival of Pizarro and the first Europeans, and show that the lashings, of hemp-rope or strips of seal hide, were fastened in grooves cut around the logs. They also show that to decrease the water resistance each log was pointed boat-fashion fore and aft. One small raft excavated by Uhle[29] and published in 1922 was fitted with a square sail of reeds similar to that used until the present day by the neighbouring mountain Indians of Lake Titicaca. It was this discovery in a grave from the primitive fisher population at Arica, dated to the first centuries AD, which made Nordenskiöld[30] conclude that 'The sail was probably known on the Peruvian coast earlier than pottery and weaving. . . .'

As earlier quoted from Inca Garcilasso, the most numerous craft along the desert coast of aboriginal Peru was the reed-raft of the individual fishermen; the wooden rafts with sail were only used for transporting heavy cargo and for regular ocean voyaging. The principal Peruvian ports for wooden rafts in Inca time were Paita and Tumbez and other villages on the northern coast near the great balsa forests of Ecuador, but until 1900 important balsa raft ports were recorded as far down as Sechura, Lambayeque, Pacasmayo, and Huanchaca, 500 miles south of Guayaquil. In Inca time the balsa rafts were employed still another 500 miles to the south, conveying guano for fertilizer from the Chincha Islands near Piaco to the various provinces of Peru. The Incas even transported balsa logs overland for the construction of buoyant rafts in remote corners of their empire. Thus, when the first Spaniards under Hernando Pizarro advanced down the highland of the Andes from Cuzco, they found in what today is Bolivia great quantities of large balsa timber transported there on the backs of native labourers to build wooden balsa rafts on Lake Titicaca for the pleasure of Inca Huayna Capac.[31]

By combining historical and archaeological information, we thus possess a fairly accurate knowledge of the construction principles and local importance of the peculiar raft which permitted aboriginal navigation in Peru and adjacent Pacific waters.

Thus, when the noted Americanist S. K. Lothrop in 1932 compiled material for his interesting paper on *Aboriginal Navigation off the West Coast of South America* he was able to give a good picture of the local balsa raft. However, in judging its sea-going ability, he stated that it 'absorbs water rapidly and loses its buoyancy completely after a few weeks. Owing to this characteristic it was necessary to take the *Jangada* [or balsa raft] apart at intervals, haul the logs ashore, and there allow them to dry out completely.'[32] Lothrop concluded that the balsa raft was unfit for oversea voyages, and that it could not travel as far as to the Pacific islands, not even to the Galapagos group a few hundred miles offshore.

Lothrop quoted Byam as his source for this information. Byam,[33] however, was a nineteenth-century British traveller who was unacquainted with balsa rafts. In his book of 1850 we find that his sailing ship met a seafaring balsa raft off Cabo Blanco in north Peru. The raft is described as merely sighted in the distance while tacking southwards against a fresh breeze, and whatever additional information Byam gave concerning its buoyancy was merely quoted as the opinion of the captain of his ship.

Lothrop's study was otherwise a valuable contribution, and few anthropologists have afterwards cared to penetrate farther into the question. Some additional material was brought up by the noted Inca authority P. A. Means[34] in 1942, in his interesting paper *Pre-Spanish Navigation Off the Andean Coast*, but referring in part to Lothrop, Means accepts the same negative view in his theoretical judgment of the balsa raft, saying: 'it was obviously a type of boat that would awake nothing but scorn in the breasts of shipbuilders of almost any other maritime people in the world.' He concludes:

'Altogether, we are justified in concluding that in Peruvian native navigation prior to the Spanish conquest, the balsa-log raft, with sails, deck-house, and cargo-space, was the least contemptible and the least inefficient type of craft known. This, admittedly, is faint praise; but, in view of the facts, it is the best that can be given to the boat-building art of those singularly unmarine-minded people, the ancient Andeans.'

The noted authority on aboriginal craft and navigation, J. Hornell, was led to bring up the same subject in 1945, first in his paper, *Was there a Pre-Columbian Contact between the Peoples of Oceania and S. America?*[35] And next in 1946 in his paper *How did the Sweet Potato reach Oceania?*[36] Hornell was confident that the early Peruvians had influenced the Polynesian island agriculture, and was therefore careful in his judgment of the balsa raft, yet he concludes:

'Certainly no ordinary, untreated balsa raft could make a prolonged oversea voyage unless the Inca's seamen knew of an effective method of treating its absorbent logs with some kind of waterproofing composition. . . .'[37]

The confident attitude among the Americanists who had actually surveyed the main principles in Peruvian boat-building had a double effect on modern anthropology. By labelling the balsa raft as 'not seaworthy,' the aboriginal Peruvians were deprived of their principal means of navigation and generally deemed a notedly unmaritime and land-locked people. This one-sided picture of the early high-cultures in Pacific South America penetrated the technical as well as the general literature, and it soon biased the study of important problems in Polynesian anthropology.

In 1932 the prominent Pacific scholar R. B. Dixon[38] succeeded in proving that the sweet potato had been carried by man from Peru to Polynesia in pre-Spanish time, accompanied by its Quechua-Peruvian name *kumara*, and pointing to the balsa rafts, he suggested that Peruvian or other American Indians had been responsible for the transfer. In the same year Lothrop published his aforesaid survey of Peruvian navigation, and two years later Dixon came back with a new publication[39] stating:

'Since we have no evidence that at any time the Indians of the Pacific Coast of South America where the sweet potato was grown, had either the craft or the skill for making long sea journeys, we are forced to conclude that the transference of the plant was carried out by Polynesians.'

Correspondingly, the noted Polynesian archaeologist, K. P. Emory,[40] had originally written in 1933 with regard to the ancient great-stone masonry of Easter Island, the Society Islands, the Marquesas, Hawaii, Tubuai, and the Tonga group:

'It is quite within reason to entertain an American origin for a cultural element so specialized as this stone facing. It is a conspicuous element localized in the part of America nearest to Polynesia, a part where currents strike out and flow in the direction of Easter Island and the Tuamotus. . . . May not one of the seagoing rafts of the early Incas have been swept into this current carrying survivors as far as Easter Island 2,000 miles to the west?'

In a subsequent publication of 1942[41] he also was led to abandon his view, since, as he states, Dixon had in the meantime pointed out to him that the balsa raft of Pacific South America quickly became waterlogged. In a publication by Morgan[42] of 1946 the author in turn quotes Emory who wrote to him on request that 'Balsa rafts become waterlogged in a few days if not taken out of the water to dry'.

At this time the verdict on the balsa raft had virtually grown into an axiom, and when Buck[43] in 1945 published his *Introduction to Polynesian Anthropology*, he eliminated one half of the Pacific border-lands by simply stating:

'Since the South American Indians had neither the vessels nor the navigating ability to cross the ocean space between their shores and the nearest Polynesian islands, they may be disregarded as the agents of supply.'

With the same confidence Weckler[44] wrote in 1943 in his monograph on *Polynesian Explorers of the Pacific* that: 'no American Indians had sea-going ships that were capable of such passages as the voyage to Polynesia.'

This belief had such a firm grip on the minds of both Americanists and Pacific anthropologists, that, when I attempted to oppose it in a publication of 1941,[45] naturally I met to response. There appeared to be in the end only one way to settle the dispute, namely to construct a replica of the craft under discussion, and to derive a satisfactory answer through a practical test. Therefore, in 1947, I organized and led what became the *Kon-Tiki* expedition.

The raft, named *Kon-Tiki*, was composed of nine two-foot-thick balsa logs, ranging in length from thirty to forty-five feet, the longest in the middle, and lashed to cross-beams supporting a bamboo deck and an open hut. A bipod mast, carrying a square sail, five *guaras* (centre-boards), and a steering-oar completed the construction. The raft was launched off Callao harbour in Peru on April 28 with a crew of six men; ninety-three days later the first inhabited Polynesian island was sighted, and passed. After a total journey of 4,300 miles in 101 days, *Kon-Tiki* grounded on the reef of Raroia Atoll in the Tuamotu Islands, with crew and nearly all the cargo safe.

The object of the expedition had been to test and study the true qualities and abilities of the balsa raft, and what was more, to get an answer to the old and disputed question whether or not the Polynesian islands were within feasible reach of the raftsmen of ancient Peru.

It proved to be an exceedingly seaworthy craft, perfectly adapted for carrying heavy cargoes in the open and unsheltered ocean. Of all the valuable qualities none surprised and impressed us more than its outstanding safety and seaworthiness in all weather conditions at sea. Next to its unique ability to ride the waves came perhaps its carrying capacity, which, however, was no surprise, since balsa rafts capable of carrying up to thirty tons or more were described by the early Spaniards.

The theoretical judgments of the balsa raft had deemed it not seaworthy because of the water-absorbent nature of the balsa wood, which would make it sink if not regularly dismantled and dried; also because it was thought that the rope lashings which kept the logs and the whole craft together would be worn through by friction when the great logs began to move at sea. The light and porous wood was also considered to be too fragile should high ocean seas lift the bow and stern up while crew and cargo were weighing upon the central part. Finally, it was considered that a one and a half foot freeboard on the flat and open raft would leave crew and cargo entirely exposed to the ocean seas.

Our experience provided the answer to these problems, and showed that the ancient culture peoples of Peru and Ecuador had their good reasons for evolving—and abiding by—this very type of deep-sea-going craft.

Dry balsa wood, as commercially distributed and generally known today, is exceedingly water-absorbent and unsuitable for raft construction, but green balsa wood, put into the sea when freshly cut and still filled with sap, is very water-resistant, and although the water gradually penetrates the sun-dried outer section, the sap inside prevents further absorption. *Kon-Tiki* was still capable of holding tons of cargo when it was finally pulled ashore for preservation more than a year after the expedition.

The balsa logs did not chafe off the rope lashings. The reason was that the surface of the logs became soft and spongy, and the ropes were left unharmed as if pressed between cork. The two-feet-thick balsa logs proved to be tough enough to resist the assault of two storms with towering seas, and even an emergency landfall on an unsheltered reef in Polynesia.

The secret of the safety and seaworthiness of the unprotected balsa raft, in spite of its negligible freeboard, was primarily its unique ability to rise with any threatening sea, thus riding over the dangerous water-masses which would have broken aboard most other small craft. Secondly it was the ingenious wash-through construction which allowed all water to disappear as through a sieve. Neither towering swells nor breaking wind-waves had any chance of getting a grip on the vessel, and the result was a feeling of complete security which no other open or small craft could have offered. Moreover the shallow construction of the raft, and the flexibility allowed by all the independent lashings, made it possible even to land directly on an exposed reef on the windward side of the dangerous Tuamotu archipelago.

During the voyage a few experiments were carried out with what the natives call *guaras*, the aforesaid centre-board. It was found that five *guaras*, six feet deep and two feet wide, when securely attached, were enough to permit the raft to sail almost at right angles to the wind. It was also ascertained that by raising or lowering a *guara* fore or aft, the raft could be steered without using the steering oar.

However, an attempt to tack into the wind failed completely, and the raft's crew therefore yielded to the generally held claim that the Peruvian balsa-raft, like just any other flat-bottomed raft, could only be sailed in the general directions of a following wind. But subsequent to the expedition the present author was gradually led to suspect[46] that this failure in our attempt to tack was probably due to the inexperience of the raft's crew rather than to limitations in the early Peruvian marine architecture, and in 1953 the experiment was renewed. Mr Emilio Estrada of Guayaquil kindly arranged for the building of a smaller test raft constructed like *Kon-Tiki* of nine balsa logs lashed together and covered by a bamboo deck. Likewise, for navigation, a square sail was hoisted on its usual bipod mast in native fashion, and similarly six *guaras* were inserted between the logs, two in the extreme bow and two in the stern. No paddles, rudder, or steering-oar were carried on the raft, which was launched from the open coast of Playas, Ecuador, with a crew of four. Our suspicion was verified: a correct interplay between the handling of the sail and the *guaras* fore and aft enabled us, after some experimentation, to tack against contrary wind, and even to sail back to the exact spot where we had set off. The *guara* method of steering a raft was astonishing through its simplicity and effectiveness,[47] and the ingenious technique involved may even be adopted with great benefit on modern life-rafts which are entirely unnavigable.

With the ability to sail and tack their capacious and seaworthy balsa rafts, through the pre-Inca invention of *guara*-navigation, the early Peruvian high cultures were very far advanced in marine matters, and an entire reappraisal of early Peruvian seamanship and navigation is necessary.

Some of the rafts actually seen by the earliest Europeans off the Andean coast carried merchants with their women and tons of cargo on board. Others were used for army transportation and the conquest and control of Puna islanders off the empire coast. Still others were used by the fishermen who went on extensive expeditions of long duration in the rapid currents and eddies of the Humboldt Current. The Spaniards even recorded Inca memories of individual merchant rafts and large organized raft flotillas that set out on direct exploring expeditions to very remote islands.

Thus, the fact that Andean watercraft was based on boat-building principles alien to our ancestors, and therefore distrusted and underestimated by us, should not be permitted to bias our judgment of the vast and diversified aboriginal population of the area. Among the local tribes and nations there were men and women who were sea-minded rather than land-locked, and who founded their existence on a long-lasting and thorough marine tradition on the north-west coast of aboriginal South America.

GUARA SAILING TECHNIQUE INDIGENOUS TO SOUTH AMERICA

To gain information on the various types of indigenous watercraft employed in the aboriginal navigation off the west coast of South America we are largely dependent on the records of the early chroniclers, and to some extent on the iconographic art of the pre-conquest population on the coast. One-man 'caballitos' and two-man reed-boats are very common motives in the ceramic art, in the tapestry, and even in the metal industry along the Peruvian coast, and large reed-ships with many passengers and cargo, often with a double deck and forked stern, are not uncommon in Mochica ceramic art. Effigy jars illustrating voyagers on rafts lashed together from straight wooden logs also occur, but specimens are rare.

The earliest written records describing aboriginal Peruvian water-craft are presented by Saamanos, Xeres, Andagoya, Oviedo, Zarate, Las Casas, Balboa, Gamboa, Garcilasso, Benzoni, and Cobo, all of whom concur in mentioning the balsa rafts and in stating that the art of sailing was indigenous to the Inca empire and employed on the balsa rafts at sea. In the highland sails were in use even on the Lake Titicaca reed-boats, but Inca Garcilasso says of the coastal population: 'They do not put up sails on their boats of rushes, . . . but they hoist sails on their wooden rafts when they navigate the sea.'

In a previous paper presented before the Congress the present author gave a synopsis on contemporary reports on the early Peruvian balsa rafts, the existence of which was made known to the Spaniards by natives in Panama before Balboa had yet reached the Pacific shore. Subsequently Pizarro's advanced party of discoverers overhauled and captured no less than six sailing balsas and sacked their Inca cargo even before the Spaniards had yet reached the first Peruvian port of Tumbez, where they met another flotilla of sailing rafts standing out to sea with Inca troops bound for Puna Island. We shall here only recall that the first of these rafts ever seen by Europeans was beating up against the wind and the strong Nino Current with more than 30 tons of cargo when captured by Pizarro's pilot. This truly difficult marine manœuvre was not accomplished by paddling, a feat which for practical reasons alone would be impossible for a broad log-raft carrying twenty men and women and thirty tons of cargo. We learn from Saamanos' pre-Conquest report to Carlos V in 1526 that this colossal cargo raft was properly equipped for regular navigation. It carried masts and yards of very fine wood, with an excellent rigging of henequen hemp, and 'cotton sails in the same shape and manner as on our own ships'.

Subsequent chroniclers also infer that Inca fishermen and merchant sailors were capable of premeditated raft voyages with successful return into the wind, a feat which has been deemed impossible by modern experts on rafts and navigation. War-time experiments with rubber dinghies and life-rafts of wood or aluminium convinced naval and civil authorities of the inaptitude of sailing rafts as means of reaching given destinations, as the flat-bottomed rafts would yield to all winds and move sideways or backwards as helpless prey to the elements. In spite of its remarkably superior buoyancy and safety in rough seas, no appliance of rudder or steering-oar could make a raft navigable such as was the case with a life-boat with hull and keel. It is the more remarkable to learn from early eyewitnesses that the Inca seamen could set sail and beat their way towards Panama, Puna Island, the Lobos and Chincha Islands, etc., or go far into the treacherous rapids of the Humboldt and Nino Currents to return after weeks of absence with heavy burdens of dried fish.

It is no secret that the Inca sailors achieved their marine exploits through the aid of *guaras*, a special form of wooden centre-boards which they thrust down in the cracks between the logs of the raft. Yet, with the appropriate number of *guaras* inserted, the members of the *Kon-Tiki* expedition were quite unable to tack or beat to windward with their balsa raft, a fact which almost ended with catastrophe upon the arrival among the atolls of Polynesia. Continued research upon my return from the expedition convinced me, however, that our lack of success in this respect was due to our own inexperience in this forgotten technique rather than to any limitations in the favourite Inca sailing system. This suspicion was finally verified by a second raft experiment off the Ecuadorian coast.

The balsa raft *guaras* vary considerably in dimensions according to the size and type of the craft and according to the dimensions of the hardwood material available. They are usually from 4 to 7 feet in length and from 5 to 10 inches wide, although off the jungle areas of Ecuador they could be as much as 3 or 4 yards in length and half a yard wide. The *guaras* are rectangular boards without shaft but with a knob or handle on the upper end. We may be dependent on the early chroniclers and on more or less conventionalized native art for information on the early Peruvian watercraft, but we are still able to inspect and study the actual hardwood *guaras* employed by the ancient local mariners. Such *guaras*, usually carved from the hard and enduring *algarrobo* tree, are among the most commonly occurring wooden artifacts in the pre-Conquest graves of coastal Peru. Thanks to the splendid art and workmanship embodied in some of them, they are very familiar objects in Peruvian museum exhibits all over the world. Most of the *guaras*, however, were crudely manufactured without ornamentation of any kind, and as these strictly utilitarian pieces failed to make impression on treasure-seeking collectors, many have been lost in the hands of *huaqueros*. It may perhaps be fair to say that the ratio between trained archaeological work and mere treasure-hunting in Peruvian coastal sites is as clearly reflected in the ratio between the plain and the exuberantly ornamented *guaras* as it is in the ratio between Peruvian plainware and decorated effigy jars found in museum collections.

The most elaborately ornamented specimens come from the Pisco, Paracas and Ica region on the south-central coast. Yet, here too, plain and crude *algarrobo guaras* are found through excavation. Whereas the ornamental *guaras* from the Chimu area on the north coast usually have no more than a bird or an animal figure carved in the free on top of the grip, like on the local paddles, the finest Paracas specimens often have grips with carved and painted birds, fishes, men, or ornamental symbols superimposed in two or three rows. The upper row is sometimes composed of six or eight men standing side by side and holding hands in such a manner that they form a wave-motive.

It has been suggested that some of the most artistic specimens are purely ceremonial emblems of rank, and this is probably true. Yet I have failed to find a single specimen which could not serve its purpose if put to use, due to the hardness of the wood employed and the carefully selected placement of the carvings which never impede the proper movement of the *guara*. The carving is always restricted to the upper grip and if, on rare specimens, it extends somewhat further down, it always follows the lateral edge of the board in such a way that it does not at all interfere with the free sliding of the board through the crack or slot between the soft balsa logs. It is indeed noteworthy that the carvings are consistently limited to that part of the *guara* which, when in use, is standing free and visible above deck, whereas the section which is left submerged below the raft, and thus is invisible to crew and passengers, is left plain and unornamented. One should expect that a purely ceremonial object might be ornamented for its full length like a ceremonial axe-handle or a staff, and not be left rude and plain for the major part of its length. In view of the function of the *guara*, which implies that the handle and upper section is standing visible and exposed to no strain or wear whatsoever except for a very slight occasional touch by a hand, we may safely assume that the great bulk even of the best ornamented specimens were actually in use too, although probably by men of rank in the coastal community.

When the first elaborately carved Pisco specimens were excavated and spread to museums and private collections in the latter part of last century, they were treated merely as fine samples of pre-Inca wood-carving art, and although they were identified by Gretzer as marine *guaras* in 1914, very little attention has been paid to their actual function ever since.

After a life-time in coastal Peru, Gretzer had adequate opportunity of observing the last lingering balsa rafts which, manœuvering with *guaras*, still carried tons of dried fish northwards to Ecuador and lumber and other cargo southwards to Peru. When he started his excavations in the valleys of Pisco and Ica and uncovered the large collection of archaeological *guaras* which are now in the Berlin-Dahlem Museum für Völkerkunde, he recognized the *guaras* for what they were. He stressed that they provided sufficient evidence to the effect that the coastal population, even in pre-Inca time, were capable of undertaking regular voyages on the ocean such as witnessed by the early Spaniards.

For anybody unfamiliar with the curious qualities of the buoyant Inca reed and balsa rafts at sea, it is difficult to perceive that the coastal population had advanced far beyond the first primitive stage in marine evolution. In reality, the early Peruvians were well familiar with dug-out canoes and boats with a hull,[48] but at sea they much preferred their specially developed types of watercraft which were marvellously adapted to meet the special requirements of the local geographical conditions. The general misjudgement of the presumably primitive totora reed-boat and the balsa log-raft may perhaps be one of the reasons for the surprisingly sparse attention paid to the existing source material on local marine activities. Even after Gretzer's publication it was not uncommon to find museum specimens of Peruvian *guaras* labelled as 'ceremonial spades' or other similar denominations, although anybody who made an attempt would soon find out that the *guara* was exceedingly unfitted for any sort of agricultural work. When specimens were excavated *in situ* and not merely obtained as stray artifacts in the hands of collectors, it became gradually evident that the peculiar boards in question were some sort of marine accessory, since they were generally interred with fishermen's equipment or other artifacts implying marine activity rather than agriculture. It was also rather striking that the special ornamentation on the grip precisely matched that of the local paddlehandles, and the *guaras* have therefore in recent years commonly been exhibited as 'a special kind of paddle' or even as 'a rudder'. A mere study of the grip will suffice, however, to show that this curious artifact could have served as neither. The principal quality of a paddle is a perfect balance: the grip must be set symmetrically on top of the central axis to prevent the blade from twisting during the stroke. The grip of the *guara*, however, is set entirely out of balance, far over on one corner of the board, in such a way that paddling or rowing is rendered quite hopeless. Nor does the *guara* have any shaft allowing a balanced grip for the second hand. Most of the south coast *guaras* have the handle carved as a mere slot for the insertion of the fingers like the carrying handle of a bag. It is obvious that the specialized *guara* handle is intended merely for a vertical one-hand raising and lowering of the wide board, and not to gain momentum through a balanced two-hand stroke. Nor does the grip of the *guara* in any way tally with—or function as—the tiller of a rudder, and we are left with the apparent fact that the practical functions of the *guara* differ from those of boat accessories occurring on common European water-craft.

(More recently Eisleb (1963) completed a systematic study of the large archaeological collection of plain and ornamented Peruvian *guaras* preserved in the store-rooms of the Berlin-Dahlem Museum für Völkerkunde. He discovered that one of the characteristics common to all these boards was that they were shaped like knives, with one edge narrower and sharper than the other, so as to enable this navigation instrument to cut the water with minimum resistance.)

When Lothrop published the first systematic study on aboriginal Peruvian navigation in 1932, he happened to be as familiar with sailing techniques and marine matters as with the local field of archaeology, and, like Gretzer, Lothrop too realized that the strange marine accessories were *guaras*, the special kind of centre-board which was still in use on the north coast until the turn of the century. Lothrop also stressed that the presence of *guaras* in early pre-Conquest graves on the Peruvian coast provides archaeological evidence of the pre-Columbian use of sail in this area. He says: 'It is obvious that a centre-board is useless unless a vessel has sails.' As opposed to a rudder or a steering-oar the movable *guara* is purely a sailing tool, superfluous and impossible on any craft propelled by oars or paddles.

The first Spaniards, arriving in caravels, showed no interest in the *guaras* as such, praising only the remarkable skill of the local mariners in the handling of their peculiar rafts. But in his early drawing of a balsa raft at Payta, Peru, published in 1619, the Dutch admiral Spilbergen illustrates two cloaked Indians standing by the sails issuing orders to three others who squat on the raft's deck, each holding the upper section of his own *guara* which is thrust down vertically in the cracks between the logs. The raft has no steering-oar or rudder. In the text Spilbergen does not comment on the *guaras* with a word, he merely states, like the Spaniards before him, that this was a very wonderful craft, adding the information that the sailing raft had been at sea fishing for two months, and now returned to Payta harbour with sufficient fish to supply all the ships of Spilbergen's fleet.

It is here important to bear in mind that the *guaras* meant nothing to the artist behind Spilbergen's interesting drawing, for the use of even regular centre-boards was an invention not yet known to contemporary Europe. Spilbergen, therefore, although leaving for posterity the very first illustration of the principles of centre-board navigation, refrained from any comment beyond the fact that the raft and sails 'were very wonderfully made'.

A hundred and thirty years more had to pass before two Spanish naval officers, Juan and Ulloa, became sufficiently intrigued by the navigation technique employed by the local Indians to look further into the mystery of the indigenous *guara*. After an excellent description of the various sizes and types of the balsa rafts they saw in Quayaquil they wrote in 1748:[49]

'Hitherto we have only mentioned the construction and the uses they are applied to, but the greatest singularity of the floating vehicle is that it sails, tacks and works as well in contrary winds as ships with a keel, and makes very little leeway. This advantage it derives from another method of steering than by a rudder, namely, by some boards three or four yards in length, and half a yard in breadth, called *guaras*, which are placed vertically, both at the head and stern between the main beams, and by thrusting some of these deep in the water, and raising others, they bear away, luff up, tack, lay to, and perform all the other motions of a regular ship. An invention hitherto unknown to the most intelligent nations of Europe . . . a *guara* being let down in the fore-part of a vessel must make her luff up and by taking it out, she will bear away or fall off. Likeways on a *guara*'s being let down at the stern, she will bear away, and by taking it out of the water, the balsa will luff, or keep nearer to the wind. Such is the method used by the Indians in steering the balsas and sometimes they use five or six *guaras*, to prevent the balsa from making leeway, it being evident that the more they are under water, the greater resistance the side of the vessel meets with, the *guaras* performing the office of leeboards used in small vessels. The method of steering by these *guaras* is so easy and simple, that when once the balsa is put in her proper course, one only is made use of, raising and lowering it as occasions require, and thus the balsa is always kept in her intended direction.'

The two authors were so impressed by this indigenous Peruvian sailing technique that they strongly recommended an introduction of the same system in Europe. Yet, when Lescalier and Charnock published their comprehensive world histories on navigation in 1791 and 1801 respectively, they could still only quote Juan and Ulloa's observations in Ecuador, and stress that the centre-board steering method was entirely peculiar to the coastal Indians of that area and not yet known in Europe. In his instructions for French naval cadets Lescalier actually made an effort of recommending *guara* navigation for European life-rafts, but with no result.

Further reports on Peruvian *guara* navigation were published by Humboldt in 1810 and by Stevenson in 1825. The latter had seen balsa rafts in Peru which, merely by means of *guara*, were 'beating up against the wind and current' for hundreds of miles, with 25 or 30 tons of cargo.

Before Paris in 1841–43 published his voluminous essay on non-European water-craft, he went to north-western South America to study the balsa rafts. He wrote, slightly more than a century ago: 'In Peru they have preserved the use of rafts as constructed by the ancient inhabitants, which are sufficiently well suited to local conditions to be still preferred to all other craft. . . .' He published an important technical drawing of a large balsa with *guaras* inserted, but he had no opportunity of seeing rafts tacking at sea. He was in fact rather sceptical as to Juan and Ulloa's eyewitness report on the unlimited possibilities of *guara* navigation, and wrote: 'We have not been able to observe these ingenious rafts sufficiently to be sure that they really do carry out all these manœuvres . . .' Yet he admitted: 'The rafts have no other means of steering in the ocean. . . .'

A few years later, in 1852, Skogman observed balsa rafts with *guaras* far into the ocean off northern Peru, and he reported that balsa rafts were visiting the Galapagos Islands, some 600 miles off the mainland.

Another twenty years were to pass before the first centre-boards were taken into use on European boats, and very little credit was then handed to the ancient people who had employed the system for many centuries. According to Lothrop, some experiments of fitting centre-boards on to certain small boat models took place in England in 1790, but the actual employment of centre-boards did first begin in England and in the United States about 1870. Until then only lee-boards had been used by European sailors, the sole function of which is to serve as a keel reducing the lee-way.

About the turn of the century, true *guara* navigation of rafts disappeared with the last lingering traits of aboriginal culture along the coasts of Peru and Ecuador. With the thorough acculturation of the twentieth century the secret of raft navigation was lost before it had spread to European life-rafts.

When the *Kon-Tiki* raft was equipped with *guaras* for its voyage in 1947, there was unanimous opinion among ethnologists and marine authorities that these would be useless for the controlled manœuvring of a raft, and although the expedition members verified that it was possible with five *guaras* intact to fall off and bear to almost at right angles to the wind, yet we failed in all efforts to turn about and tack the raft against the wind. We returned from the expedition sharing the impression of Paris and subsequent scholars that the raft could only be navigated before the wind.

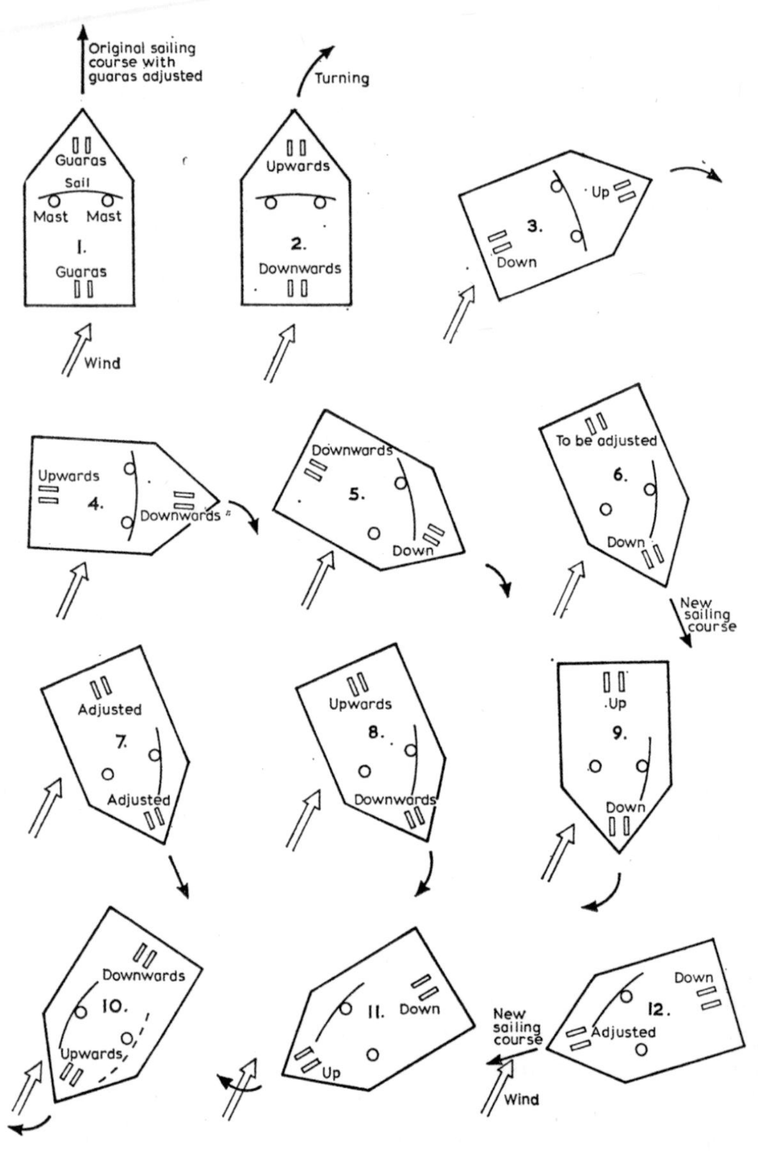

Guara Navigation

In 1953, with the kind aid of Mr Emilio Estrada of Guayaquil, it was possible to resume practical tests with a regular size balsa raft off the bay of Playas in Ecuador, where tiny three-log rafts of the Brazilian *jangada* type were still employed by local fishermen.

This time the whole secret of how the Incas could sail their rafts into the wind was rediscovered, and like all ingenious inventions the trick was exceedingly simple once it was known. It was found, by a crew consisting of Estrada, the two archaeologists Reed and Skjölsvold and the present author, that by quickly turning the sail and equally rapidly reversing the ratio of submerged *guara* surface respectively fore and aft of the mast at the very critical moment when the turning raft was taking the wind straight abeam, then the raft would willingly turn all about and resume a new course into the contrary wind. A consistent interplay between the turning of the yard and the lowering and raising of the *guaras* was required, and the yard had to be even with the junction of the bipod mast to swing freely from one side to the other. The moment the trick of turning a raft all about was rediscovered, the *guaras* were mely to be readjusted, and the raft sailed easily into the wind, tacking at the same angle as could be expected by a regular sail-boat. Once at its new course it was, as before, only the ratio between the *guaras* submerged fore and aft which would dermine the direction taken by the raft.

In conclusion we know today, that for practical reasons, there is no limit to the range of indigenous Peruvian water-craft in the Pacific Ocean. We may well understand, then, that Pizarro's advanced party ran into a merchant's balsa bound for Panama, and we can no longer deny the likelihood of very distant marine activities of the coastal Peruvian population since their ingenious invention of *guaras* in pre-Inca time.

CHAPTER 6

ARCHAEOLOGY IN THE GALAPAGOS ISLANDS

EDITORIAL NOTE. *Dr Heyerdahl has shown that the Indians possessed sea-worthy vessels and nautical knowledge which were quite sufficient to carry them to the South Sea Islands. And so the next task is to find traces of their presence there, be it in the form of specific cultural traditions or of archaeological remains. In his interpretation of such cultural traditions Dr Heyerdahl has always had this end in view. As early as 1937 he was examining archaeological material in this light. The first of the two next expeditions which he organized and led brought him and his team of scientists to the Galapagos Islands, which are only 600 miles from the coast of Peru and Ecuador. As the reader already knows, these islands play an important part in the interpretations placed on the Inca reports: due to their volcanic cactus landscape, however, they were not permanently settled.*

In various parts of the Galapagos group the archaeologists on the expedition excavated a considerable number of pottery fragments. Although these constituted their principal find, they also discovered remnants of other artifacts of Indian origin. These objects were sent to the United States National Museum in Washington, where they were traced back to various Indian cultures on the coast of ancient Peru and Ecuador. It is certain that a considerable number of these objects were made not only in pre-Spanish but also in pre-Inca times.

Later Dr Heyerdahl was obliged to combat a theory advanced by certain of his opponents, who maintained that these objects had been brought to the Galapagos by pirates, who had plundered Peruvian graves. But we have no knowledge of any such desecration of Peruvian graves by pirates; moreover, the fragments found on the Galapagos were for the most part cooking vessels with no ornamentation. Such vessels could have held no more interest for buccaneers than the spindle whorl, the earthenware flute and the primitive cutting tools of flint and obsidian, which were also found on the Galapagos.

What is more, many of the fragments came from types of pottery which were characteristic only of the inhabitants of the coastal jungle of Ecuador, a district where pirates never strayed. There is also the further fact that these fragments from Peru and Ecuador were found at various places on various islands in the Galapagos Group, which would tend to support the comprehensive view which the experts in the National Museum in Washington finally arrived at: the archaeological finds on the Galapagos Islands furnish proof that South American Indians frequently visited these islands over a long period in pre-European times.

The lecture on which this article is based was entitled Archaeology in the Galapagos Islands *and was given before the Xth Pacific Science Congress at the University of Honolulu, Hawaii, which took place between August 21 and September 6, 1961.*

Archaeological investigations of the Galapagos group have until recently been neglected on the assumption that the area has been outside the range of aboriginal craft from either South America or Polynesia. It is noteworthy, however, that the Galapagos group was considered within the reach of aboriginal craft from Peru and Ecuador by observers from the sixteenth to the nineteenth century who were personally familiar with *guara*-operated balsa rafts, whereas the confidence in this remarkably ingenious water vehicle disappeared with the craft itself at the turn of the present century. Discussions on the possibility of pre-Spanish visits to the Galapagos have all admittedly been biassed by the writers' attitude toward balsa rafts.

When Miguel Cabello de Balboa and Pedro Sarmiento de Gamboa independently recorded the sixteenth-century Inca versions of Inca Tupac Yupanqui's enduring ocean voyage by balsa rafts to distant islands in the Pacific, they were both personally familiar with the type of rafts in question, which they also describe. Although Polynesia was still unknown to Europeans, Bishop de Berlanga had by then drifted so far out as to discover the Galapagos group, and Balboa suggested that these were perhaps the islands visited by the Inca's armada of rafts. Sarmiento de Gamboa, however, who was himself a keen navigator, inquired about the old sailing directions still preserved among some of the Peruvian raftsmen, and concluded that the inhabited islands known to the coastal raftsmen and only revisited by Inca Tupac's armada were in the South Pacific on a line west-south-west from Callao and at a distance of about 600 leguas (2,000 miles). He was so confident in this specific position that he talked the Viceroy into organizing the first Mendaña expedition which was actually sailing straight into the waters immediately surrounding Easter Island when Mendaña, to Gamboa's disgust, altered course and, instead, discovered other islands further away from Peru, first Melanesia, and, on a subsequent voyage, Polynesia.

The remarkable capacity of balsa sailing rafts and the expertness of their crews in navigation were unanimously praised by the contemporary chroniclers (see Chapter 5).

In 1619 the Dutch admiral Spilbergen had his whole fleet at Payta, Peru, supplied with dried fish from a sailing raft that had been out fishing for two months in the open ocean between Payta and the Galapagos group. The raft is illustrated with a native crew navigating with characteristic *guara* boards sunk between the logs fore and aft.

In 1680 the buccaneer Captain Sharp cruised in the local waters, trying as well to land in the Galapagos. His sailing vessel first followed the coast towards Peru, but turned into the open ocean off Punta Parina to avoid being detected by the Spaniards. Out there, where the impact of the Humboldt Current strikes out towards the Galapagos, and in the midst of what the buccaneers describe as a very stiff off-shore gale, they encountered a merchant balsa raft under sail. Their own pilot advised them not to meddle with its native crew, 'for it was very doubtful whether we should be able to come up with them or not. . . .' We learn from the same early buccaneer record that these aboriginal balsa rafts 'sail excellently well for the most part, and some of them are so big as to carry two hundred and fifty packs of meal from the valleys [of Peru] to Panama without wetting any of it.'[1]

In 1736 two Spanish naval officers, Juan and Ulloa, made the first technical study of the ingenious *guara* method which permitted the Indians to steer their rafts into the open ocean irrespective of the direction of the winds. Archaeological specimens of *guara*, dating back to pre-Inca times, are still preserved in desert graves from the Chimu area and as far south as Paracas and Ica in south central Peru, and, ethnographically, *guara* were commonly in use in northern Peru and Ecuador during Juan and Ulloa's investigations in the Guayas region. They reported that Ecuadorian balsa rafts, from seventy-five to ninety feet long, with entire families on board, and often a cargo of twenty to twenty-five tons, resisted the rapidity of the currents in the open ocean off Puna Island and northern Peru.[2]

Humboldt, Stevenson, and Paris continue to praise the amazing sailing abilities and seaworthiness of the balsa rafts surviving in the nineteenth century, and in 1832 Morrell reported seeing them fifty miles from land and able to 'beat to windward like a pilot boat . . .[3] Skogman on his world cruise in 1854 reported that deep sea-going balsa rafts even visited the distant Galapagos group, and he met them at sea navigating with bipod masts and long *guaras* sunk between the logs fore and aft.[4]

About the turn of the century the balsa rafts disappeared, and the directly associated and ingenious technique of *guara* navigation was ignored and forgotten. Archaeological *guara* were common, but often ignorantly labelled as agricultural tools, while writers who have realized it was a former navigational device have judged the *guara* to be a kind of rudder or a usual centre-board serving merely as a substitute to a keel to reduce the leeway on a raft.

At this time the first scholarly discussions of possible pre-Spanish visits to the Galapagos began. Historians of Inca history from Markham in 1907 to Means in 1942 have been so impressed by the obviously historic aspect of Inca Tupac's ocean voyage that they believed his raft armada to have visited the Galapagos, since these were the nearest oceanic islands. Hutchinson (1875) had by then termed the balsa raft a 'floating bundle of corkwood', and Means, although believing the Inca had reached the Galapagos, underestimated the raft which had taken him there, stating it was 'obviously a type of boat that would awake nothing but scorn in the breasts of shipbuilders of almost any other maritime people in the world'.

Lothrop (1932) made a more comprehensive study of the practical aspects of such a voyage, but was misled by an erroneous nineteenth-century source to believe that the Galapagos could never have been reached by balsa rafts. He referred to Byam (1850), an English traveller a century ago, who also saw a balsa beating against the wind off northern Peru, and who was told by his captain that these rafts could tack much closer into a contrary wind than a European whale-boat, but that they went slower through the water, and that in a few weeks they lost their buoyancy and had to be taken ashore to dry. From the latter statement Lothrop concluded that a balsa raft was unable to remain afloat at sea long enough to complete a voyage to the Galapagos, and he suggested that Tupac may rather have transported an army by sea and plundered the mainland to the north of Guayaquil.

Hornell (1946) wrote: 'Certainly no ordinary, untreated balsa raft could make a prolonged oversea voyage unless the Inca's seamen knew of an effective method of treating its absorbent logs with some kind of waterproofing composition. . . .' He found it likely, however, that the early Peruvians used some preparation of gum, resin or wax in some solvent to rub over the logs, and that this had helped the Inca rafts remain afloat to the Galapagos.

However, the erroneous verdict of the balsa rafts had now spread into the general Pacific literature, and deprived archaeologists of any stimulus to investigate the arid and uninhabited Galapagos. General visitors to the group, rather than being alerted to the possibility of finding pre-Inca vestiges, denied it absolutely. For example, von Hagen (1949) was led to assert: 'Whatever islands the Inca sailed to, he did not sail to the Galapagos.' He backed this assertion by citing presumably authoritative statements to the effect that the Andean seaboard dwellers were 'majestically inept' in marine matters, and concluded that any Inca landing in the Galapagos 'was a manifest impossibility'.

Subsequent events have shown that the modern verdict on balsa rafts has been erroneous and directly misleading. (In the two decades since the *Kon-Tiki* crossing in 1947, seven manned sailing rafts have left Peru and Ecuador propelled by the tradewinds and ocean currents. Five of them left the central coast of Peru and landed safely well inside Polynesia, whereas the remaining two, which started respectively on the north coast of Peru and the Guayaquil Bay area of Ecuador, landed in the Galapagos group, from where they later headed too far north and became becalmed in the doldrums north of the equator, having finally to be rescued because the illusive Counter-Equatorial Current proved useless in aiding them back to America.)[6]

Of more importance still, renewed experiments with the *guara* technique carried out by Estrada, Reed, Skjölsvold, and the writer in a balsa raft off Ecuador in 1953, resulted in the rediscovery of the functional system of this exceedingly ingenious navigational invention, verifying all the discredited early records to the effect that, through a correct interplay between *guara* fore and aft, the balsa will turn around and tack along any chosen course regardless of wind direction. Other experiments have shown that balsa rafts of green timber will retain perfect buoyancy for two years and probably more.

Accordingly, the Galapagos are located far within the feasible range of aboriginal Peruvian and Ecuadorian navigation.

With this knowledge in mind, an expedition organized to search for possible archaeological sites was led to the Galapagos by the writer in 1953, with E. K. Reed and A. Skjölsvold as participating archaeologists. No attempt was made to accomplish an exhaustive survey of the group or any single island, and areas for investigation were selected according to apparent geographical possibilities for aboriginal occupation combined with primitive landing facilities.

Four pre-Spanish occupation areas were located on three different islands. The largest site was on the plateau above James Bay on Santiago Island, where eight different aboriginal camp sites were located. A mountain ridge separated these from another site at Buccaneer Bay on the same island. The two other sites were encountered respectively at Whale Bay on Santa Cruz and at Black Beach on Floreana. An additional prehistoric site was located at Cabo Colorado on Santa Cruz by Mr J. C. Couffer and Mr C. Hall subsequent to the departure of our expedition.

The combined sites yielded in all 1961 aboriginal ceramic sherds, representing at least 131 pots, probably more. Of these, forty-four pots were identifiable with known ceramic wares from the coasts of Ecuador and northern Peru and thirteen additional pots are probably identifiable with ware from the same area. The remaining seventy-four pots represent aboriginal ware of which sixty-seven are unidentified merely because of insufficient characteristics in the limited material preserved, whereas seven pots are unidentifiable in spite of striking characteristics in the remaining sherds. Some sites produced only Peruvian sherds, while others yielded both Peruvian and Ecuadorian material. The ceramic types from the North Coast of Peru were studied by C. Evans and B. J. Meggers of the Smithsonian Institution, the United States National Museum.

La Plata Moulded ware is represented by three pots from two different localities in James Bay. San Juan Moulded is represented by one pot from another locality in James Bay. Queneto Polished Plain is represented by two pots from two different localities in James Bay. Tiahuanacoid ware is represented by three pots from two different localities in James Bay. San Nicolas Moulded is represented by one pot from James Bay. Tomaval Plain is represented by at least fifteen pots from James Bay, Buccaneer Bay, Whale Bay, and Black Beach. Another five pots from three sites were probable Tomaval Plain. Castillo Plain is represented by at least ten pots from James Bay, Whale Bay, and Black Beach. The latter site also produced a Mochica-type clay whistle. Another six pots were probable Castillo Plain. The other identifiable pots were characteristic plainware of the Guayas area in Ecuador. The material is reported in detail by Skjölsvold and the writer in Memoir no. 12 of the Society for American Archaeology.

With the exception of three pots of hitherto unknown non-European type, represented by 377 rim, handle, and body sherds of a very thin ware with thick, glossy red slip and complex form, no distinctly new types of ceramic were encountered. In other words, the material collected as such is in itself of scant scientific value. Its only importance is embodied in the fact that it has been left behind in the Galapagos Islands, from 600 to 1,000 miles from its identifiable mainland points of origins.

Naturally, then, the question arises: to what extent may some of these remains have found their way to these oceanic islands in post-Columbian times? It may be useful therefore to review very briefly the early history of the Galapagos.

The group was accidentally discovered by Europeans in 1535, when Bishop Tomás de Berlanga was caught by the strong off-shore set of the combined El Niño and Humboldt Current while sailing from Panama bound for Peru. A day was spent on one island and two on another in futile search for water, whereupon the Spaniards barely managed to tack back to Ecuador against the strong westbound currents. Coming from Panama, however, the Bishop and his party could hardly have brought aboriginal Peruvian or Ecuadorian ceramics to the Galapagos.

A second visit to the group occurred in 1546, when Captain Diego de Rivadeneira stole a ship at Arica, present Chile, and set sail for Guatemala. He rediscovered the Galapagos, and a brief and futile search for water was made on one of the smaller islands, whereupon the ship immediately left the group without setting foot ashore on any of the other islands. Under these circumstances this party could not have left the sherds under discussion.

We know that some extremely few other Spanish caravels sailed into the Galapagos Sea in the latter part of the sixteenth

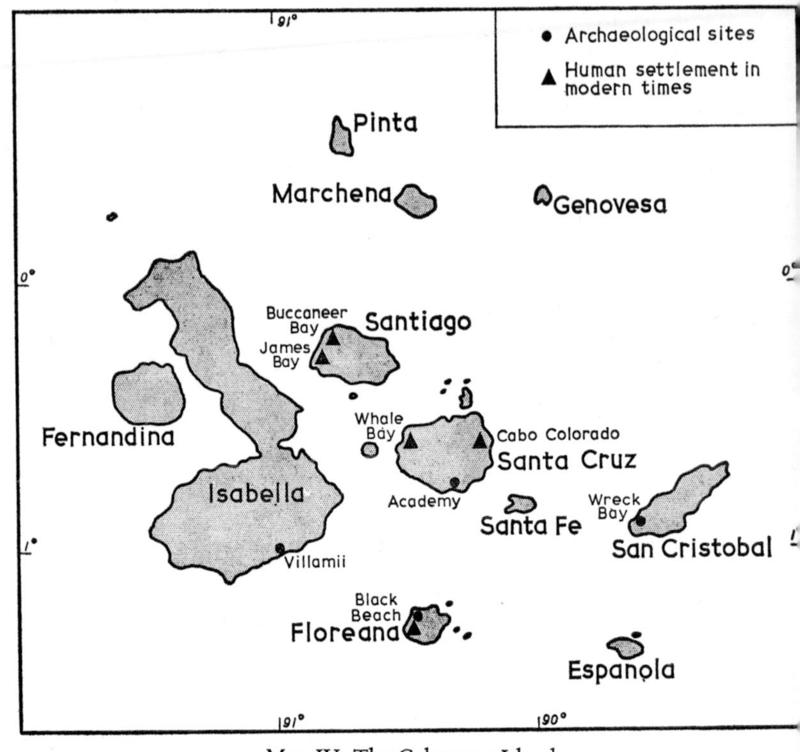

Map IV. The Galapagos Islands

century, but it is also known that they made no use of the islands, which they found to be desert and without fruit or water. It is possible that some of these caravels carried some Indians on board, and that some of the latter went ashore with ceramic pots, some of which were broken there, but it is hardly possible that they carried a minimum of 131 aboriginal pots ashore, and broke them all. Nor would they even have brought along such variety of ware, representing widely separated geographical regions and cultural epochs in aboriginal Peru and Ecuador.

Although first referred to as Galapagos on a map by Ortelius in 1570, this remote group in the treacherous Humboldt Current remained *Las Islas Encantadas* to the Spaniards, until the British buccaneers found it a convenient hide-out towards the end of the seventeenth century. As cited above, the buccaneer Captain Sharp, who described merchant balsa rafts carrying cargo between the valleys of Peru and Panama, attempted to call at the Galapagos in 1680, but the currents prevented him even from landing. Four years later, in 1684, Europeans got a brief foothold ashore for the first time, when a group including Cowley, Dampier, Davis, Wafer, Ringrose, and John Cook anchored for twelve days in James Bay on Santiago, while dividing their spoils. A British Museum manuscript by Cowley reflects the isolation of the group until then: '. . . wee sailed away to the Westwards to see if wee could find those Islands called the Galipoloes, which made the Spaniards Laugh at us telling us that they were inchanted Islands and that there was never any but Captaino Porialto that had ever seen them but could not come neare them to Anchor at them, and they were but Shadowes and noe reall Islands.'[7]

A curious incident is that this buccaneer party in 1684 stored a strange booty in James Bay, including eight tons of quince marmalade. The Viceroy of Peru detected their hide-out, all the huge jars were destroyed, and countless sherds of thick, wheel-made 'Spanish jars', first noted by Colnett in 1798,[8] are still found over all the local plateau. An interesting point is that some of these sherds were seen by us imbedded in the large black lava flow part of which covers a main portion of the local valley, thus showing that this major volcanic outburst on Santiago Island post-dates AD 1684.

These pioneering British buccaneers were followed in 1700 by a French expedition under Beauchesne-Gouin which remained a month, whereas the Spaniards arrived to explore and map the group under Torres in 1789, a visit which is recorded to be the first of any consequence by a Spaniard since Berlanga's brief visit of discovery.

There is, accordingly, no foundation for a hypothesis of post-European introduction of the aboriginal refuse in various sites in the Galapagos group. The identification by Evans and Meggers of the Peruvian ware shows that the local deposits consist of material dating back through Estero, La Plata, and Tomaval periods on the mainland, which means that refuse from at least two of the Galapagos sites are datable to Coastal Tiahuanaco times.

The discovery of sherds from a minimum of 131 aboriginal pots broken and left behind in the Galapagos implies a considerable human activity in precolonial times. It is quite obvious that our cursory survey failed to encounter all sites, and only uncovered part of the material still available. Owing to the general scarcity of soil on the coastal cliffs, much of the refuse is also washed into the sea. It is also clear that we are dealing with repeated visits rather than permanent habitation, as the latter would have left thicker deposits and a more homogenous ware. A local development would scarcely have succeeded in achieving an independent evolution in pottery that closely followed the mainland pattern from Castillo and Tomaval Plain ware through polychrome Tiahuanacoid, San Nicolas Moulded, and finally the three characteristic types of Chimu blackware as represented by Queneto Polished Plain and San Juan and La Plata Moulded. The refuse deposited represents ceramic types from the Guayas area of Ecuador down to the Casma Valley near the transition to the Central Coast of Peru, 1,000 miles away.

To summarize: The use of the Galapagos Islands probably as a fishing outpost is not a practice of European origin, but the continuation of an aboriginal pattern that appears to date at least as far back as the Coastal Tiahuanaco period in the Peruvian archaeological sequence.

CHAPTER 7

THE COCONUTS ON COCOS ISLAND

EDITORIAL NOTE. *Cocos Island, which is only 300 miles south-west of Costa Rica, was said by its first visitors to be a lovely isle, even though it was uninhabited. There was such a wealth of idyllic coconut groves that this volcanic island crowned by steep crags was named after them. Dr Heyerdahl's second archaeological expedition found the island completely overgrown by virgin forest; all that remained of its previous wealth are isolated palm trees. This transformation was the starting point in a chain of reasoning which led to the production of new circumstantial evidence for the nautical prowess of the ancient American tribes. The ethno-botanical ideas, which were presented in Chapter 3, are now further considered in the light of a concrete example.*

The one day visit which was made to the island in order to gain a general impression of the situation there was enough to persuade the members of the expedition of the desirability of future archaeological excavation.

This chapter is based on 'Notes on the Pre-European Coconut Groves on Cocos Island' which appeared as Part 17 of the 2nd volume of Reports of the Norwegian Archaeological Expedition to Easter Island and the East Pacific. (*Monograph of the School of American Research and the* Kon-Tiki *Museum, No. 24, Pt. 2, 1965.*)

This small and uninhabited oceanic island was visited by the expedition July 25–26, 1956, while en route from the Marquesas to Panama. Located at 5° 35′ N. and 87° 2′ W., the isolated island lies in mid-ocean between the Galapagos Islands and Costa Rica, about 450 miles north-east of the former and 300 miles south-west of the latter. Covering an area of about 45 square kilometres (18 sq. miles), the interior highlands rise to an altitude of 911 meters (*ca.* 3,000 feet), surrounded on all sides by vertical coastal cliffs, which attain a height of 100–200 meters around most of the island. Its geology has been described by Chubb.[1]

Only at the north end of the island have the cliffs been broken through by two permanent streams where mouths have become embayed to form, respectively, Wafer and Chatham bays, each with a mountaingirt valley running part way inland.

The rainfall is very heavy, creating innumerable waterfalls that leap directly from hanging valleys or from the tops of the cliffs into basins they have hollowed out of the shore shelf. The steep valley walls as well as the inland plateaux and ridges are covered by dense and impenetrable tropical jungles, and verdant moss and foliages cover most of the vertical cliffs around the coast. Penetration of the interior other than part way up the two main river-beds is impossible without clearing a passage.

The general vegetation has greatly changed since the island was first named and described by Europeans. Coconut palms are today so sparse that the name of Cocos Island seems truly far-fetched in comparison with other islands nearer to the Isthmus or farther out in the Pacific. That the island formerly merited its descriptive name, however, is apparent from the verbal accounts given to Captain Dampier by the contemporary Spanish discoverers. Dampier[2] writes:

'The Island Cocos is so named by the Spaniards, because there are abundance of Coco-nut Trees growing on it. They are not only in one or two places, but grow in great Groves, . . . This is the account that the *Spaniards* give of it, and I had the same also from Captain Eaton, who was there afterwards.'

Among the very first visitors was Captain Wafer[3] who called at the island in 1685, and whose name was given to the landing place:

'Our Men being tolerably well recover'd, we stood away to the Southward, and came to the Island *Cocos*, in 5 Deg. 15 Min. N. Lat. 'Tis so called from its Coco-Nuts, wherewith 'tis plentifully stor'd. 'Tis but a small Island, yet a pleasant one: For the Middle of the Island is a steep Hill, surrounded all about with a Plain, declining to the Sea. This Plain, and particularly the Valley where you go ashore, is thick set with Coco-nut Trees, which flourish here very finely, it being a rich and fruitful Soil. They grow also on the Skirts of the Hilly Ground in the Middle of the Isle, and scattering in Spots upon the Sides of it, very pleasantly. But that which contributes most to the Pleasure of the Place is, that a great many Springs of clear and sweet Water rising to the Top of the Hill, are there gathered in a deep large Bason or Pond, the top subsiding inwards quite round; and the Water having by this Means no Channel whereby to flow along, as in a Brook or River, it overflows the Verge of its Bason in several Places, and runs trickling down in many pretty Streams. In some Places of its overflowing, the rocky Sides of the Hill being more than perpendicular, and hanging over the Plain beneath, the Water pours down in a Cataract, as out of a Bucket, so as to leave a Space dry under the Spout, and form a kind of arch of water; which together with the Advantage of the Prospect, the near adjoining Coco-nut Trees, and the Freshness which the Falling Water gives the Air in this hot Climate, makes it a very charming Place, and deleightful to several of the senses at once.

'Our Men were very much pleas'd with the Entertainment this Island afforded them: And they also fill'd here all their Water-Casks; for here is excellent fresh Water in the Rivulet, which those little Cataracts form below in the Plain, and the Ship lay just at its Outlet into the Sea, where there was very good Riding: So that 'tis as commodious a Watering-place as any I have met with.

'Nor did we spare the Coco-nuts, eating what we would, and drinking the Milk, and carrying several Hundreds of them on board. Some or other of our Men went ashore every Day: And one Day among the rest, being minded to make themselves very merry, they went ashore and cut down a great many Coco-trees; from which they gather'd the Fruit, and drew about 20 Gallons of the Milk. Then they all sat down and drank Healths to the King, and Queen, & c. They drank an excessive Quantity; yet it did not end in Drunkenness: But however, that Sort of Liquor had so chilled and benumb'd their Nerves, that they could neither go nor stand: Nor could they return on board the Ship, without the Help of those who had not been Partakers in the Frolick: Nor did they recover it under 4 or 5 Days Time.'

The presence of these extensive pre-European coconut groves on Cocos Island will have to be explained through local activity of planters arriving either from America or Polynesia, or else through natural dispersal with the ocean current. All three hypotheses have been expounded. As so often in Pacific botany, the conclusions of botanists, of great importance to anthropological reconstructions, have to a great extent been founded on current ideas on human movements. The question of the origin of *Cocos nucifera* has not yet been finally settled by botanists.

The coconut palm was known to the Europeans from India and Indonesia long before the discovery of America. Apollonius of Tyana saw this palm in Hindustan at the beginning of the Christian era, when it was regarded as an Indian curiosity.[4] Its arrival in continental Asia from the Malay archipelago was probably not much before that time. The earliest Chinese descriptions are from the ninth century of our own era, and in Ceylon the introduction is ascribed to an almost historic epoch.[5]

When Columbus discovered Cuba on his first voyage to America, his Journal states that they found a beach with many very tall palms and 'a large nut of the kind belonging to India'. As the Spaniards next reached the Isthmus of Panama, Oviedo recorded in 1526: '... there is both in the firm land and the ilandes a certain tree called Cocus, ...' whereupon he proceeds to give a most detailed description of the coconut and its uses.[6]

Botanists of the seventeenth century often continued to regard the coconut palm as an Asiatic species, but in the nineteenth century, Martius (1823–50) and Grisebach (1872) arrived at the conclusion that the plant, for botanical reasons, must be of New World origin. De Candolle originally shared their view, but in *Origin of Cultivated Plants*[7] he altered his opinion and says that the question of origin remains obscure. His arguments are anticipatory of later discussions. He shows that strictly botanical evidence is in favour of an American origin, since eleven related species of the genus *Cocos* are American, whereas none at all is Asiatic. His arguments in favour of Asiatic origin, however, are of ethnographic and historic nature, such as its early pre-Columbian distribution, many local uses, multiplicity of forms, and a variety of names. The trade winds do drive floating objects from tropical America to tropical Asia, he admits, but: 'The inhabitants of the islands of Asia were far bolder navigators than the American Indians. It is very possible that canoes from the Asiatic Islands, containing a provision of coconuts, were thrown by tempests or false manœuvres on to the islands or the west coast of America. The converse is highly improbable.' De Candolle assumed that the coconut palms of Cocos Island might have been brought there by Polynesian voyagers.

Nothing fundamentally new has later been added to De Candolle's arguments in either direction. The small-fruited fossil species, *Cocos zeylandica*, discovered in the late Tertiary of northern New Zealand, is not a true coconut (*C. nucifera*) and, while entering into the species count, which still points overwhelmingly to America, it has no bearing on human migrations.[8]

A number of scholars have followed De Candolle in his theory on the spread of the coconut, resting heavily on ethnographic arguments, whereas others have equally consistently followed Martius and Grisebach in pointing to the absence of related species in Indonesia and continental Asia.[9] The most active defender of an American home of this species was probably Cook[10] who brought Cocos Island into the centre of the discussion:

'If the coconut could be submitted as a new natural object to a specialist familiar with all other known palms, he would without hesitation recognize it as a product of America, since all the score of related genera, including about three hundred species, are American. With equal confidence the specialist would assign the coco-nut to South America, because all other species of the genus Cocos are confined to that continent, and he would further locate it in the north-western portion of South America, because the wild species of Cocos of that region are much more similar to the coconut than are those of the Amazon Valley and eastern Brazil. Thus, from a purely biological standpoint, it is reasonable to suppose that the vigorous and productive coconut palms reported by Humboldt in the interior districts of Venezuela and Colombia may have been growing near the ancestral home of the species.' And: 'The uses of the coconut have been most highly developed in the Pacific islands because lack of other plants has compelled the inhabitants to depend on it more and more. Necessity has given rise to the multiplicity of uses, but the palm itself had to be brought from the only part of the world where such palms grew—South America.'

'The presence of large numbers of coconuts on Cocos Island in the time of Wafer (1685) and their subsequent disappearance should be considered as evidence that the island was formerly inhabited, or at least regularly visited, by the maritime natives of the adjacent mainland.' 'Even without a permanent population the coconuts may have been planted and cared for by natives of the mainland for use during fishing expeditions, a plan followed in some localities in the Malay region. The serious disturbances that followed the arrival of the Spaniards in the Panama region would naturally tend to interrupt such visits. Ethnologists may find in this hitherto unsuspected primitive occupation of Cocos Island an additional evidence of the maritime skill of the Indians of the Pacific coast of tropical America, and thus be more willing to consider the possibility of prehistoric communication between the shores of the American Continent and the Pacific islands.'

Hill[11] comments:

'Cook also attaches importance to the occurrence of coconut palms on Cocos Island. . . . After considering the various suggestions made by Cook, there seems to be nothing against the view, held by De Candolle, that the coconut palms on this island might have been brought there by early Polynesian voyagers. From this island, or more possibly by the landing of some of these early voyagers on the Pacific coast of Central America, they became established on the mainland and were in the course of time carried far and wide.'

Sauer[12] says: 'Probably only two palms in the New World were truly domesticated in aboriginal culture, the coconut and pejibaye. The others appear to be unmodified wild species, . . .' Stating that we have 'adequate and explicit' eyewitness evidence that the coconut palm was already established 'in great groves in Panama, Costa Rica, and on Cocos Island' when the first Spaniards arrived, he adds: 'It is possible that such groves of coconuts existed as far north as the coast of Jalisco [Mexico].' Further: 'The earliest known groves in the New World were in part along the coast and in part at some distance inland, but then, as now, apparently always as groves, and not scattered through the native jungle or brush.' Sauer takes no standpoint in the diverse opinions on the original home and prehistoric spread of the coconut palm, but says of Cook's approach to this problem. 'These studies are still the most significant contribution to the subject even though the conclusions are not sustained in toto.' And: 'The complete hypothesis of Cook has met with resistance, especially because it requires an ancient skill in navigation and because the coconut has little significance in American economy, as compared with that of Indonesia.'

The strongest opposition to Cook's views on the spread of American cultigens into the Pacific came for years from Merrill.[13] Carter's[14] comment on this controversy is that Cook was so intent on proving American origin of agriculture that he was incautious in some of his argumentation. Merrill, on the other hand, 'was either so incensed by Cook's special pleading or so allergic to trans-Pacific contacts (or both) that the violence of his reaction blinded him to the virtues of Cook's arguments'.

A few years after, Merrill,[15] too, listed for the first time the coconut palm as one of the plants that had crossed the Pacific through human agency prior to the arrival of Europeans. He now writes:

'That there were occasional and accidental associations between the peoples of Polynesia and America, and even occasional ones between the American Indians and the eastern Polynesian islands, actually must be accepted; but most certainly there was no "Pacific Regatta" in either direction.' And: '. . . it is most certain that the Polynesians introduced the coconut on the west coast of America between Panama and Ecuador, not too long before the Spaniards arrived'. 'The last word has not been yet said as to where the species originated nor as to when and how it attained its present wide distribution. One thing is certain: the coconut palm was thoroughly established along the wet Pacific coast of Panama and adjacent Columbia before the arrival of the Spaniards.'

The lack of general agreement on the centre of domestication of *Cocos nucifera* is without direct importance to the problem under discussion, as is the fact that the majority of botanical opinion increasingly inclines to the view that America is its homeland. Whereas the opinion on origin and domestication is still divided, general agreement has been reached on the fact that the coconut palm was thoroughly established both on the mainland to the east and the islands to the west of Cocos Island prior to the arrival of Europeans. Therefore, the geographic distribution pattern alone cannot answer the question as to whence the coconut palm spread to Cocos Island in pre-Spanish times.

The enduring buoyancy of a coconut has never been doubted.

Its ability to germinate upon oceanic drift depends solely on the resistance of the eyes to sea-water and fouling organisms, and the topography, soil conditions, and existing density of vegetation on the terminal end of the drift voyage. The suspected need of human aid in the spreading of this useful palm over major ocean stretches was further accentuated when Edmondson (1941), experimenting in Hawaii, and the writer, making independent tests in 1947 during the *Kon-Tiki* raft voyage, discovered that sea-water slowly penetrates the area of the coconut eyes, causing micro-organisms to affect and destroy the germinating ability after a couple of months at sea, even if the seed is granted ideal conditions by being properly planted in a cleared area and in sand mixed with soil. Self propagation of coconut palms across such extensive spans of ocean as that which separates Polynesia from Cocos Island is therefore highly improbable. If the coconut palm reached Cocos Island on a direct dispersal from Polynesia, this must have happened through the agency of man.

The nearest possible Polynesian source from which coconuts could have been brought to Cocos Island is the Marquesas group. It would be reasonable to ask if there is any legendary memory within Polynesia as to the existence of any island east of the Marquesas. On the remarkably correct chart made for Captain Cook by Tupia of Ulitea, there is actually marked to the east of the Marquesas group an unidentified island named Utu [in English spelling *Ootoo*]. Captain Porter[16] was also independently told by natives of the Marquesas that there was an island to the east of their group, known to them as Utupu [Ootoopoo]. He writes:

'None of our navigators have yet discovered an island of that name, so situated; but in examining the chart of *Tupia*, . . . we find nearly in the place assigned by the natives of *Nooaheevah* [Nukuhiva] to Ootoopoo an island called Ootoo . . . this chart, although not drawn with the accuracy which could be expected from our hydrographers, was, nevertheless, constructed by Sir Joseph Banks, under the direction of Tupia, and was of great assistance to Cook and other navigators in discovering the islands he has named. . . . Of the existence of Ootoo or Ootoopoo there cannot be a doubt; Tupia received such information from the accounts of other navigators as enabled him to give it a position on his chart nearly fifty years ago, and the position now ascribed to it by Gattenewa [of Nukuhiva], differs little from that of Tupia.'

What is remarkable, however, is that the only memory recorded by Porter as associated with the easterly island was that this was the place from which the early Marquesans had originally obtained the coconut: 'The coco-nut tree, as I before remarked, was said to have been brought from Ootoopoo, an island which is supposed by the natives to be situated somewhere to the windward of La Magdalena.'[17]

There is, accordingly, no traditional support for a theory that Polynesian voyagers established coconut groves on Cocos Island, on the contrary, they do claim to have received the first coconuts by voyagers from an island to the east of the Marquesas.

Whereas the penetration of sea-water and micro-organisms would have damaged the eyes of a floating Polynesian coconut long before any current could have carried it 4,000 miles to the vicinity of Cocos Island or the New World, the three hundred miles separating the same island from the American mainland is within feasible range for natural drift. This, admittedly, is the more apparent since the winds are favourable, in contrast to the doldrums and confused eddies of the equatorial belt farther west.

What remains to be ascertained, then, is whether coconuts arriving through drift from the American mainland would encounter conditions permitting natural propagation on the shores of Cocos Island. The object of our brief visit to the island was to become acquainted with such details of the local topography and vegetation as is not available in the sparse published literature and rather sketchy maps.

A cruise around the island showed clearly that the high cliffs and steeply rising sides surrounding the entire coast of the fortress-like island would not give the least foothold for a seaborn coconut anywhere except at the two narrow river-mouths of Chatham and Wafer bay on the north coast. The expedition ship anchored off Chatham bay, and landings were effected both there and at Wafer bay.

The change of vegetation since Wafer's visit in 1685 was so pronounced that it would have been tempting to suspect that he had visited another island, had he not given an exact position which precludes confusion. Whereas Wafer's party found the island 'a pleasant one', and apparently had no difficulties in visiting the plain surrounding hilly ground in the middle of the island, our party had considerable difficulty in penetrating merely the overgrown valley where Wafer landed.

During the single day we had at our disposal on the island, none of the expedition party reached farther than to the steeply rising walls at the bottom of Wafer valley, or the ridges near the landing. We also noted that Chubb,[18] during his geological survey of the island, states that he was unable to explore the interior sufficiently to investigate the existence of a possible crater lake such as suggested by Wafer's description. Undoubtedly, a determined effort to cut a trail uphill and inland is fully possible, but it does not appear that this was needed during the early visit of the Englishmen, when the inland plain and the valley where they went ashore were 'thick set with Coco-nut Trees, which flourished here very finely. . . .'

Unquestionably, the jungle had, during more than two and a half centuries, encroached upon the existing coconut groves, and recaptured the former clearings. Our reconnaissance, with a view inland, revealed that, in the elevated interior forest area, and at widely separated points on top of the jungle-covered ridges, were crests of single isolated coconut palms, kilometres apart. Some very few isolated palms also emerged from the compact roof of the jungle in the interior of the two valleys. Only a very small piece of level land next to the beach in Wafer bay preserved a cluster of coconut palms, large enough to be considered a very small grove. This area near the beach showed evidence of recent clearing, and some of the palms had been chopped down, possibly during the brief local establishment of a Costa Rican penal colony.

If we were not provided with Wafer's original description of extensive former inland groves, it might have been tempting to suspect that, on Cocos Island, *Cocos nucifera* was not a littoral plant but a truly wild palm that grew spontaneously as an integral part of the rain forest. This, then, would have been the only locality where *Cocos nucifera* was found to be grown in a truly wild state, and the question of New World origin would have been satisfactorily answered.

The cluster of palms near the beach in Wafer bay might well have been the result of drifts from Costa Rica or the Panama region prior to Wafer's visit. From this beach the coconut palms might have spread inland along the bottom of the ravine through natural propagation, provided the present jungle was not there to arrest and suppress the progress of the extremely sun-craving young palms. A professional copra planter, A. Kinander, who accompanied the expedition group from the Society Islands, was thoroughly convinced that sprouting coconuts would be completely choked by the dense canopy before it would be able to penetrate the local jungle roof. In fact, nowhere in the underbrush did we observe a sprouting nut or young palm, except in the clearing near the beach. All the sporadic coconut palms observed were old and had their lofty crests above the close grasp of the jungle. The dense jungle of the inland plateaux and ridges are separated from the two lowland ravines by steep mountain sides completely surrounding these two blind alleys in such a way that a falling coconut could not without human aid reach the lofty interior parts of the island, where Wafer had seen extensive groves and we still witnessed individual palm crests far apart.

Unless we ignore Wafer's report, and assume that *Cocos nucifera* is a wild plant native to Cocos Island, it seems evident enough that man had cleared considerable areas in the bottom of the ravines and on the interior plateaux and ridges, utilizing the clearings for coconut plantations of quite considerable extent or distribution prior to the arrival of Europeans.

Apart from the coconut palms, many of which were seen from a distance, no other evidence immediately suggesting aboriginal activity was seen during our brief visit, with the possible exception of Chatham bay. Excavations were not attempted. A more detailed inquiry near the mouths of the two rivers and in the overgrown interior highland may be worth while for future archeological investigators.

At Chatham bay two very small and disconnected beaches were separated by a high and dominating promontory, with its steep sides and artificially levelled crest all covered by an extremely dense grass taller than a man and interwoven with creepers. This vegetation formed a marked contrast with the surrounding jungle, and the evidence of former human activity at this point was evident, although it might have been of post-European date. The tall and strong grass of this steep slope could only be penetrated with the aid of machetes, and several small terraces formed by cut and fill were encountered *en route*. Their function remains obscure, unless they were constructed to support small dwellings. The levelled and equally overgrown summit plateau, which measured about 60 m. in width and about twice as much in length, could not have been formed without a considerable amount of labour. A vertical cut about four meters high through the rock and soil on the inland side formed the western limit of the levelled area, and the masses removed along the originally narrow crest had been utilized as fill to widen the artificial plateau. On the north side a deep and wide ravine came up the slope and cut into the plateau like a natural moat. In a few quite recent clearings old sheets of corrugated iron and other remains of camp sites revealed the activities of recent visitors, possibly modern treasure hunters.

At the time of our visit it was known that a Costa Rican penal colony had been stationed for a short period on the island, and it seemed possible that the terraced promontory was the site of this establishment, which seemed the only plausible alternative to aboriginal activity. It has later been ascertained that the penal colony was on the island from 1878 to 1881, and that it was not located in Chatham bay, but in Wafer bay. In a report of a local visit, Prof. Anastacio Alfaro[19] writes:

'On the day of our disembarkation in Chatham bay, March 14, my brother Rafael and I accompanied Sr. Pittier in his passage overland to Wafer bay, where the houses of the colony were. . . . On the path we followed were frequently seen the tracks of great pigs which had been in confinement in two hogsties in Wafer bay. . . . The greatest number of tracks were seen in the pasturages and coffee and cashew-nut plantations close to the site where the house of the old penitentiary was, of which scarcely remain some rotten timber and some rusty sheets of corrugated iron.'

There is no known record of agricultural or constructural activity in the area of Chatham bay,[20] and with the penetentiary located in Wafer bay it is difficult to ascribe the major project of levelling and terracing the Chatham bay promontory to the historic period. Other than the period of the penal colony, and the brief and casual visits by treasure hunters, Cocos Island has been reported as uninhabited by all visitors throughout its historic period.

Test pits from old and recent treasure hunting parties were encountered everywhere near the beaches of Chatham and Wafer bays, and in clearings near the outlets of the two rivers. The latter adventurers, paying a set fee to the Costa Rican government, were authorized to dig for a supposed treasure, and have been the only regular visitors to the island, which, due to its impenetrable jungle and precipitous coastline, has held no other commercial or tourist attraction. All accessible terrain in the limited level area near the landing places had been dug and re-dug, some of it even blown up by dynamite, and wild pigs have continuously aided in the havoc by turning over loose stones and mouldy soil, destroying all original features.

At Wafer bay, some fifty metres from the sandy beach and

parallel to the foot of the hill, the remains of two short rows of boulders deeply set in the soil had escaped destruction, but the surrounding soil was too disturbed to permit identification of the original function, which was difficult to associate with any practical purposes. The penal colony, however, had been near this locality.

To ascertain the degree of antiquity of the artificial features in Chatham and Wafer bays would require more time than allotted to our brief call upon an already overcrowded archaeological programme, and sufficient evidence to suggest prehistoric human occupancy of the island was deduced only from the many vestiges of former clearings for coconut plantations.

In conclusion, prehistoric planters may have found the location of Cocos Island sufficiently favourable and important to be worthy of the vast amount of labour spent in clearing the natural jungle for the planting of coconuts. It is difficult to see why Polynesians, unless involved in considerable trade and contact with the Panama region, of which there is little or no evidence, should go to this amount of labour on an island some four thousand miles or more from their own settlements. It is equally difficult to see why American Indians should go to the same trouble in clearing large jungle areas on a remotely off-shore island, when the coconut was of secondary importance in their own diet, and there was ample space for clearing in their own jungle territory on the mainland coast.

It is the opinion of the present writer that the extensive coconut groves on early Cocos Island would be of little use to anyone unless we assume that the island was either densely inhabited or else favourably located for voyagers who frequented the area and were in need of convenient supplies. From personal experience I can testify that no natural product is better suited as provision for primitive seafarers than newly picked, scarcely mature coconuts, which will withstand almost any amount of water-spray and rough storage, and yet yield fresh liquid and substantial food for weeks of navigation. According to Ferdon's personal observations, large quantities of husked green coconuts were still being used as the primary water supply for ocean-going *Imbabura* dugouts sailing from northern Esmeraldas, Ecuador, to Tumaco and Buenaventura, Colombia, in 1943 (verbal statement); and green coconuts were immediately brought as the only water supply by the Ecuadorian raftsmen who floated Watzinger and the writer down stream to Guayaquil in 1947 with the balsa logs for the *Kon-Tiki*.

In recent years there has been an increasing tendency among archaeologists to explain the rapidly accumulating evidence of cultural contact between Guatemala and Ecuador or North Peru as the result of direct oversea trade between the two areas.[21] A glance at the map (p. 196) will show that Cocos Island is located direct on the sailing route between them. The presence of archaeology in the Galapagos group,[22] the aboriginal knowledge of *guara* navigation with sailing rafts in north-western South America,[23] and the dearth of concurring archaeology in the coastal bend in between, are strong arguments in favour of Cocos Island having an ideal location as a port of call and supply station providing water and coconuts to pre-Spanish navigators in the open sea off Panama.

The moist climatic conditions, with verdant rain forest and rapid accumulation of humus, typifying Cocos Island, are markedly different from the dry and barren conditions in the Galapagos. Future archaeological work will probably have to be organized as a major task, with the disturbed areas near the river mouths, and the level highland areas once covered by coconut groves, being the regions most likely to produce possible archaeological sites.

CHAPTER 8

THE STATUES OF EASTER ISLAND

EDITORIAL NOTE. *Those readers who are acquainted with* Aku-Aku *(which is the best introduction for the layman to the following chapters) will no doubt also welcome this opportunity of refreshing their memories of Easter Island, whose archaeological exploration was the primary objective of the 1955–56 expedition. The account presented here is based on the systematic geographical and historical survey of the island complied by Dr Heyerdahl and printed under the title* An Introduction to Easter Island *in the first volume of the Reports of the Norwegian Archaeological Expedition. The survey itself was too detailed for inclusion in this book.*

Easter Island lies 2,300 miles off the coast of Peru and Northern Chile and 1,200 miles from Pitcairn Island, the nearest of the East Polynesian Group. It first came into being as a result of a series of volcanic eruptions from the seabed. Craters, fields of lava and a remarkable variety of volcanic rocks bear witness to the island's geological past. But on Easter Island—in contrast to the Galapagos Islands—this formative process had been completed long before the arrival of the first human beings. Of the numerous caves, to which Dr Heyerdahl makes frequent reference, many were formed by bubbles of volcanic gas.

This small island, which measures 22 by 11 kilometres, is roughly triangular in shape. Many parts of the coast are steeply shelved and in front of the cliff face there are only a few small islets. There are no coral reefs. The climate is sub-tropical (longitude 109 degrees 25 minutes, latitude only 27 degrees 8 minutes) and the rainfall adequate. Flora and fauna are nonetheless distinctly sparse, a fact which was said to be due to the great distances which separate the island both from the mainland and from the Polynesian archipelago. The almost total absence of trees

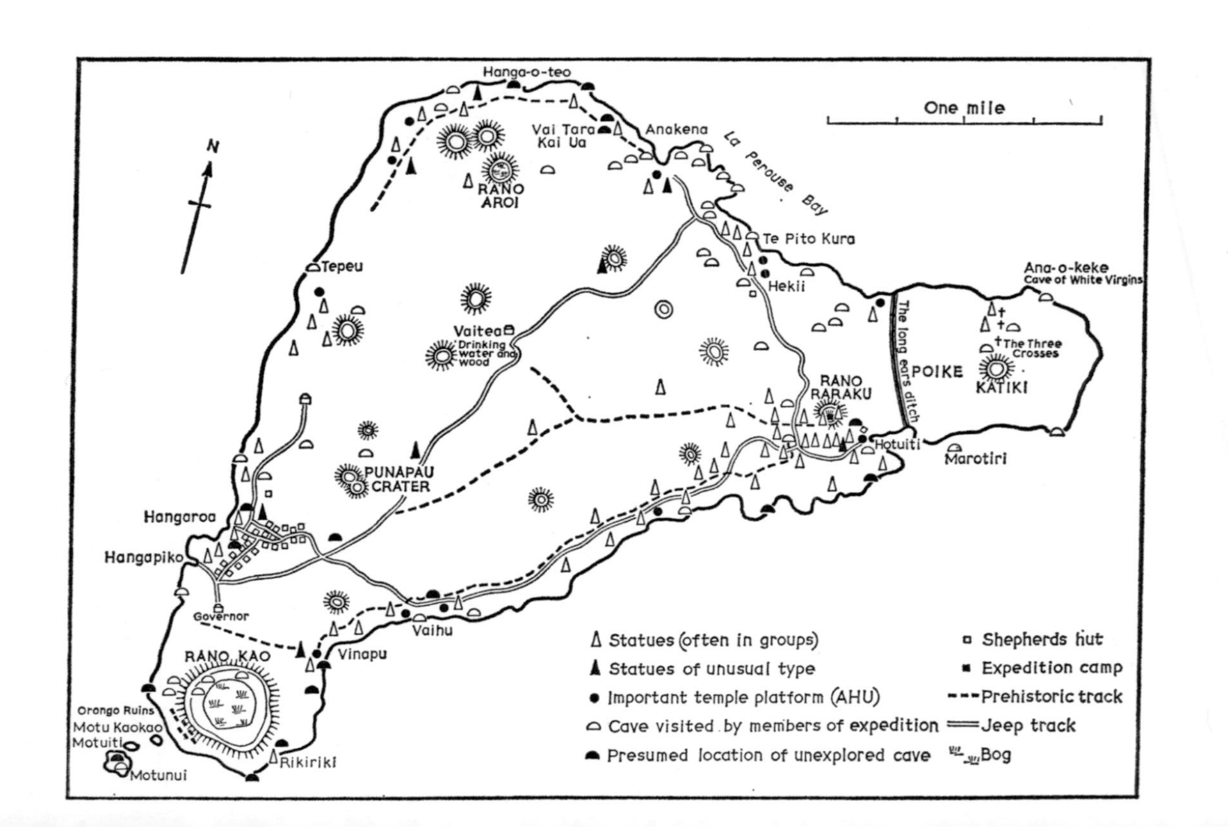

One mile
N
Hanga-o-teo
Vai Tara
Kai Ua
Anakena
La Perouse Bay
RANO
AROI
Te Pito Kura
Hekii
Tepeu
Ana-o-keke
Cave of White Virgins
The Three
Crosses
Vaitea
Drinking
water and
wood
The long ears ditch
POIKE
KATIKI
RANO
RARAKU
Hotuiti
Marotiri
PUNAPAU
CRATER
Hangaroa
Hangapiko
Governor
Vaihu
Vinapu
RANO KAO
Orongo Ruins
Motu Kaokao
Motuiti
Motunui
Rikiriki
Statues (often in groups)
Statues of unusual type
Important temple platform (AHU)
Cave visited by members of expedition
Presumed location of unexplored cave
Shepherds hut
Expedition camp
Prehistoric track
Jeep track
Bog

is especially characteristic—although when the expedition investigated this particular phenomenon it produced a surprising result.

A number of plants and animals, including species essential to agriculture, were introduced by man. This we already know about from Dr Heyerdahl's Aku-Aku. *In the following pages he furnishes further information.*

The dearth of plant and animal life is in marked contrast to the great wealth of stone objects which bear witness to the island's past. Stone house foundations were found in various places and buildings made entirely of stone were described by the first Europeans to discover the island. But it was the human statues of truly megalithic proportions which made the greatest impression on these explorers. The earliest drawings show the statues standing on stone platforms which contained burial vaults. The giant statues had red stone wigs balanced on their heads. The production and transportation of these statues were clarified by Dr Heyerdahl in 1956. The achievements of the indigenous people of Easter Island, who worked within the limitations imposed by Stone Age techniques, were quite tremendous.

Later visitors discovered that the last of these statues had been toppled from their platforms, the ahus, *in the course of the wars which had been fought between the different tribes living in the island. During these wars the richest areas of the island must have changed hands many times over. The last great battle took place in the interval between two different visits by Europeans. In the end the island drifted into an unhappy phase, in which attacks by Europeans and slave-hunting all but extirpated the native population.*

But this period of internal warfare is well documented and so we naturally ask ourselves how it was that, with war constantly flaring up between the rival groups of tribes, the people of the island found the time and the leisure to erect so many and such enormous statues.

The natives themselves say that the statues were all erected in a time of peace, when their own ancestors were the servants of another race. They describe this other race in detail. Confirmation of the existence on an island relatively close to South America of a racial group which differed widely from the Polynesians would afford valuable support to Dr Heyerdahl's theory.

Shortly before, however, Métraux, the prominent French ethnologist, who died recently, had declared that the native reports were legends which simply served to explain something which had become incomprehensible in a period of decline. The phenomenon, he said, was a common one. According to Dr Métraux the original Easter Islanders had been Polynesians, who, after settling on this treeless island, from which—since they lacked the materials with which to make seagoing vessels—they could scarcely hope to escape, had achieved great things in order to make their lives on this barren stage worth living. These achievements ranged from the erection of the statues, which were prompted by impulses similar to those observed on certain other islands in the East Polynesian Group, to wars, which were prompted by ambition. Dr. Métraux even considers the emergence of a system of writing, the only one in the whole of Polynesia, within this context.

His thesis was accepted, not only because it fitted what appeared to be the facts, but also because it was in harmony with the leanings of certain ethnological schools. To-day there is a marked tendency to seek the explanatory principle underlying the formation of a given culture in the environment (this concept is capable of a very broad interpretation) and to pay as little attention as possible to historical development, which it is in any case often almost impossible to establish in the case of primitive peoples.

But the whole of Dr Métraux's artificial construction fell to the ground when Dr Heyerdahl's expedition introduced trained archaeologists to proceed with systematic excavations. These were: E. N. Ferdon, then permanent archaeologist at the Museum of New Mexico, now Assistant Director of the State Museum of Arizona, USA; W. Mulloy, then already Professor and Head of the Department of Anthropology at the University of Wyoming, USA; A. Skjölsvold, then Director of the Department of Archaeology at the Stavanger Museum, to-day Chief Archaeologist in the Collection of Antiquities at the University of Oslo, Norway; C. S. Smith, then already Professor and Head of the Department of Anthropology at the University of Kansas, USA; and finally G. Figueroa and E. Sanchez, both archaeologists at the University of Santiago, Chile.

The archaeologists on the Norwegian expedition showed that Dr

Métraux's conception was surely incomplete. It restricted reality by setting up what was virtually an artificial horizon.

There was a previous population on the island and it underwent a development which lasted for more than a thousand years. The starting point of this development was a culture which was distinctly non-Polynesian in character. It was only later that points of resemblance with the people on the other islands began to emerge as a result of what would appear to have been a gradual process of assimilation that was promoted by sporadic immigration. And it was only then that those elements appeared which Dr Métraux regarded as the original Polynesian stock. In the final period of development the Polynesian element gained the ascendency. This process became even more pronounced at the time of the transportations and immigrations which took place under the Europeans (it was primarily the Christian Mission which introduced new people to the island). And so a solution was found to the mystery of Easter Island which fitted in very well with the theory put forward by Dr Heyerdahl.

Of the many articles which Dr Heyerdahl has devoted to Easter Island and its problems we now present the one in which he deals with the statues. These statues are more than mere symbols, for their creation and subsequent fate clearly reflect the lives and chronological sequence of different peoples which inhabited the island. The man who discovers the source of the inspiration which led to their erection holds the key to the mystery of Easter Island.

The article shows the further development of Dr Heyerdahl's ideas since he recorded his first impressions in Aku-Aku. *It also provides us with a synopsis of the history of research into the island and its close connection with the tragic events which destroyed the last island culture.*

This chapter is based on a lecture given before the Swedish Society for Anthropology and Geography in Stockholm which was printed in 1962 under the title 'Statuene på Paskeöen: problem og resultat' in the journal Ymer, *Book 2, pp. 108–24.*

Geography and archaeology each offers specific peculiarities on Easter Island which, when seen together, form a paradoxical combination. Although dry and barren and less accessible than any other island in the Pacific Ocean, this isolated speck of land contains more outstanding archaeological monuments crowding its restricted surface than any of the larger, truly fertile and more readily accessible islands and archipelagos farther west. It is of course to be expected, as a consequence of the geographical layout, that the Pacific Ocean with its countless inhabitable islands widely scattered over half the earth's surface, present more problems to the anthropologist than any other ocean. But it seems rather unjustified, and even unreasonable, that the most remote and inaccessible of all the innumerable local islands should become the very one among them to attract the attention of the entire world due to the presence of an abundance of spectacular archaeological remains. It is perhaps as surprising that this island, with its geographical and archaeological key position in the Pacific, had never been subject to systematic archaeological excavation prior to the arrival of the expedition to be dealt with below.

When lay brother Eugène Eyraud was landed on Easter Island in 1864 as the first European to settle ashore, he and his missionary colleagues soon managed to turn the last page of the aboriginal Easter Island history. With him the curtain dropped for the final tragic act of one of the strangest dramas ever to take place on a lonely oceanic isle, thousands of miles from any eye-witness.

The first acts were not seen by any outsiders. The drama was well into the final act before the audience reached Easter Island. We depend on archaeology and other means of prehistoric research to reconstruct the main features of Easter Island's period of greatness. Although not previously known, today we may state with certainty that nothing but the last phases of a tragic postscript was witnessed on Easter Island when the first European stepped ashore for some hours to become hailed by us as the island discoverer. This was the Dutch Admiral Jacob Roggeveen who approached Easter Island in the evening twilight of Easter day, 1722.[1]

As the sun rose above the sea next morning the Dutchmen brought their ships closer inshore, and observed people of different skin colours who had lit fires in front of some enormous statues standing in a row. The people ashore were squatting in front of the statues, with their heads bent while they alternately raised and lowered their arms. When the sun rose they prostrated themselves on the ground facing the sunrise, their fires still flickering in front of the stone colossi. The statues were even at that early time so old and eroded that Roggeveen with his bare fingers could break off a piece from the decomposed surface, wherefore he concluded that the giant figures were simply moulded from clay and soil mixed with pebbles. The Dutchmen left the island after a single day's visit.

Nearly fifty years passed before the Spaniard Felipe Gonzalez and his companions rediscovered the same island from Peru in 1770. The Spaniards were not satisfied by merely watching the eroded surface of the statues, they hit them with pickaxes so hard that the monuments flew sparks, and thus discovered that the statues had been carved from a very hard and heavy stone. They recorded that the thirty feet tall monolithic statues carried large cylinders of a different stone at the summit of their heads, on top of which lay human bones, wherefore they concluded that the monuments served the double function of being gods as well as receptacles for burials.

The Dutch and Spanish visitors concurred in pointing out that Easter Island was lacking timber and ropes large enough for erecting such colossal monuments. As stated, Roggeveen believed he possessed the solution to this riddle by arguing that the statues were made from clay, but the Spaniards disproved this assertion and brought to a wondering world the first reports of the huge monoliths in human form which stood erect in great numbers among primitive aborigines on a barren island short of forest, thousands of miles from the rest of the world. During the two centuries to follow the mystery of Easter Island solidified its grip on the human imagination throughout the world.

Four years after the Spaniards, Captain James Cook reached

the same island, and after him the French arrived under La Pérouse. All of these early visitors emphasized very strongly that the Easter Island monuments represented relics of extremely great antiquity, and they stressed that the poor and primitive contemporary island population had had no hand in their production. Cook was the first to note that many of the statues lay overturned on the ground next to their destroyed altar-like masonry foundations, and he pointed out that the contemporary islanders did not even keep up maintenance of the old structures.

Cook brought with him a Polynesian interpreter who had the greatest difficulties in understanding the local language, but he understood sufficiently to learn that the numerous statues represented deceased kings and chiefs. There was no further evidence of worship of the stone images such as witnessed by the Dutch, but the English and French concurred with the Spaniards in finding skeletal remains strewn about the statues, and therefore described them as funeral monuments.

Regardless of whatever the statues might have signified to the contemporary population, they continued to overthrow them from their old foundation platforms. The Russian Lisjanskij was the next visitor to Easter Island, in 1804. He reported that four statues still stood erect on their masonry platforms in Cook's Bay, and seven more in Vinapu. Twelve years later, in 1816, another Russian expedition called under Kotzebue. He found all the statues in Cook's Bay overturned, and out of the seven in Vinapu only two remained standing.

The last report on statues still balancing erect on top of their masonry platforms derived from Du Petit-Thouars who observed nine standing statues north of Cook's Bay in 1838. During the subsequent years they, too, were overthrown, and when Eugéne Eyraud arrived in 1864 to settle ashore as the first European, there was not a single statue left erect on the numerous local image platforms; all were overturned from their former foundations, many were broken during the fall, and the large stone cylinders they had supported on their heads had often tumbled like heavy steam rollers down the nearby slopes. The only standing statues that none had managed to capsize were the unfinished ones that Captain Cook's advanced party had first discovered partly buried in the descending silt at the foot of the overgrown and long abandoned image quarries on the slopes of the Rano Raraku crater.

Eyraud and his missionary colleagues were the first to learn to converse with the aborigines on Easter Island. They attempted through direct queries to get the answers to the riddles of Easter Island. The contemporary natives could give no better explanation than narrating that once upon a time all the statues had walked by themselves to the various *ahu*-platforms, on orders from the creator god, Makemake.

Seven years later the missionaries were once more driven from the island. Shortly afterwards the Tahitian sheep ranger Tati Salmon arrived, and subsequently a Chilean meteorologist, Martinez. Both of them were to live in intimate contact with the local aborigines, and through them some highly interesting traditions have survived.[2]

According to the earliest recorded traditional memories, the ancestors of the surviving population were distinguished as 'Short-ears' and had reached Easter Island with a chief named Tuu-ko-ihu who came from another island far towards the west, *i.e.* in the direction of Polynesia proper. On their arrival they had discovered that this island was already inhabited by a different people, the 'Long-ears'. This earlier population had reached the island under the leadership of the true discoverer, King Hotu Matua, who had come from the opposite direction, from the east, reaching Easter Island upon a 60 days oversea voyage from a huge country in the direction of the sunrise, where it was so hot that the vegetation in certain seasons was scorched and shrivelled up by the burning sun. The Long-ears, arriving first, had raised *moai*, or statues, ever since they landed with Hotu Matua; while the Short-ears, arriving subsequently, had assisted the Long-ears for two hundred years in building *ahu* walls and long-eared statues, until the peaceful coexistence ended in a disastrous civil war where the Short-ears massacred all but one of the Long-eared men in a pyre lit in an extensive defensive trench across the Poike peninsula. The one Long-ear was saved to continue the propagation of his kin. During the period that followed these massacres, the tribal feuds continued among the surviving Short-ears on Easter Island, and all the statues were gradually overthrown through undermining and pulling with ropes, according to the same traditions.

In 1914 archaeology was introduced on Easter Island when the English Mrs Catherine Scoresby Routledge arrived with a private yacht. No professional archaeologist participated in the expedition, and Mrs Routledge's own scientific notes were unfortunately lost prior to publication, but her popular book on the visit contains most important scientific observations and has so far been the principal source of general information on Easter Island archaeology.[3]

Twenty years later, in 1934, the island was visited by a Franco-Belgian scientific team, but unfortunately the French archaeologist died *en route* and his Belgian colleague Henri Lavachery was therefore left alone to study the vast quantity of prehistoric remains. He concentrated all his efforts on his own important discovery of a large number of hitherto unknown petroglyphs,[4] whereas the French ethnologist Alfred Métraux made an equally important study of the ethnology of Easter Island.[5] As had been the case with the Routledge party the Franco-Belgian expedition, too, neglected systematic excavation as it was a general opinion that Easter Island had no humus that might cover up unknown evidence from the past, since the barren grass-covered island had no forest.

Routledge suspected that an unknown and later exterminated people, possibly of Melanesian origin, had inhabited Easter Island prior to the present Polynesians, but Métraux and Lavachery rejected this suspicion, and asserted categorically that no human beings had visited this isolated island before the Polynesians arrived about the twelfth or thirteenth century AD. They advanced the theory subsequently generally accepted that the inhabitants of Easter Island had started erecting giant statues because they had reached a naked and barren island where they found no material permitting them to continue with wood carving which was practised in the other forest-covered islands in Polynesia proper. This theory seemed sufficiently plausible to discourage further archaeologists from visiting the island, and stratigraphic excavations were never attempted.

Had Easter Island been as barren as assumed by the anthropologists at the time the first aboriginal voyagers settled ashore? This was one of the most important questions we hoped to answer by bringing modern equipment for pollen borings to the island.

To-day I am glad to report the first summaric result of the pollen analytic borings which we undertook around the crater lakes in the extinct volcanoes Rano Raraku and Rano Kao on Easter Island, and which produced a rich paleo-botanical material which is analysed by Professor Olof H. Selling at the National Museum of Natural History in Stockholm. It has been possible to reveal that the natural environment found by the first people to settle on Easter Island was different from the one we know to-day, different from the one that has been characteristic of Easter Island ever since its discovery on Easter day 1722. This island which is now poor in vegetation had formerly a richer flora including even trees of families which have later become extinct on Easter Island. Between the trees were bushes of various species. It was a vegetation which in certain ways must have resembled the original lowland vegetation on for instance the leeboard side of Hawaii or the Marquesas islands, although many species differed. Before the stone sculptors started their work in the crater walls of the now completely barren volcano Rano Raraku, the slopes of this volcano must have been covered by palms of a species unknown on the island today, the pollen of which filled every cubic millimetre of the bottom strata in the crater lake. One of the most surprising discoveries was the pollen of a shrub related to the coniferae (*Ephedra*), which was so far unknown throughout the Pacific, but which is closely related to, if not directly identical with, a South American species. Dr Selling has found pollen of the same species in the Marquesas islands as well.

It is possible to follow the gradual disappearance of this original vegetation on Easter Island in our series of 8 metres (*c.* 26 feet). deep borings containing identifiable pollen. While trees still surrounded the old and open crater lakes, the American fresh water species *Polygonom amphibium* suddenly appeared for the first time, probably brought as a medical plant from the coast of South America by the first settlers to arrive, and from now on soot particles began to appear in certain pollen strata simultaneously with a rapid impoverishment of the original flora. The soot particles are probably vestiges of vegetation fires sending clouds of smoke across the crater lakes. These fires were evidently caused by the aboriginal immigrants as the population increased and they needed land for settlement and cultivation, subsequently perhaps even as deliberate ravage during warfare. The destruction became so effective that in the upper strata hardly anything survived from the original vegetation, whereas grass and ferns gradually intruded the barren landscape.

This local scene-shifting on Easter Island represents a discovery that has more than botanical interest. It shows that we have had wrong conceptions concerning life on Easter Island during the first local period of cultural bloom. The stone masons that went ashore and began to cut and join enormous blocks of basalt had not reached a barren and grass-covered island where they could drag their enormous monoliths about the plains at will, they first had to cut down trees and clear land to get access to quarries and freedom of movement for themselves and their monuments. This discovery immediately invalidates the long accepted argument that the people of Easter Island began to carve the mountain side because they landed on an island where they could not carve in wood as on the other islands in Polynesia. The environment in which the first Easter Islanders settled was essentially the same as on the other islands, and it is accordingly the more striking to note the peculiar cultural characteristics which, as shown below, they brought along at their first arrival.

Another and entirely different contention, also generally accepted, had made problems pertaining to the statues of Easter

Island unduly complicated while it proved to be based on a series of misinterpretations of one of the observations by the Routledge expedition. Routledge had sand and gravel removed from the lower portion of some of the statues partly buried in silt at the foot of the Rano Raraku quarries. She wrote in her narrative of the expedition that a particular one among these statues proved to have a pointed base, and she assumed that it was carved in this way because it was intended to be set in the earth and not to balance on top of an *ahu*-platform like all the other statues, scattered about the island.[6] Métraux and Lavachery interpreted this discovery to mean that each of the sixty statues which stood partly buried in the silt at the foot of the quarries had a similarly pointed base. Without further examination Métraux writes in his monograph on the ethnology of Easter Island that there are two fundamentally different classes of statues on the island, one with a peg-shaped base, to be set in the ground, the other with a wide flat base, carved to stand free on top of one of the enormous *ahu* walls of the island.[7]

Sir Peter Buck, the leading authority on Polynesian culture, who never visited the island, increased the confusion by believing that Métraux meant that even the 170 unfinished statues which lay exposed in the open shelves of the quarry proper had pointed bases and accordingly had been designed to be set in the earth. One single statue, which actually proved to be merely defective, had thus become 230 statues in the published literature, and in 'Vikings of the Sunrise', the most diffused publication on Polynesian problems, Buck draws the following far-reaching conclusion: 'The images with pegged bases were never intended to be placed on the stone platforms of the temples, but were to be erected in the ground as secular objects to ornament the landscape and mark the boundaries of districts and highways. Because the images remaining in the quarry all had pegged bases, it would appear that the orders for the platforms had been filled and that the people had embarked on a scheme of highway decoration....'[8]

It was a simple matter for our expedition to ascertain that not a single one among all the statues that remained in the quarries had a pointed base in spite of the fact that Arne Skjölsvold,[9] who led the investigations in Rano Raraku, discovered about fifty statues in addition to those that had been known so far. When we initiated the excavations of the partly buried giants standing at the foot of the quarries, we discovered that each of these, too, except one defective specimen, had a full body with long arms and slender fingers placed at the lower end next to a wide and flat base, which was in no way pointed to be sunk in the ground, but on the contrary was designed to stand fully exposed on a platform.

Our investigations disclosed that all the 600 or so statues so far known on Easter Island represented one basically homogenous type including unfinished specimens representing different stages of work on that same type. The statues could be recognized and divided into four main stages of production. In the first stage the statue had its back still attached to the crater wall, whereas the front and the sides were partly or completely finished, sometimes to the very last detail, a perfect surface polish; only the concavities of the eyes were lacking. In the second stage the back, too, was detached and the statue was temporarily erected in the refuse silt at the foot of the quarries in such a manner that the back could be carved into shape and receive its final polish including in some instances symbols in low relief. On the steep slopes of the volcano the statue was readily tipped upright with its wide flat base standing on an excavated terrace crudely paved with unworked lava boulders. At the third stage, when the statue was completely finished except for the concavities of the eyes, it was laid down once more and transported away from the volcano along the paved roads, and only at the fourth stage when it was lifted on to its specific *ahu*, did the statue receive its excavated eye concavities with, in addition, a large red stone cylinder on top of its head, referred to by the local natives as *pukao*, or the 'top-knot'. With this discovery the entire problem was simplified; none of the statues represented landscape or highway decoration. The stone carvers had been engaged in a single enterprise: to produce homogeneous monuments with red 'top-knots', erected side by side on *ahu*-platforms around the entire coast.

But other problems of Easter Island still remained to be solved. While Skjölsvold directed the excavations at Rano Raraku, William Mulloy[10] and Carlyle Smith[11] began the first systematic investigations and excavations of the *ahu* ruins on which the statues had formerly been standing. They discovered that the masonry covered earlier structures which had subsequently been partly rebuilt and partly extended and strengthened. The original constructions had not been designed to carry heavy monuments, and in addition they represented a different architecture and a different technique of stone work.

As excavations advanced it was clearly seen in the various stratified structures that the prehistory of Easter Island could be divided into three distinctly separate epochs, which the archaeologists denominated as Early, Middle and Late Periods. In the Early Period there was no production of true *ahu* images. The temples were altar-like elevations of very large, mutually dissimilar, and most precisely cut and joined stones, and they had their façade towards the ocean, and a sunken court on the inland side. Astronomically oriented, they were constructed by highly specialized stone-masons who studied the annual movements of the sun and incorporated these observations in their religious architecture. During the Early Period different types of smaller sculptures were erected on the ground inside the temple court.

Not until the next cultural period, the Middle one, were the well known type of giant statues carved and placed on terraced stone platforms. By this time the original temple constructions had been partly destroyed or altered, and superimposed by a different masonry to form the later well-known *ahu*. These *ahu* were built without astronomical orientation, and were designed for the first time to support rows of giant monuments, which had their backs to the ocean while facing the old inland court.

The third and final period, the Late one, was initiated by the sudden end of all work in the Rano Raraku quarries, and the

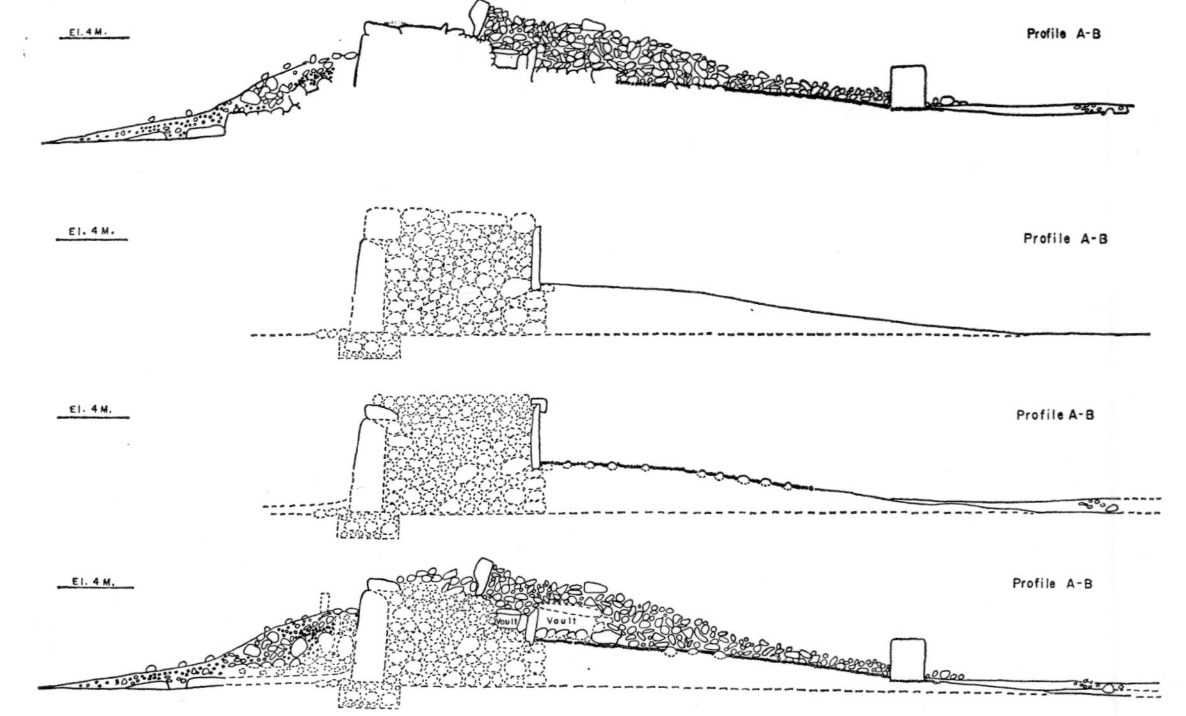

Structural development of an *ahu* as demonstrated on *ahu* No. 2 in Vinapu; reconstructions made after the 1955/56 excavations.

First drawing: Condition of *ahu* prior to excavation (sectional view); Second drawing: Reconstruction of tranverse section of *ahu* at close of Early Period; Third drawing: Reconstruction of transverse section of *ahu* at close of Middle Period; Fourth drawing: Reconstruction of tranverse section of *ahu* at close of Late Period. Note the burial vaults which simultaneous interruption of the transport of statues along the roads. During this period the statues were one by one overthrown from the *ahu* and a primitive sect of wood carvers, lacking abilities in megalithic sculpture or masonry, buried the dead underneath piles of unworked boulders thrown together in formless heaps on top of the destroyed *ahu*, or in large multi-burial chambers roughly constructed underneath the bellies or faces of the overturned giants. The Late Period was everywhere marked by decadence, warfare, and destruction. Thousands of spear points of obsidian characterize all strata of this final period, whereas weapons did not occur, or were extremely rare, in each of the two earlier periods.

Whereas the architects and image sculptors in the Middle Period concentrated all their energy and interest in erecting their enormous monuments of Rano Raraku tuff, the earliest population on Easter Island, in the Early Period, were far better experts in the art of shaping and fitting together vast polished blocks of hard basalt, forming their altar-like religious structures.

This discovery not only disclosed a stratification of heterogenous cultures on Easter Island, but caused the local evolution previously hypothesized for Easter Island to be reversed. Routledge[12] had merely suspected that the Easter Island *ahu* had been rebuilt, and that they originally had been of a different appearance, but Métraux[13] and Lavachery[14] had rejected this and claimed that the Easter Island culture was homogeneous and without any sign of stratification. All observers had concurred in pointing out the striking similarity existing between the largest and best preserved *ahu* façades on Easter Island and corresponding structures in the Andean area. They had assumed, however, that the best walls on Easter Island were of late date and represented the result of independent local evolution. Polynesians were assumed to have reached Easter Island ignorant of this specialized type of stone masonry, but, as time passed on this tree-less island, they gradually became the equals of the foremost experts in South America in carving and joining megalithic blocks. This picture, however, now suddenly had to be reversed. It was the first settlers on Easter Island who had started to build the best walls of the same type as found in Peru and the adjoining sections of the Andean area, after first clearing the trees away from quarries and temple sites. The people in the second period did not master this specialized masonry technique at all, and merely erected their giant statues. Furthermore, the third period showed no signs of evolution in any type of stonework and was typified by decadence, mass destruction, and deterioration of everything created by the two earlier cultures. Hence the situation was completely reversed, and an influence from the characteristic stone carving cultures of South America could no longer be excluded, since there was no other region in the entire Pacific from where the earliest immigrants might have brought along their already developed knowledge of this specialized stone masonry.

The heterogeneous nature of the Easter Island cultures proved to extend beyond religious structures and burial customs, and to include the secular dwellings of the aboriginal population. Upon the initial surveys of the local surface archaeology, Edwin Ferdon[15] began to suspect that there were vestiges of entirely different types of houses in various sections of the island. Ethnologists and archaeologists had so far agreed that, apart from underground caves, there existed only one house type on Easter Island: *i.e.*, long, lenticular reed houses resembling a boat turned upside down. A frame of arched poles supporting a thatch of reed and

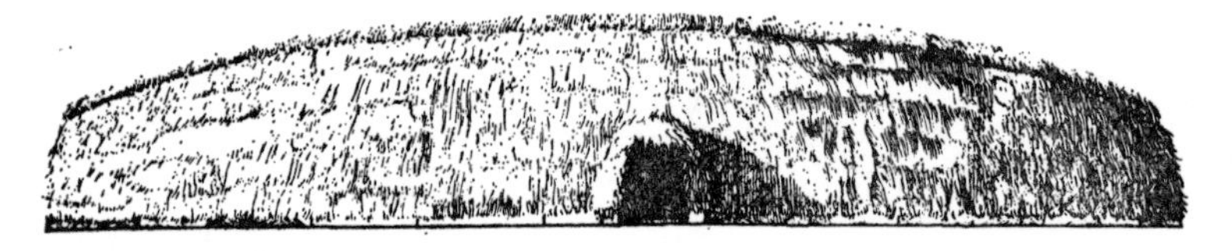

Reconstruction of an elongated reed hut shaped like an upturned boat

grass was set into narrow drill holes in a boat-shaped foundation wall of dressed stone. The expedition's archaeologists first excavated a considerable number of these house foundations, all of which proved to originate from the time immediately before or after European contact, i.e. within the span of the Late Period. Subsequently Ferdon[16] and Skjölsvold[17] turned their attention to certain circular masonry walls remaining in large quantities in various sections of the island. Earlier ethnologists and archaeologists had accepted the information from the present population, which claimed that these structures represented the garden plots of their ancestors, and that the circular walls were built to protect the *mahute* plantations against the wind on the barren island. The Swedish botanist Carl Skottsberg who visited Easter Island in 1917 confirmed that the circular walls were used as garden plots, and he illustrated them as such in a publication on the flora of Easter Island,[18] later adopted and reproduced in Métraux's work on the ethnology of the island.[19] Our excavations revealed that this function of the circular walls was entirely secondary, and began in the Late Period of the island. Actually these structures represented the thick masonry walls of circular houses which had been covered by reed roof, and through excavations we found the floor filled with refuse and tools from a long-lasting occupation. A cooking place was located either in the centre of the floor or immediately outside the wall, and in one instance Skjölsvold encountered an oven filled with charred remains from baked sweet potatoes and sugar cane that had been abandoned in a hurry. Radio carbon datings disclosed that this utterly non-Polynesian house type had been in use on Easter Island during the Middle Period, when the large statues were erected, and in some cases this type continued into the Late Period together with the entirely unrelated boat-shaped pole-and-thatch dwellings. Ferdon, who was personally well familiar with South American archaeology, recognized these circular stone houses—unknown throughout Polynesia—as concurring with a type characteristic for the adjacent slopes of the Andean region directly facing Easter Island.

Our excavations on the plains of Vinapu disclosed a third, and also entirely divergent house type, with a solid slab roof covered with earth. It was secondarily used for the burial of a decapitated person. An entire village of similar stone houses remains on the summit of the highest volcano on Easter Island, and has been known ever since the arrival of the missionaries as the most important ceremonial centre, named Orongo. In this village the whole population of the island gathered each year at the period around spring equinox. They then sat here as spectators and judges during the annual competition where the participants swam with small reed boats to the bird islets off the coast in search of the first egg, while struggling to gain the title as the sacred birdman of the year.

Routledge and Métraux had both paid considerable attention to this peculiar annual ceremony at Orongo which had continued well into historic times, but no one had regarded the stone houses at Orongo as more than a purely ceremonial village unique to Easter Island, since this form of crypt-like masonry dwelling was unknown throughout the rest of the Pacific. Ferdon[20] while directing extensive excavations at Orongo, encountered the same cultural stratification at this site, and discovered that these peculiar houses, which had survived as ceremonial structures on top of the volcano, actually represented the continuation of a building form which had previously served as dwellings in the Early Period on Easter Island. This corbelled house type, too, unknown elsewhere in Polynesia, could be retraced to ancient Peru and to adjacent sections in the Andean area.

Projecting barren rocks in the Orongo village were entirely covered by birdmen carved in relief. They represented the local well-known figures with human bodies and limbs, but with bird heads and long hooked beaks. One birdman was embracing a realistic incision of the sun. In excavating some of the low and frequently caved-in ceremonial houses, Ferdon[21] discovered several unknown fresco paintings on the smooth slabs of the walls and ceilings. The dominating motives were reed boats, double-bladed paddles, and the 'weeping eye' motive characteristic of American high cultures. None of these traits reappear elsewhere in Polynesia. Ferdon's stratigraphic excavations disclosed that, with short interruptions, this village on top of the highest of Easter Island's volcanoes had represented a ceremonial centre throughout the three cultural epochs of the island. At the bottom layer he exposed a solar observatory which registered the sun's position at sunrise both at December and June solstices and at equinox. Sun symbols which included petroglyphs as well as a small, hitherto unknown statue of entirely aberrant type were exposed in direct association with the solar observatory. The sun-measuring structure represents the first of its kind ever known inside Polynesia. Once more it was necessary to turn to the Andean area for comparable features.

In the Middle Period the beautifully faced and fitted masonry of the solar observatory was superimposed by an *ahu*-like temple structure. The stone house village was now constructed in the intimate vicinity, and the birdman cult was suddenly introduced in a ready developed form and mixed with the earlier sun worship, gradually to displace the latter almost entirely. A comparatively small, beautifully executed stone statue of dark basalt [historically known as Hoa-haka-mana-ia, now in the British Museum] which probably represented the sun god during the Early Period, and carried the sun and rainbow symbols in relief on its back, was at the beginning of the Middle Period incorporated as inventory inside the largest and most important stone house in the cult centre of Orongo village. Primitive birdmen and double-bladed paddles were secondarily cut across the original sun symbols on its back, an observation that had first been made by Routledge, although she had not attempted an explanation. This important Orongo statue differed from all the well-known statues of Easter Island in having a convex rather than flat base, and in not being carved from the usual yellowish-grey tuff, but rather from hard, black basalt, wherefore it could not have come from the stone quarries in Rano Raraku. As later will be shown this statue may possibly represent the prototype for all the *ahu* images subsequently erected during the Middle Period on the island.

As excavations advanced on the lowland below, statues of hitherto unknown types were encountered there as well. Some of these earliest statues were found deliberately broken, and their fragments were used as masonry blocks in the walls of the circular stone houses of the Middle Period. Others were dishonoured by being set face into the wall as mere construction blocks in the crude *ahu*-platform supporting the large statues of the Middle Period. Some of these early, demolished and dishonoured statues, were carved from dark basalt like the statue at Orongo, others were of various types of red scorea, and still others of the yellowish-grey tuff from Rano Raraku. However, all were unlike the common type of Easter Island statue so far known.

These newly discovered statues from the earliest period could be divided into four different types, out of which three were not previously known in the Pacific area.[22] Type I was represented by flattish, rectangular stone heads without body, like the head in the sun temple at Orongo; Type II was a pillar-like unrealistic figure with full body and rounded rectangular cross-section; and Type III was a most realistic kneeling figure with goatee beard, which sits on its heels with the hands clasping the projecting knees and gazing slightly upwards. All three types, unknown on the other islands, belong to three categories of monuments shown by Bennett[23] to be characteristic for the pre-Inca cult centre at Tiahuanaco in the Andes. Type IV of Easter Island, however, is a conventional truncated bust, with long fingers meeting in front above the groin. It seems to be an entirely local art conception, approaching noticeably that of the subsequently homogenous type of giant statue of Easter Island's Middle Period.

The correspondences in detail between the kneeling statue from Easter Island's earliest period, excavated by Skjölsvold from the refuse silt covering the oldest part of the Rano Raraku quarry, and the kneeling statues in Tiahuanaco which are dated by Bennett to the earliest pre-Classic period in this important culture centre, is so marked that Skjölsvold concludes[24] that it can scarcely be put down to chance, 'but must be ascribed to a close relationship, which implies that there is a connection between these two examples of ancient stone sculptures in the Andes and on Easter Island. . . .'

Type IV in the earliest period of Easter Island, *i.e.* the stiff, truncated busts, which have no obvious counterpart either in Polynesia or in South America, is apparently a locally developed variant from the later part of the Early Period. Its primitive prototypes are to be found in red scorea as well as in black basalt and in its final classic form it is represented during the Early Period by the smallish basalt statue from the stone house at Orongo. All the statues mass-produced during the next epoch of Easter Island, the Middle Period, are carefully executed repetitions of the traits of this smallish statue. They are merely carved to much larger proportions, sculptured from Rano Raraku tuff rather than from harder basalt, and have a flat base rather than a convex one to be able to balance on top of *ahu*.

Against the background of these diverging types it is possible to visualize a clear evolution behind the Easter Island *ahu* monuments. So far only the homogeneous giants from the Middle Period had been known, and they had no similarity whatsoever to statues either on the islands to the west or to those on the continent to the east. This was one of the reasons why their isolated occurrence on Easter Island had created such an enigmatic problem. The new discoveries show that, during a still earlier period hitherto not recognized, the earliest population had experimented with various qualities of rock on Easter Island, and with various types of anthropomorphic monuments, out of which three were well-known early forms in the most important culture centre on the nearest mainland to the east. In addition, a fourth and purely local Easter Island form had been developed on the island towards the end of the Early Period. The latter type was subsequently unanimously accepted as a norm for the several hundreds of giant monuments erected on the rebuilt *ahu* during Easter Island's next epoch.

Why was this? To obtain an explanation for the evolution and the peculiar subsequent local stagnation demonstrated by the archaeologists, we have to resort to assistance from ethnology. There is no reason to doubt the verbal information from the surviving aborigines of the Late Period, as obtained by Cook,

La Pérouse, and other earlier visitors while several of the statues still stood erect on their *ahu*: the statues represented no idols in the true sense of the word, they were monuments of kings, chiefs, and other important persons, set up on or near their burial sites. Each single statue was erected in honour of a certain deceased person, and even subsequent to the tribal feuds which involved the overturning of the statues during the Late Period, several among the old natives could remember the name of specific *ariki* or chiefs represented by certain statues. Our excavations revealed that prepared tombs and other burials were restricted to the *ahu* during the very last part of the Middle and the entire Late Period, while we found no evidence of burial in the astronomically oriented altar-like structures without statues in the Early Period. On the other hand, crematories with multi-burials were excavated in front of the façade of the finely dressed and fitted and astronomically oriented temple walls. This, too, was a surprising discovery since it was not previously known that cremation had ever been part of the burial tradition on Easter Island.

Another question naturally emerges. Why did all these powerful chiefs in the Middle Period of Easter Island want their mortuary monument to be stereotype copies of the smaller model in the Orongo stone house? Was this Orongo statue of some particular significance? To the latter question we may undoubtedly answer affirmatively. The smallish statue in Orongo with its convex base was not merely the only one on the island to be erected on the floor inside a building, but it was also the only statue on the entire island to survive all the three cultural periods without anybody attempting to overturn or damage it. In addition, it was the only statue on Easter Island which was known to have been the object of worship and religious attention from the entire island population irrespective of family or tribe. All the other statues belonged to separate families together with the *ahu* on which they stood, and for this reason they were all overthrown and demolished as an act of revenge in the savage tribal feuds of the Late Period. Even some of the unfinished statues standing at the foot of the Rano Raraku quarries had deep scars from attempts at decapitation by aborigines who had been unable to overturn them because most of their bodies were deeply buried in silt. But that one statue in the Orongo stone house was left untouched throughout the entire Middle and Late Periods, and it was still the object of fertility worship in important rituals for all the inter-combatant tribes on the island when the missionaries arrived in the later half of the last century. Our excavations revealed that large quantities of charcoal from ceremonial fires were accumulated in front of the entrance to the large central stone house which had enshrined this important little basalt figure.

In all probability this statue in the house on top of the highest island volcano had originally been associated with the local sun rituals during the Early Period. It had the symbol of the sun and the rainbow carved in relief on its back until it was moved into a newly constructed stone house during the Middle Period when the birdman symbols of this new period were crudely added to the earlier symbols on its back. Yet it resumed its central position in the cult of the island as a sort of creator or fertility god, worshipped at ceremonies during the annual spring equinox. Whereas the other statues, which the people of the Middle Period now began to erect on family *ahu*, represented deceased human individuals, the Orongo statue continued to be a common deity venerated by all families on the island. In view of the fact that the kings of Easter Island, as elsewhere in Polynesia as well as in Peru, counted their descent in direct line from the supreme deity, it is understandable that they wished their portrait to resemble to the greatest possible extent this divine ancestor-model known to them all through the common ceremonial centre at Orongo. While maintaining the physical resemblance to this omnipotent progenitor the only divergency they allowed themselves in their own sculpture was, to an ever increasing extent, to make their mortuary monuments as large and as towering as possible to show off their own power and importance.

With regards to the long renowned giant images of Easter Island, their chronological position in the complicated local history did now seem clear: they all belong to the Middle Period of the island; their inspiration can be traced locally in older and smaller monuments from the Early Period; their production terminated abruptly at the end of the Middle Period; and they were finally, without respect, overthrown from their burial *ahu* during the Late Period which extended well into historic times.

The natural question now emerging is whether it may be possible to identify the approximate dates for these three heterogeneous culture periods. In an attempt to answer this question the expedition archaeologists did their utmost to detect organic remains associated with the various period of building structures and serviceable for radio carbon datings. All previous attempts to date the earliest settlement on Easter Island were based on the legendary genealogies of local kings recorded from aboriginal island informants. The earliest royal lines, which could be counted as far as 57 generations back to the first immigrant king, had been discarded in favour of a shorter royal line comprising between 20 and 30 names, since it was generally assumed that Easter Island had been discovered from Asia and for this reason and due to its geographical position nearest South America would have to be the last occupied island in the entire Pacific.

Routledge[25] believed that two unrelated immigrations had reached Easter Island, of which the Polynesians arrived about AD 1400. Knoche[26] similarly suspected that two different people had reached the island, the first between the eleventh and the thirteenth centuries AD. Lavachery[27] and Métraux[28] both held the opinion that the Easter Island culture was young and homogenous, and that the island remained undiscovered until between the twelfth and the thirteenth centuries AD. Englert[29] shared the view that there was apparent evidence of a local conglomeration of two cultures, but he believed that neither of them had reached the lonely Easter Island until about AD 1575. Our excavations indicated that Easter Island was inhabited by a considerable population occupied in constructing extensive defensive works as early as about AD 380 plus or minus 100 years. This was more than a millennium earlier than anybody had hitherto suspected, and represented the earliest date up to that time reported for any island inside Polynesia. It was possible through the discovery of stratigraphically placed charcoal and bone material to produce seventeen different carbon-14 datings from Easter Island. Two of the most interesting derived from the ditch of legendary renown which divided the peninsula Poike from the rest of the island. According to claims consistently repeated by the island population from the time of the earliest historic records, this was a man-made ditch where the final decisive battle between their own ancestors and the 'Long-ears' had taken place, and in which the latter were cremated alive in a defensive pyre at the bottom of the nearly two-mile-long trench.

However, geologists had so far concurred with anthropologists in suspecting that the Poike ditch was but a natural geological depression,[30] and both Métraux and Lavachery[31] had concluded that the natives invented the tradition to explain a natural geological phenomenon. In consequence the associated tradition about the 'Long-ears' and the 'Short-ears' was also commonly discarded as a mere fable. As soon as we sank test pits into the Poike ditch, however, it was found that it contained large quantities of charcoal from a huge and intensive fire, and the carbon-14 tests dated this fire to about AD 1676 plus or minus 100 years. This was in remarkable agreement with AD 1680, the date estimated in advance by Father Sebastian Englert[32] on the basis of aboriginal tradition which insisted that the battle along the Poike pyre took place twelve generations ago.

Smith's excavations[33] showed that this defensive ditch was not built in haste during the feuds resulting in the pyre of about 1680: when this pyre was lit the ditch was already an old structure partly blown full of aeolian dust and drifting sand. Smith found obsidian flakes at the very bottom of the ditch. The latter proved to be a natural depression which had once been artificially transformed and extended to a depth of twelve to fifteen feet and a width of thirty-five to forty feet, while being nearly two miles long, severing the peninsula from the rest of the island. Gravel and débris dug up from the bottom of the ditch had been used to build a defensive embankment along its up-hill side, and during this procedure charcoal from a fire had become imbedded beneath the displaced débris, disclosing that preparations for defence of the precipitous peninsula were in progress as early as about AD 380. This would seem to indicate local feuds at that early period, or perhaps, rather, a fear of pursuit by enemies from the original homeland, since references to such a pursuit actually form an important element in all the earliest legends of the island.

At the foot of the Rano Raraku quarries lay a row of grass-covered hillocks and sloping ridges, which had hitherto been considered natural formations. On top of one of the highest of these was the foundation wall of what had been the sacred dwelling of the annually elected birdman, a structure which Routledge and Métraux associated with the earliest rituals of Easter Island. Skjölsvold's excavations[34] revealed that these hillocks, too, were entirely artificial. They constituted enormous rubble mounds composed of débris, broken basalt picks, and ashes transported down from the quarries located in the mountain side above. Remains from early fires imbedded in this refuse made possible the dating of a portion of the Middle Period when work still went on in the Rano Raraku quarries; and the discovery of the true nature of these artificial hillocks disclosed that the superimposed house of the birdman was a purely secondary contrivance, built during the Late Period on top of refuse from the Middle Period, after the abandonment of work in the image quarries.

As a result of the various radio carbon dates the expedition archaeologists established the following three cultural periods for Easter Island:[35] the Early Period from some time prior to AD 380 to about 1100, the Middle Period from about 1100 to 1680, and the Late Period from 1680 to the full introduction of Christianity in 1868.

To obtain a basis for chronological and typological comparisons, our expedition, upon leaving Easter Island, visited Pitcairn and Raivavae, as well as Hivaoa and Nukuhiva in the Marquesas group, the only four islands in the whole Pacific outside of Easter Island where monumental stone statues occur.

Pitcairn and Raivavae formerly possessed a limited number of smaller statues evidently of comparatively recent origins, and no attempts have ever been made to suggest that these had inspired the ancient sculptors of Easter Island. On the other hand, Buck[36] and others have thought to see the primitive forerunners of the sophisticated Easter Island monuments in the roughly man-sized but plump and diabolic stone images on two temple sites in the Marquesas, the latter group being located as far from Easter Island towards the north-west as is Peru towards the east. Skjölsvold succeeded in finding charcoal at two different levels underneath the masonry platform supporting the Hivaoa statues, and Mulloy and Ferdon[38] excavated charcoal below the foundations of the Nukuhiva statues, revealing that the Marquesan monuments were erected as recently as during the thirteenth, fourteenth, and fifteenth centuries respectively: i.e., far into the Middle Period of Easter Island. The possibility that they might have inspired the first artists of Easter Island may therefore be disregarded, since, as we have seen, statuary art was an important element during Easter Island's Early Period, too, which antedated the Marquesan images by a millenium. Stylistically or chronologically these thirteenth- to fifteenth-century Marquesan products could not have influenced the mass producers of *ahu* images even during Easter Island's Middle Period, since it began about AD 1100. On the other hand, the possibility of an influence spreading in the opposite direction, i.e., from Easter Island to the Marquesas, cannot be excluded on chronological grounds.

As has been described elsewhere,[39] the modern descendants of Ororoina, the sole survivor of the 'Long-ears' during the massacres in the Poike ditch, showed our expedition through practical demonstration how the large statues were carved from the hard crater walls of Rano Raraku until twelve generations ago, by means of roughly pointed hand-picks of hard andesite; furthermore, how a few hundred men could transport the giant monuments across the terrain, and how twelve islanders with no other expedients than two logs, cord, and a pile of crude boulders could erect a twenty-ton giant on the upper platform of an *ahu* in a matter of eighteen days.

Let us finally attempt a summaric reconstruction of our present knowledge concerning the mystery of Easter Island.

At some unidentified date prior to AD 380, that is more than fifteen centuries ago, the first settlers landed on Easter Island. They found a verdant island covered by various species of trees and shrubs, including palms. They therefore had to make clearings for their own settlements, for their religious masonry structures, and for their various image quarries. Although there was thus no shortage of wood on the island, they did not build their dwellings in Polynesian manner from pole and thatch, but they opened quarries and selected stone to construct circular masonry houses and boat-shaped dwellings of corbelled slabs. These dwellings were either slab-roofed or thatched with *totora* reed, a plant necessarily transported as root stock from an irrigated field on the desert coast of South America, and planted by the settlers in the freshwater crater lakes together with the equally American medical plant *Polygonum amphibium.* In spite of the local presence of wood they also built peculiar water craft from *totora* reeds, following again the characteristic construction principles of the inland Tiahuanaco waterways and the Pacific desert coast of ancient Peru. They cleared, and finally exterminated, the indigenous palms covering the verdant slopes of the extinct Rano Raraku volcano, to get across to the solid tuff below the soil. This selected rock, as well as scoria and basalt in other quarries, was attacked with remarkable expertness and experience, using non-Polynesian hand-picks of American type to shape colossal blocks which they dressed and fitted in a variety of forms and yet designed to match each other so precisely that not a knife's edge could be squeezed in between them.

Their highly specialized masonry technique was unknown elsewhere in Polynesia, but was of the type characteristic for ancient Peru from the Cuzco Valley to Tiahuanaco. The religion brought by these early immigrants must have been a form of solar cult, since their impressive religious structures were altar-like megalithic platforms precisely oriented to the movement of the sun. They also chose the highest mountain peak for constructing a solar observatory and a cult site for the sun. Rather than carving wood in customary Polynesian fashion they sculptured statues both from very hard basalt and from different kinds of tuff and scoria, and these statues were erected in the earthen temple courts. The statues included specialized types unknown throughout the Pacific island area but characteristic of the dynamic culture centred on Tiahuanaco. A defensive structure was built across the Poike peninsula, perhaps for fear of enemy pursuit from the original homeland to this isolated refuge.

What finally happened to the founders of this Early Period culture is not known. Archaeological evidence at Vinapu and Orongo seems to indicate a temporary abandonment of the local temple structures, and the entire island might perhaps have been abandoned for a period interjacent between the Early and Middle Period. What seems evident, however, is that the people subsequently occupying the island was hostile to its predecessors, tore their temples apart and rearranged the building blocks with no regard for the original fitting of their exquisitely shaped and dressed surfaces, and without interest in the annual movements of the sun. The old stone images were also broken and dishonoured, their remains serving as crude building material in the walls of a new architectural manifestation: the image *ahu*.

In spite of hostility and marked difference in religious concepts, the new culture was sufficiently related to the old one to make it reasonable to suspect arrivals from the same general geographical region. It is thus possible that the whereabouts of Easter Island was not unknown to the immigrants marking the commencement of the Middle Period. On their arrival about AD 1100 the birdman cult was suddenly introduced to dominate religious activities. Intimately associated with the birdman cult the newcomers venerated their own deceased ancestors. Large ancestor statues became the central feature in their architectural development and dominated all creative efforts, and the many different burial sites became the private cult centra of the respective families. During a period of less than six hundred years, more than six hundred giant ancestor statues were sculptured from the now naked crater walls of Rano Raraku, where man had long since cleared the verdant slopes until the Rano Raraku palm forest had been transformed to windblown ashes. As time passed, the acquisition of a mortuary statue became a matter of prestige, and successive generations, protected through isolation from disturbant outside wars, became increasingly ambitious in exceeding each other in the dimension of their individual family images. At the end of the Middle Period the treeless island had thus become entirely surrounded by *ahu*-platforms supporting mortuary stone giants, all facing the inland temple court with their backs to the ocean. At the end of this period, too, cremation burials in front of the *ahu* seem to be replaced by multiple burials in or on top of the *ahu*, a custom that became almost universal throughout the Late Period.

When image production reached its peak—immediately prior to the disruption of the Middle Period—the island engineers were able to erect statues up to forty feet tall, that is one-piece sculptures with the height of a four-storey building. The largest statue lifted on to an *ahu* platform far from the quarries weighed more than eighty tons, and although it was more than thirty feet tall it balanced a red stone cylinder weighing twelve tons, i.e. the weight of two grown elephants, on top of its own head. It is difficult to visualize how this evolution would have ended. A monolithic statue seventy feet tall, i.e., as tall as a seven-storey building, was left almost completed by the sculptors in the quarries when the catastrophe occurred, about AD 1680. The work in the quarries, along the roads, and on the *ahu*, was momentarily arrested, and was never again reassumed. Thousands of obsidian spear points were now manufactured for the first time, and they dominate all culture levels throughout the following era. The *ahu* images were overthrown, the reed houses burnt, and walls torn down.

The victor who remained alive was Polynesian, he was not a stone mason or a carver of stone monuments, he built pole-and-thatch houses and gathered drift wood along the coast to make wooden figures like those elsewhere in Polynesia. On Easter Island his most important traditional wood carving, still today produced by the hundreds for commercial purpose, is a peculiar emaciated person with goatee beard, strongly aquiline nose, and long ear-lobes pending to the shoulders. Thus, the Easter Islanders claim, was the appearance of the people found by their ancestors on the island and exterminated in the Poike pyre.

The Polynesians who came to Easter Island did not bring with them the *poi* pounder or the *tapa* beater, the two most important household implements characteristic of the pan-Polynesian culture. There is indeed little or no material evidence to mark the time of their arrival. It is as if they had come in a very modest manner and quietly adopted the local non-Polynesian beliefs and customs. From which island they had departed cannot yet be stated with certainty. Their own tradition as collected last century insisted that they arrived *karau-karau*, i.e. 200 years, prior to their own uprising which led to the battle of Poike. This would agree well with the estimates of Routledge and others based on the shortest of the two distinct Easter Island genealogies (twenty-two generations whereas Hotu Matua was said to have come from the east fifty-seven generations ago).

There are many indications suggesting that they did not come to isolated Easter Island to assist the long-eared engineers of their own free will. The possibility is present that they may have been fetched by Middle Period Easter Islanders, assuming that the latter actually visited the Marquesas group about the fourteenth century AD.

At any rate, history found them living alone among war-ridden ruins on the bare stage of Easter Island—reportedly with remnants of an alien race in their midst—when Roggeveen raised the curtain for European spectators once the main play had long since ended and the leading actors had already left the stage.

CHAPTER 9

THE COMPOSITE CULTURE OF EASTER ISLAND

EDITORIAL NOTE. *Now that archaeological explorations have revealed the existence on Easter Island of more than one cultural level we would do well to recall that other scientific disciplines (such as physical anthropology, linguistics and ethnology, each of which approached the problem from a different viewpoint), have long since indicated the presence of a non-Polynesian component in the culture of Easter Island.*

There was, indeed, a period when those who raised such voices were ignored due to Métraux' suggestive substitute for history which gained approbation in the face of better knowledge: the conception that nothing but a variant of the Polynesian stock had here—in complete isolation—reached paramount heights. The conception of a creative achievement, carried beyond all sensible bounds to end in self-destruction, was too fascinating.

Today, however, minds are once more open for an unbiased consideration of available evidence.

The text of this chapter is taken from a lecture entitled 'How far is Easter Island Culture Polynesian?', which Heyerdahl gave before the VIIth International Congress for Anthropology and Ethnology in Moscow in 1964.

A series of controlled excavations initiated by the Norwegian Archaeological Expedition to Easter Island in 1955–56, and subsequently followed up by William Mulloy and Gonzalo Figueroa under the auspices of the University of Chile, has revealed a superimposition of cultures on Easter Island. At least a thousand years, and possibly more, before the period formerly assumed to represent that of the first local arrivals, a people whose religious and architectonic concepts were quite different from those of the subsequent period, had left their lasting traces.[1] This discovery makes it relevant to re-examine Easter Island's historic culture in search of aberrant elements which may represent inheritance from archaeological levels with independent culture traditions. The fact that a Polynesian people speaking a Polynesian dialect inhabits the island today becomes particularly significant when we note that their cultural inheritance comprises an array of traits not at all conforming with Polynesian characteristics.

The idea that lonely Easter Island represents a melting pot of cultures was not born of recent excavations. The Dutch discoverers in 1722, and the Spanish rediscoverers in 1770, describe different racial types living together on the island and representing a strong and numerous population.[2] Next, when Cook arrived, he found in 1774 a war-ridden and decimated population of obvious Polynesian affiliations, whom he firmly dissociated from the monolithic sculptures in their midst, which he identified as vestiges from an earlier island era.[3] When the first Europeans settled ashore and became able to communicate directly with the Easter Islanders, the latter immediately told them of two different local arrivals, one from the east and one from the west, and they most consistently stressed that after a period of peaceful co-existence their forefathers had almost exterminated the other local people which had a different culture.[4] Thomson,[5] upon interviewing the local natives with the early settler Salmon as his aid, was the first to suggest that there might have been more than one immigration to the island. Knoche[6] observing diversity in the local culture, concluded that a non-Polynesian stratum had preceded the now dominant population. He rejected Sir Clements Markham's view (1870) of a possible connection with Tiahuanaco, arguing that South American rafts were incapable of any voyage in the open ocean, and he postulated instead a pre-Polynesian substratum from distant Melanesia. Balfour[7] concluded categorically that Easter Island culture was composite, with at least one pre-Polynesian arrival, probably from Melanesia. Balfour's view was developed further by Haddon[8] who proposed that three separate migrations had reached this lonely island, respectively from Australia, Melanesia, and Polynesia. He based this view on the craniological studies of Volz, Hamy, Joyce, Pycraft, and Keith, all of whom had pointed to non-Polynesian features in the Easter Islanders.

Next Routledge[9] arrived to carry out the first systematic archaeological surface survey. Her scientific notes were lost, but in her popular book she argues that a very strong alien element underlies the Polynesian culture on Easter Island, and she adds: 'It is obvious that we are dealing with a mixed race. . . .'

Shapiro[10] approaching once more the problem within the field of physical anthropology, failed to find any unanimity of opinion, but his personal conclusion was that, 'the association of Easter Island with Melanesian or Australian stocks . . . does violence to the known facts'. This dismissal of a Melanesian element was considered conclusive by Métraux[11] and in his monograph on the ethnology of Easter Island he claims that an examination of the archaeological remains had convinced him 'that Easter Island culture is one'. However, Métraux's companion, Lavachery,[12] the only professional archaeologist who had visited Easter Island prior to 1955, stressed that their work had been restricted to surface investigations. They had omitted stratigraphic excavations due to the current belief that the local soil was stabile, and cultural remains from different periods were therefore thought to be juxtaposed on the surface rather than superimposed. Lavachery cautiously concluded: 'The Polynesians probably found Easter Island devoid of monuments and uninhabited; but this statement lacks proof.'

In 1941 the present writer revived the arguments for cultural complexity, but instead of resorting to a Melanesian sub-stratum suggested one from the confining Andean culture area.[13] Subsequently Englert[14] reassumed the archaeological surface surveys and challenged the conclusions of Métraux and Lavachery. He reverted to the view of Routledge and others who had proposed a racial and cultural sub-stratum underneath the Polynesian, but modified the old hypothesis of a voyage from Melanesia by pointing as well to existing parallels in ancient Peru.

This brief survey of opinions shows that, prior to our introduction of stratified archaeology on Easter Island, various fields of science had lent themselves to arguments for cultural complexity.

Linguistically there was less reason to suspect an alien substratum. Englert,[15] however, who made the most thorough study of modern Easter Island language, refers to the traditional claim that an earlier and alien people on the island had a different way of speaking, and he says that some synonymous words which still exist may have their origin in this difference of languages.

The first vocabulary of 94 Easter Island terms was collected in 1770 by Agüera[16] of the Spanish expedition. The list contained many characteristic Polynesian words, and some which were equally obviously non-Polynesian. Among the foreign words were the numerals, recorded from one to ten. They were, with the present Polynesian numerals of the island mentioned in brackets:

Coyana (etahi)
Corena (erua)
Cogojui (etoru)
Quiroqui (eha)
Majana (erima)
Feuto (eono)
Fegea (ehitu)
Moroqui (evaru)
Vijoviri (eiva)
Queromata (angahuru).

To account for the seemingly uncalled for foreign words, Ross[17] and Métraux[18] suggest that they probably have a meaning entirely different from that assumed by the recorder. If this were so, these words, including the numerals, are equally foreign to the Polynesian language, as they have no other meaning.

As shown by Englert[19] the disastrous Hotu-iti war must have raged over Easter Island about 1772–4, immediately prior to the arrival of Cook. The plantations had been destroyed and some disorganized groups of war-ridden Polynesians living in extreme poverty were all there was left to greet the disappointed Englishmen, who could not even obtain provisions. Cook and his companions were well aware of the marked difference between the few hundred surviving Easter Islanders seen by their expedition, and the flourishing population of mixed types described by the earlier visitors. Both he and Forster recognized the Polynesian element, but describe the survivors as small, lean, timid, and miserable, and believe a catastrophe to have hit the island, leaving only harassed monuments as witnesses of the past.[20] Modern observers have usually overlooked this drastic transfiguration in the local overall picture between the two European visits of 1770 and 1774. Nevertheless archaeology supported by tradition, indicate another similar annihilation of a major population group as early as about 1680, prior even to Roggerveen's visit.[21]

To what extent non-Polynesian terms survived at the time of Cook's visit we do not know, since Cook[22] and Forster[23] for the sake of comparison collected only a small list of such specific words as were recognized by them and their Tahitian interpreter as having equivalents in Tahiti, whereas terms they did not recognize were disregarded. That Cook's selected list of twenty-eight Tahitian-kindred words was not representative of the contemporary Easter Island language was admitted by the author himself, as he says of the first Easter Islander who boarded the ship, while the Tahitian interpreter Otiti was present: '. . . nevertheless his language was, in a manner, wholly unintelligible to all of us.'[24]

In 1864, before the local language had been recorded, Eyraud settled ashore as missionary with a group of Mangarevens and the only survivors from the disastrous Peruvian slave raids, who were repatriated by way of Tahiti. Tahitian language was now introduced to the decimated Easter Island population both in speech and writing. Some years later Roussel (1908) compiled a Rapanui vocabulary, published post-mortem, but during Roussel's local sojourn Palmer[25] recorded: 'Their language has so much altered that it is impossible to say what it was originally." The adjustment to Tahitian speech augmented further in 1871, when most Easter Islanders moved to Mangareva and Tahiti, while Polynesian-speaking sheep rangers and catechists came to settle among the remaining Easter Islanders, whose total number in 1877 had sunk to 111.[26] Most Easter Island vocabularies have been obtained from their descendants, whose schooling continued to be in Tahitian. No wonder that Churchill wrote in 1912[27] when comparing his own much quoted vocabulary with the Rapanui text recorded by Thomson on Easter Island a generation earlier: 'Of the text we need but say that it is not such language of Rapanui as is recorded in the pages of this vocabulary, nor is it consistently the known speech of any Polynesian people, but a jumble of several.'

Regardless of the otherwise split opinion on the validity of glottochronology, calculations based on existing Easter Island vocabularies are full of pitfalls, and should be handled with utmost care.[28]

The intrepid Tahitian-speaking groups that imposed their own language on the small and susceptible Easter Island stock were all converted Christians, and did not bring the vocabulary of their former mythology to the island. As a result the gods and goddesses of Easter Island were never confused or affected by those dominating Polynesia proper. The supreme pan-Polynesian deities, Tu, Tane, Tangaroa, Tiki, and Maui, played no part in the religion of the Easter Islanders. Hiro, Rongo, Tangaroa, and Tiki existed only as traditional names but were not worshipped or venerated. With due reason Métraux[29] stresses: 'The most striking feature of Easter Island religion is the unimportance of the great gods and heroes of other Polynesian religions.' Métraux[30] suggests that: 'The importance given in the Easter Island mythology to gods whose names are unknown in the rest of Polynesia shows that the emigrants who settled on the island substituted for some of the principal Polynesian deities lesser gods who took their rank and attributes.'

However, there are no lesser gods in Polynesia with the names that were worshipped on Easter Island. The supreme god of the Easter Islanders was Makemake, and, with him, Haua was the only deity to receive offerings and prayers.[31] Neither Makemake nor Haua were known, not even by name, in any other part of Polynesia. It would seem more likely that these non-Polynesian gods were adopted from another cultural tradition on the same island than to assume that the Polynesian emigrants upon arrival on an empty island discarded all the prominent pan-Polynesian gods to sacrifice to some self-conceived novelty unknown to their own ancestors. Such an act would be utterly un-Polynesian. Makemake was indeed no deified man, but the supreme god of Easter Island, who created earth and ocean, sun, moon, stars, man and all living creatures. He rewarded the good and devoured the spirit of the evil after death, while he made his anger known by thunder. Ferdon[32] has demonstrated that the Makemake symbols were closely associated with the sun-measuring device and other vestiges of solar worship on top of the highest local mountain, at Orongo. The ceremonial village of Orongo with its masonry buildings was the nucleus of the Makemake worship and of all pan-Easter Island religious activity; and yet the entire structure as well as the local ceremonies were as clearly non-Polynesian as was Makemake himself. The prepared solar observatory, designed to measure the sun's position at the time of the equinox and summer and winter solstices, has no known parallel in Polynesia or adjacent island territories. Such prepared devices were common in Peru on the mainland next to Easter Island, however, where they, as on Easter Island, were associated with sun ceremonies and special fires.[33]

We have stated that, even in architecture, the paramount ceremonial village of Orongo is not Polynesian. Nowhere in Polynesia is this concept of joining different houses into a compact unit repeated. This is a common feature in ancient Peruvian architecture both in the highlands and on the coast. As unique in Polynesia is the specialized building technique of each individual Orongo house, with its masonry walls, corbel-vaulted roof, and slab cribwork at the corners. Although nothing parallel is known in Polynesia, stone houses with the technique of corbelling, or false arch construction, and slab cribwork are architectural features of nearby Peru and adjacent regions of western South America.[34]

Archaeology reveals that the Makemake worship associated with the sun was later supplemented by, or assimilated with,

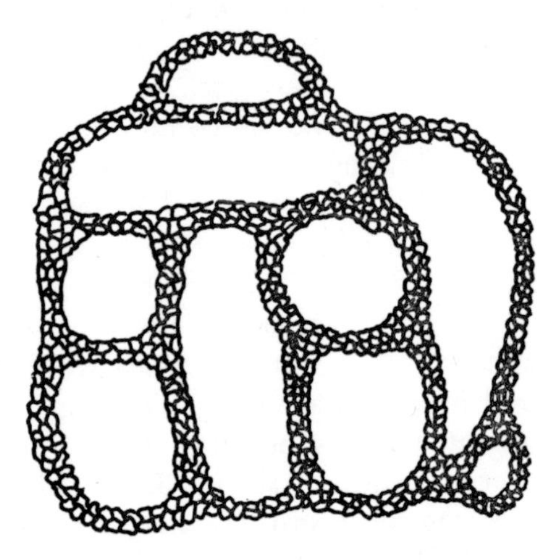

Groundplan of a settlement on Easter Island showing houses built as a unit with common walls

the subsequently all-important bird-man cult, where the non-Polynesian deity Haua played a principal part. From the Middle Period of Easter Island history all rocks around Orongo were covered by human figures with a hook-beaked bird's head. The bird-man rites involved the annual swimming on tusk-shaped *totora* reed floats to an off-shore islet in search of the first bird's egg, the winner becoming the sacred bird-man of the year with almost unlimited social privileges. Métraux[35] writes: 'The importance of the bird cult cannot be denied in the face of the Orongo ruins and the numerous images of bird-men carved on the rocks. Traditions, testimonies of early missionaries, and records of travellers confirm the exceptional importance of the cult ritual as well as the social order built on this annual competition. . . . The complex of the bird cult . . . has no parallel in the rest of Polynesia . . . nowhere else was there open competition resulting in the election of a sacred man.' Ferdon[36] writes: 'although the artistic representations of Easter Island bird-men at present appear to be unique, the evidence of a bird-man cult at Tiahuanaco, Bolivia, and another in the Chimu culture of northern coastal Peru, suggest an American origin for the Easter Island cult.'

The tusk-shaped reed floats used in the bird-man competition embody another non-Polynesian feature. Reed-bundle vessels were formerly used in New Zealand, but they were not tusk-shaped and were made from local *Phormium tenax* which became quickly water-logged.[37] Tusk-shaped reed-boats of the size and type used in Easter Island, and of the very same reed, were the most common water-craft of ancient Peru. On Lake Titicaca, and especially along the Pacific coast, reed-boats occasionally took on prodigious dimensions, and it is noteworthy that bird-men, with long hooked beaks as on Easter Island, are frequently navigating reed vessels in Early Chimu art.[38] Skottsberg[39] has now shown that the aboriginal Easter Island reed is the non-Polynesian *Scirpus riparius*, an American aquatic plant dependent on human aid for its transfer from irrigate areas in coastal Peru to the fresh-water lakes on Easter Island. Ferdon[40] asserts that the occurrence on Easter Island of the South American type raft and the very plant from which it was made 'is strong evidence of American contact and suggests the means by which American-derived traits could have reached Easter Island'.

Large and small reed-boats play an important part in the mural paintings on the slabs of the Orongo houses. Among them are also the conventionalized mask of the double-bladed paddle of Easter Island. Double-bladed paddles did not exist elsewhere in Polynesia, not even for religious dances as on Easter Island, but were widespread in America and used on reed-floats in ancient Peru.[41] The Orongo masks are, moreover, characterized by the weeping-eye motif, repeatedly occurring in Easter Island art.[42] The weeping-eye motif is not found elsewhere in Polynesia, but is a diagnostic feature of early cultures in Peru and in wide areas of adjacent America, typical for instance on the bird-men at the Gateway of the Sun in Tiahuanaco.[43]

The supreme god Makemake was at Orongo also carved as a feline figure. Thomson[44] thus said of some Orongo rock-carvings which he estimated to antedate all others: 'the most common figure is a mythical animal, half human in form, with bowed back and long claw-like legs and arms. According to the natives this symbol was intended to represent the god "Meke-Meke" . . .' He claimed it bore a 'striking resemblance' to a form he had seen in Peruvian art. A feline figure with arched back, drawn-up abdomen, tall legs, and a round head with gaping mouth is incised with bird-men on the Easter Island tablets.[45] Jaussen's[46] theory that this animal is a rat is dictated by the fact that feline animals do not exist on any Pacific island, yet it was present and used from Mexico to Peru since Tiahuanaco times, and precisely as symbol of the creator god.

In addition to the important inter-tribal cult centre at Orongo, each extended family had its individual image platform, that served for ancestor commemoration. In its historic phase this image *ahu* has much in common with religious structures elsewhere in south-eastern Polynesia. But excavation reveals that the *ahu* is built over an early structure with different plan and purposes. The earlier structure had its front where the image *ahu* has its back, and it did not contain burial chambers nor was it designed to support giant statues, the two sole purposes of the subsequent image *ahu*. The image *ahu* with its additional wings could face in any direction, and was built for strength, of boulders and re-used blocks, whereas the earlier structures were astronomically oriented altars consisting of core filling covered up and elegantly faced with exquisitely shaped and fitted blocks. All the numerous statues of the image *ahu* were consistently turned to face *inland*,

and the inland plaza was the centre of ceremonial attention. In the Early Period, however, the ceremonial attention was in front of the high *seaward* wall, which was carefully oriented to the yearly movements of the sun. Here irregularities in the huge rectangular and multiangular blocks were patched with scrupulously matched angular or loaf-shaped stones, and surfaces were ground smooth and slightly convex. This highly specialized masonry technique has no known counterpart in Polynesia. Walls of fitted blocks do occasionally occur on some islands, but the finishing is not the same, and they are not oriented to the sun. Core-filled walls oriented to the sun and fitted and finished with the specialized Early Period Easter Island technique occur over wide areas in pre-Incaic Peru from the Cuzco Valley with Rumi-Kolke to Ollantay-Tambo and Tiahuanaco.[47]

Buck[48] suggested that the Easter Island statues have their inspiration from the few life-size stone figures in the Marquesas. This hypothesis is no longer valid in view of recent excavations and carbon datings. The Marquesan image structures in question post-date the commencement of the *Middle* Period statue making on Easter Island[49] and when the numerous *Early* Period statues were carved on Easter Island, there were no monolithic monuments in human form in any part of Polynesia, nor in Melanesia or Micronesia; whereas giant stone men raised in the open were common and characteristic of the contemporary cult sites in the adjoining areas of north-western South America. Three out of four Early Period statue types excavated on Easter Island have close counterparts in specialized early Tiahuanaco types.[50]

The complexity of burial customs on tiny Easter Island is particularly noteworthy, and was augmented by Mulloy's excavation of contiguous cists with numerous cremation-burials first found in front of the sun-oriented wall at Vinapu, and subsequently in front of other Easter Island *ahu*.[51] Cremation is reported from New Zealand, but is unknown elsewhere in Polynesia, and has only a sporadic occurrence respectively in Melanesia and in some western regions of South America.[52] Equally unknown throughout Polynesia is the oval masonry tomb with its central tube for secondary burials, so common on Easter Island;[53] and also the cylindrical and corbelled masonry tower known on the island as *tupa*, which in all its details is a duplicate of the South American burial tower, known there as *chulpa*, and abounding in the regions around Tiahuanaco.

Proceeding to dwellings, we encounter the same non-Polynesian picture. Ferdon[54] in a special study of Easter Island house types, writes: 'One of several features that makes the Easter Island material culture complex stand out as markedly different from those of other Polynesian islands is its variety of dwelling structures . . . the fact that every one of these buildings, in their total construction, appears to be unique in Polynesia, presents a further problem that is not immediately answerable in terms of independent invention.'

One of the principal types of early dwelling on Easter Island, the remains of which are found in vast quantities especially on the eastern side, are circular stone houses with thick, low, core-filled masonry walls, built-in storage cists, and entrance through a presumably conical, thatched roof. Such circular stone houses are sometimes clustered together in contiguously walled units, forming regular village patterns.[55] They do not have any relationship to Polynesian architecture, but reappear, even to the detail of the entrance through the roof, in the circular and thick-walled contiguous-room houses of the Pacific slopes below Tiahuanaco.[56] As important as the core-filled circular houses were the long, boat-shaped slab-houses built with masonry cribwork at the pointed ends, corbel-vaulted roof, and tunnel-shaped side entrance. The ceremonial village at Orongo is the best preserved sample of this remarkably non-Polynesian architecture, although single buildings and ruins of an extensive village of this type exist elsewhere on the island.[57] The Easter Island reed house, rather than being rectangular or oval as the pole and thatch houses of Polynesia, follows the lenticular plan of the ancient cribwork stone houses where the pointed ends were dictated by constructural needs. Thus, in its peculiar ground plan, and also in being built from the South American *totora* reed, with its poles resting in drill-holes in elaborately cut and fitted curbstones, even the historic house of Easter Island differs from dwellings elsewhere in Polynesia.[58] The ever-present basaltic curbstones, *paenga*, are among the most characteristic archaeological remains on Easter Island, and have no counterparts in Polynesia.[59]

The Easter Island masonry cooking place, quite unlike the pan-Polynesian earth-oven, is built from rectangular slabs or blocks set on edge half above the ground in square or pentagonal shape, thus duplicating a well-known pattern in ancient Peru.[60]

It has been customary to ascribe the unexpected presence of stone houses, fitted megalithic walls, and giant statues to a special evolution on Easter Island encouraged by the local lack of wood for carving and construction. This theory is no longer tenable. Pollen borings reveal that the island was formerly covered by now extinct species of trees and shrubs, even palms, and that the original settlers immediately started to clear the woods with fire to create openings for their Early Period stone quarries and masonry structures.

In what is left of this chapter I shall add only a summary reference to the artifact complex.

The principal weapon and most common artifact is the *mataa*, a tanged obsidian spear-head of non-Polynesian characteristics. Only two *mataa* are found outside Easter Island, both in an aboriginal burial near the coast of Chile. Their local origin is unexplained.[61] (Since the above was written further obsidian *mataa* indistinguishable from the Easter Island specimens have been uncovered from two additional archaeological sites on and near the coast of Chile, i.e. at Zapallar and on Mocha Island.)

Double-bevelled axes, or celts, are not considered a Polynesian feature. Yet they have been found in datable Middle Period contexts. Single and double pointed *coups de poing* are numerically in the majority on the island, due to the stone-work. Yet they are not reported as a Polynesian element, whereas, like the celt, they are common in America.

A most prominent element in the heterogeneous Easter Island fishhook complex is the one-piece stone fishhook, which has no counterpart in Polynesia or the territories beyond. It reappears for some strange reason in archaeologic deposits on islands off California, and stone fishhooks were otherwise only manufactured on the nearby South American coast below Tiahuanaco.[62]

A principal element in all Polynesian cultures is the stone *poi* pounder. It is conspicuous through its complete absence on Easter Island although taro is grown, and *poi*, the pan-Polynesian staple, is locally an unknown dish.[63]

Kava, the pan-Polynesian ceremonial beverage, considered diagnostic of Polynesian culture, was entirely unknown on Easter Island.

The grooved wooden or whale-bone *tapa* beater, the most impor-

Map VI. Easter Island in relation to the nearest South Seas Islands and the South American coast

tant domestic tool throughout Polynesia beside the *poi* pounder, was unknown on Easter Island until introduced in missionary times. The Easter Islanders used rounded and polished beach stones for beating their *mahute* bast into strips which were fastened together in a non-Polynesian manner, with needle and thread.[64] As is shown by Métraux[65] Easter Island is the only place in Polynesia where bark-cloth is made by sewing. As a result a small bone needle with eye is a principal culture element, of which 163 specimens were encountered by our expedition. The type is exceedingly rare in Polynesia, but reappears in an identical form in ancient Peru.[66]

The only household furniture were mats of South American *totora* reed, and a locally characteristic and non-Polynesian incised stone pillow. This universal use of a stone pillow on the island has been wrongly ascribed[67] to the formerly assumed shortage of wood.

Hitherto unobserved is a commonly occurring and quite un-Polynesian grinding stone morphologically appearing like American *metates*, but of unknown use; and an equally non-Polynesian small hemispheric and polished basalt bowl of a type common on the north coast of Chile.[68]

The personal ornaments and badges of Easter Island, like the wooden *rei miro* and the *tahonga* pectorals, are not Polynesian features; and the highly important *moai kavakava*, *moai paapaa*, with the entire series of wooden figurines representing the backbone of Easter Island art and ceremonial activity are all unknown in Polynesia, and have nothing in common with the *tiki* neither morphologically nor functionally.

The array of Easter Island elements lacking in Polynesia, and Polynesian elements lacking on Easter Island, could be extended, but does already cover the principal traits in local customs and beliefs. It shall suffice here to conclude by pointing to the much disputed *rongorongo* tablets. Script is not a Polynesian art, yet Easter Island with its extreme geographic position stands out as the only Pacific island where it existed.

The Easter Island script was incised in boustrophedon on

wooden tablets, and the text was chanted by the reader. At present the artistic signs of this script are unique, but the Cuna Indians of Panama had an aboriginal script which they, like the Easter Islanders, incised in boustrophedon on wooden tablets and chanted at ceremonies.[69] Easter Island is not farther away from the Cuna territory than it is from central Polynesia. Although archaeological support is wanting, Ferdon[70] points to the vestiges of boustrophedon script in the Titicaca region; and the early chroniclers Sarmiento,[71] Molina[72] and Montesinos[73] state that the Inca *amautas* taught reading and writing on 'certain boards', an art later substituted by *quipu*. (Since the above was written, the Russian *rongo-rongo* expert, J. V. Knorozov, has discovered that the writing system known as 'reversed boustrophedon' has been in use in only two areas in the entire world, namely on Easter Island and among the early historic Indians in the Lake Titicaca region near Tiahuanaco.[74] The script of the Easter Island tablets are still completely undeciphered, and island natives as well as European investigators who have claimed to be able to read the contents of the tablets since their first discovery by missionaries a century ago, have all failed completely when put to a scientific test.)

It is difficult to explain the complex history of Easter Island by dogmatically ignoring the New World cultures which were as near towards the east as was nuclear Polynesia towards the west.

NOTES

CHAPTER 1

1. The arguments in favour of a migratory route from South-east Asia to Hawaii by way of North-west America are dealt with at greater length in Heyerdahl (1952a, pp. 71–178).

CHAPTER 2

1. Merrill (1946, p. 344).
2. Merrill (1950, p. 9).
3. Merrill (1954, p. 213).
4. Merrill (1954, p. 212).
5. Merrill (1954, p. 255).
6. Merrill (1954, p. 195).
7. Merrill (1954, pp. 278–9).
8. Merrill (1954, p. 338).
9. Merrill (1954, p. 242).
10. Newsweek, February 19, 1962, p. 49.
11. Greenman (1963, pp. 41–91).
12. The raft *Kon-Tiki* crossed from Callao, Peru, to Raroia in the Tuamotu group in 1947; the raft *Seven Sisters* (William Willis) crossed from Callao to Samoa in western Polynesia in 1954; the raft *Tahiti Nui II* (Eric de Bisschop, who had previously failed in his attempt to reach South America by raft from Polynesia) crossed from Callao to the Cook Islands in west-central Polynesia in 1958; the raft *La Cantuta II* (Eduard Ingris, who had reached the Galapagos but ended becalmed in the doldrums north of the equator on a previous voyage from Talara, North Peru) crossed from Callao to Matahiva north of Tahiti in 1959; the raft *Age Unlimited* (William Willis) crossed once more from Callao to Samoa in 1963 and proceeded thence to Australia in 1964; and the raft *Tangaroa* (Carlos Caravedo Arca) crossed from Callao to Napuka and Fakarava in the Tuamotu group in 1965.
13. Bisschop (1939, pp. 57–8).
14. The same experience was repeated in 1966–67 by the survivors of an international group of balsa-raft voyagers lead by Vital Alsar Ramirez,

which first sailed from Ecuador to the Galapagos group and thence went on north of the equator where they got becalmed in the doldrums. Like Ingris and his companions, this group, too, tried in vain to get back to America with the Equatorial Counter Current and, after 143 days drifting helplessly in circles they, too, had to be rescued and brought back to Panama by ship.

CHAPTER 3

1. Candolle (1884, p. 461).
2. Merrill (1937, p. 282).
3. Merrill (1946, p. 344).
4. Merrill (1954, p. 213).
5. Candolle (1884, p. 433).
6. Guppy (1906, p. 413).
7. Merrill (1954, pp. 195, 267).
8. Nordenskiöld (1931, p. 269).
9. Buck (1938a, p. 315).
10. Buck (1945, p. 11).
11. Eames and St John (1943, p. 256).
12. Merrill (1950, p. 9).
13. Merrill (1954, p. 255).
14. Merrill (1954, p. 278).
15. Hutchinson, Silow and Stephens (1947, p. 79).
16. Sauer (1950, p. 537).
17. Carter (1950, p. 169).
18. Merrill (1954, p. 338).
19. Merrill (1954, p. 190).
20. Merrill (1954, p. 242).
21. Skottsberg (1934, p. 278).
22. Skottsberg (1920–56, pp. 407, 412; 1957).
23. Thomson (1889, p. 456).
24. Bertoni (1919, p. 280).
25. Brown (1931, p. 137).
26. Degener (1930, p. 88).
27. Bryan (1935, p. 67).
28. Hillebrand (1888, p. 14).
29. Carter (1950, p. 173).
30. Prain (1895, p. 325).
31. Fedde (1909, p. 280).
32. Stokes (1932, p. 599).
33. Yacovleff and Herrera (1935, p. 41).

34. Carter (1950, pp. 172, 179).
35. Brown (1935, p. 190).
36. Brown (1935, p. 49).
37. Brown (1935, p. 79).
38. Brown (1935, p. 336).
39. Baker (1893, p. 192).
40. Cook (1903, p. 490).
41. Clausen (1944, p. 29).
42. Yacovleff and Herrera (1934, p. 283).
43. Cook (1903, p. 483).
44. Cook (1903, p. 496).
45. Guppy (1906, p. 413).
46. Steward (1949, p. 744).
47. Sauer (1950, p. 513).
48. Carter (1950, p. 165).
49. Brown (1931, p. 158).
50. Jakeman (1950, p. 32).
51. Brown (1935, p. 174).
52. Cook and Cook (1918, p. 156).
53. Cook and Cook (1918, p. 169).
54. Merrill (1920, p. 195).
55. Carter (1950, p. 164).
56. Carter (1950, p. 181).
57. Körnicke (1885, p. 136).
58. Wittmack (1880, p. 176).
59. Wittmack (1886; 1888).
60. Hutchinson, Silow, and Stephens (1947, p. 138).
61. Sauer (1950, p. 502).
62. Stonor and Anderson (1949, p. 392).
63. Whitaker and Bird (1949, p. 2).
64. Sauer (1950, p. 499).
65. Merrill (1950, pp. 9–10).
66. Barrau (1963, pp. 1–2).
67. For further discussions on ethno-botanical evidence for human migrations in the Pacific, see papers by Carter, Conklin, Heyerdahl, Nishiyama, Robbins, Spencer, Yawata, Yen and others in: Barrau, 1963; also Heyerdahl, 1952a, pp. 427–98).

CHAPTER 4

1. Amherst and Thomson (1901, Vol. 1, p. XVII).
2. Sáamanos (1526, p. 196); Murphy (1941, p. 17).

3. Las Casas (1559, Chap. 41, pp. 78–9).
4. Lizarraga (1560–1602, pp. 32–3).
5. Valverde (1879, p. 179).
6. Sáamanos (1526, p. 196).
7. Andagoya (1541–46, p. 36).
8. Oviedo (1535–48, Vol. 4, Bk. 46, Chap. XVII)...
9. Zarate (1555, Bk. 1, Chap. VI).
10. Pizarro (1571, p. 157).
11. Garcilasso (1609, p. 432).
12. Cobo (1653, Bk. 12, Chap. XXXII).
13. Garcilasso (1609, Vol. 1, Bk. 3, Chap. XVI).
14. Sarmiento (1572, p. 135).
15. Balboa (1576–86, p. 501; 1586, Chap. VII, p. 81).
16. Betanzos (1551, Chap. III).
17. Sarmiento (1572, pp. 32, 186).
18. Balboa (MS from 1576–86).
19. Stevenson (1825, Vol. 1, p. 394).
19. Stevenson (1825, Vol. 1, p. 394).
20. Oliva (1631, translation by Bandelier, 1910, p. 325).
21. Acosta (1590, Vol. 1, p. 56).
22. Heyerdahl (1952a, pp. 550–5; 1957); Eisleb (1963).
23. Amherst and Thomson (1901, Vol. 2, pp. 463–8).
24. Agüera (1770, p. 109).
25. Amherst and Thomson (1901, Vol. 1, pp. IV–V).
26. Amherst and Thomson (1901, Vol. 1, p. VI).
27. González (1770, p. XLIV).
28. Amherst and Thomson (1901, Vol. 1, pp. 6–7, 84–5, 97–8, 161–2, 217–18, 461).
29. Amherst and Thomson (1901, Vol. 1, pp. 83–5).
30. Amherst and Thomson (1901, Vol. 1, p. 8).
31. Christian (1924, p. 525).
32. Rivet (1928, pp. 583, 603; 1943, p. 124).
33. Buck (1938b, p. 22).
34. Buck (1938b, p. 453).
35. Heyerdahl and Skjölsvold (1956).
36. Beechey (1831, Vol. 1, pp. 186–8).

CHAPTER 5

1. Heyerdahl (1941).
2. Hutchinson (1875, pp. 426, 454).
3. Lothrop (1932, pp. 229–56).

4. Means (1942).
5. Hornell (1945, pp. 167–91).
6. Sáamanos (1526, p. 196).
7. Sáamanos (1526, p. 196).
8. Pizarro (1571, p. 138).
9. Las Casas (1559, Chap. XLI, pp. 78–9).
10. Oviedo (1535–48, Vol. 4, Bk. 45, Chap. 17).
11. Andagoya (1541–46, p. 41).
12. Zárate (1555, Bk. 1, Chap. 6).
13. Benzoni (1565, p. 242).
14. Garcilasso (1609, Vol. 1, Bk. 3, Chap. XVI).
15. Lizarraga (1560–1602, pp. 32–3).
16. Balboa (1586, p. 81).
17. Sarmiento (1572, p. 135).
18. Cobo (1653, Chap. XIV, p. 218).
19. Spilbergen (1614–18, p. 83).
20. Juan and Ulloa (1748, Vol. 1, p. 189).
21. Lascallier (1741, Vol. 1, pp. 458–63).
22. Charnock (1801, Vol. 1, p. 12).
23. Humboldt (1810, p. 295).
24. Stevenson (1825, pp. 222–3).
25. Blaxland (MS).
26. Paris (1841–43), p. 148).
27. Lothrop (1932, p. 240).
28. Bennett (1954, Figs. 89, 90).
29. Uhle (1922, p. 49).
30. Nordenskiöld (1931, p. 265).
31. Valverde (1879, p. 179).
32. Lothrop (1932, p. 238).
33. Byam (1850, p. 200).
34. Means (1942, pp. 15, 18).
35. Hornell (1945).
36. Hornell (1946).
37. Hornell (1946, p. 54).
38. Dixon (1932).
39. Dixon (1934, p. 173).
40. Emory (1933, p. 48).
41. Emory (1942, p. 129).
42. Morgan (1946, p. 80).
43. Buck (1945, p. 11).
44. Weckler (1943, p. 35).
45. Heyerdahl (1941).

46. Heyerdahl (1952a, p. 606).
47. Heyerdahl (1954, pp. 1039–44).
48. Cobo (1653, Chap. XIV, p. 218).
49. Juan and Ulloa (1748, pp. 189 ff.).

CHAPTER 6

1. Sharp (1704, pp. 58, 64).
2. Juan and Ulloa (1748, pp. 189 ff.).
3. Morrell (1832, p. 120).
4. Skogman (1854, Vol. 1, p. 164).
5. Hagen (1949, p. 178).
6. See also Footnotes 12 and 14 of Chapter 2. At the time of writing (September 1967) the author has been approached independently by three further groups of potential balsa raft voyagers, all of whom want to sail from Peru to Polynesia.
7. Cowley (1684).
8. Colnett (1798).

CHAPTER 7

1. Chubb (1933, pp. 25–30).
2. Dampier (1729, Vol. 1, p. 111).
3. Wafer (1699, pp. 379–81).
4. Candolle (1884, p. 435).
5. Candolle (1884, p. 435).
6. Oviedo (1535–48); Kerchove (1878, p. 147).
7. Candolle (1884, pp. 429–35).
8. Berry (1926, p. 184).
9. Cf. Heyerdahl (1952a, pp. 453–68).
10. Cook (1910–12, pp. 293, 304, 318, 340).
11. Hill (1929, p. 151).
12. Sauer (1950, p. 524).
13. Merrill (1920, 1930, 1946, etc.).
14. Carter (1950, p. 181).
15. Merrill (1954, pp. 190, 195, 267).
16. Porter (1815, Vol. 2, p. 139).
17. Stewart (1832, p. 177) reports that the particular *atua* who brought the coconut to the Marquesas had crossed the ocean in a 'stone canoe'. N. A. Rowe (*Personal communication*, April 16, 1950) points out that this peculiar information was first recorded in a manuscript journal by the early mis-

sionary William Pascoe Crook who worked in the Marquesas in 1797 and 1798, and he adds with reference to this obscure type of water craft: 'I had wondered for many years what this could mean, but I see now of course that it was a reference to a raft or *pae-pae*. *Pae-pae* can also mean stone platform: hence the confusion.'
18. Chubb (1933, p. 26).
19. Alfaro (1898, p. 33).
20. Dr. Doris Stone (*Personal communications*, March 17, 1965).
21. Coe (1960, pp. 384–6, 390, etc.).
22. Heyerdahl and Skjölsvold (1956).
23. Gretzer (1914); Lothrop (1932); Heyerdahl (1958); Eisleb (1963).

CHAPTER 8

1. For more detailed reports on observations by the various early European visitors, see: Heyerdahl 1961, pp. 45–89.
2. For more detailed reports on the Easter Island traditions recorded by the early visitors, see: Heyerdahl, 1961, pp. 33–43.
3. Routledge (1919).
4. Lavachery (1935, 1939).
5. Métraux (1940).
6. Routledge (1919, pp. 186–7).
7. Métraux (1940, p. 293).
8. Buck (1938a, p. 234).
9. Skjölsvold (1961, Report 14).
10. Mulloy (1961, Report 1).
11. Smith (1961, Report 2).
12. Routledge (1919, pp. 171–2).
13. Métraux (1940, pp. 414–16).
14. Lavachery (1936, p. 393).
15. Ferdon (1961, Report 13).
16. Ferdon (1961, Report 10).
17. Skjölsvold (1961, Report 9).
18. Skottsberg (1920, Fig. 2).
19. Métraux (1940, p. 157).
20. Ferdon (1961, Report 3).
21. Ferdon (1961, pp. 236–40).
22. Heyerdahl (1961, pp. 502–12).
23. Bennett (1934, pp. 460–75).
24. Skjölsvold (1961, pp. 361–2).
25. Routledge (1919, pp. 295–9).
26. Knoche (1925, pp. 313–14).

27. Lavachery (1936, p. 392).
28. Métraux (1940, pp. 88–94).
29. Englert (1948, p. 156).
30. Chubb (1933, p. 33).
31. Métraux (1940, p. 7 and Lavachery 1935, pp. 346–7).
32. Englert (1948, p. 157).
33. Smith (1961, Report 16).
34. Skjölsvold (1961, pp. 291–2, 343–5).
35. Smith (1961, pp. 218–19).
36. Buck (1938a, p. 232).
37. See Heyerdahl (1965, pp. 136–8).
38. Ferdon (1965, Report 9).
39. Heyerdahl (1957, Chap. 5).

CHAPTER 9

1. Heyerdahl, Ferdon *et al.* (1961).
2. Behrens (1722, pp. 134, 136; Aguera 1770, p. 96).
3. J. Cook (1777, Vol. 2, p. 296).
4. *cf.* the original translations collected by Heyerdahl in 1961, pp. 33–43).
5. Thomson (1889, p. 532).
6. Knoche (1912, pp. 876, 877; 1925, pp. 309–12).
7. Markhams (1870).
8. Balfour (1917, pp. 377, 378).
9. Haddon (1918, pp. 161, 162).
10. Routledge (1919, pp. 221, 295–9).
11. Shapiro (1940, pp. 24–30).
12. Metraux (1940, pp. 414, 415).
13. Lavachery (1935, pp. 324, 325; 1936, p. 393).
14. Heyerdahl (1941b, pp. 18, 21, 22).
15. Englert (1948, pp. 88, 101, 156, 157).
16. Englert (1948, pp. 121, 122).
17. Aguera (1770, pp. 109, 110).
18. Ross (1936).
19. Metraux (1940, p. 31).
20. Englert (1948, pp. 139–47; see also Heyerdahl and Ferdon 1961, pp. 30, 39, 40).
21. J. Cook (1777, Vol. 1, p. 290; Forster 1777, Vol. 1, pp. 564, 584, 585).
22. Smith (1961, pp. 385–91).
23. J. Cook (1777, Vol. 2, p. 364).
24. Forster (1778, p. 284).
25. J. Cook (1777, Vol. 1, p. 278).

26. Roussel (1908).
27. Palmer (1870, p. 109).
28. Pinart (1878a, p. 238).
29. Churchill (1912, p. 5).
30. Bergsland and Vogt (1962; Englert 1948, p. 327).
31. Metraux (1940, p. 309).
32. Metraux (1940, p. 315).
33. Geisler (1883, p. 131; Ferdon 1961, pp. 250–3).
34. Ferdon (1961, pp. 250–4).
35. Roggeveen (1722, p. 15; Behrens 1722, p. 133; Ferdon 1961, p. 534).
36. Ferdon (1961, p. 534).
37. Ferdon (1961, p. 534).
38. Metraux (1940, pp. 340, 341).
39. Ferdon (1961, p. 534).
40. Ferdon (1961, p. 535).
41. See illustration, Plate 9a, top.
42. Heyerdahl (1952a, Pl. 81, Fig. 588).
43. Skottsberg (1956, pp. 412, 497; 1957, p. 3).
44. Ferdon (1961, p. 535).
45. Heyerdahl (1952a, p. 583).
46. Thomson (1889, Pl. 23; Routledge 1919, Fig. 105; Ferdon 1961, Fig. 65, p. 535).
47. Heyerdahl (1952a, Pl. 82).
48. Thomson (1889, pp. 481, 482).
49. Heyerdahl (1952a, pp. 505, 506).
50. Jaussen (1894, p. 261).
51. Ferdon (1961, p. 534; Heyerdahl 1961, pp. 328, 497–502).
52. Ferdon (1961, p. 535).
53. Buck (1938a, p. 232).
54. Smith (1961, pp. 217, 218); Heyerdahl (1961, p. 507).
55. Skjölsvold (1961, pp. 360–2; Heyerdahl 1961, pp. 462–9, 502–12).
56. Mulloy (1961, pp. 100, 128, 130, 133–5).
57. Ferdon (1961, p. 535).
58. Geiseler (1883, pp. 30, 31; Ferdon 1961, pp. 381–3, Fig. 12b).
59. Ferdon (1961, pp. 329–38).
60. Skjölsvold (1961, pp. 295–303; Ferdon 1961, pp. 305–11).
61. Ferdon (1961, p. 338; Bruyne 1963).
62. Thomson (1889, p. 486; Ferdon 1961, pp. 329–31).
63. Mulloy (1961, pp. 138–45; Smith 1961, pp. 287–9; Skjölsvold 1961, pp. 291–3).
64. Heyerdahl (1961, pp. 448–9).
65. Heyerdahl and Ferdon (1961, pp. 449, 450, Pl. 80 a–d).

66. Izumi and Sono (1963, Pl. 24).
67. Smith (1961, pp. 270, 271; Mulloy 1961, pp. 151–3; Heyerdahl and Ferdon 1961, pp. 398–400, 481, 482).
68. Heyerdahl and Ferdon (1961, pp. 415–38, 485–7).
69. Heyerdahl and Ferdon (1961, pp. 448, 484, 485).
70. Metraux (1940, p. 215).
71. Heyerdahl and Ferdon (1961, pp. 412, 413, 484); Izumi and Sono (1963, Pl. 101 b5, 102 b6, 164).
72. Metraux (1940, p. 201).
73. Heyerdahl and Ferdon (1961, pp. 438–48, 487, 488).
74. The subject of the still undeciphered Easter Island script is dealt with in detail in Heyerdahl (1965, Report 16, pp. 345–60, with appendices by T. Barthel, J. V. Knorozov, I. K. Fedorova, and A. M. Kondratov).

a

b

. Young Maori girl from New Zealand; **b.** Girl of the Douglas tribe, British Columbia; **c.** Young Indian from the North-west Coast, Kitimat, British Columbia; **d.** Young Polynesian from Fatuhiva in the Marquesas.

c

d

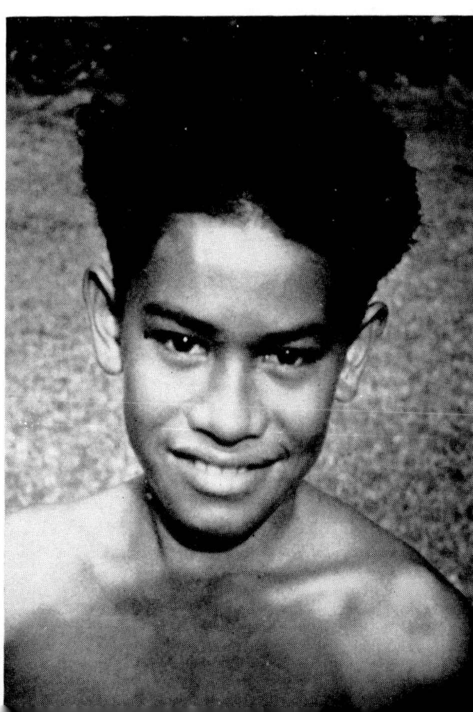

a b c

2a & c. Stone figurines from the American North-west Coast (left Salish, right Kwakiut
b. Stone figurine said to be a precious heirloom of the Maoris which was brought fr
the land of their ancestors.

d. Kwakiutl house-post, North-west Coast;
e. Maori housepost, New Zealand.

d e

a b

Carved wooden pillar, New Zealand; **b.** Corresponding pillar on the North-west Coast with head-decoration said to be the man's topknot.

a

4a. Polynesian gourds; **b.** A fishing net with floats made of gourds from the North Peruvian coast deriving from the pre-ceramic period. This piece has been dated at least a thousand years before the first sea-crossing to Polynesia. The gourd in the foreground on the right still shows traces of the original binding.

b

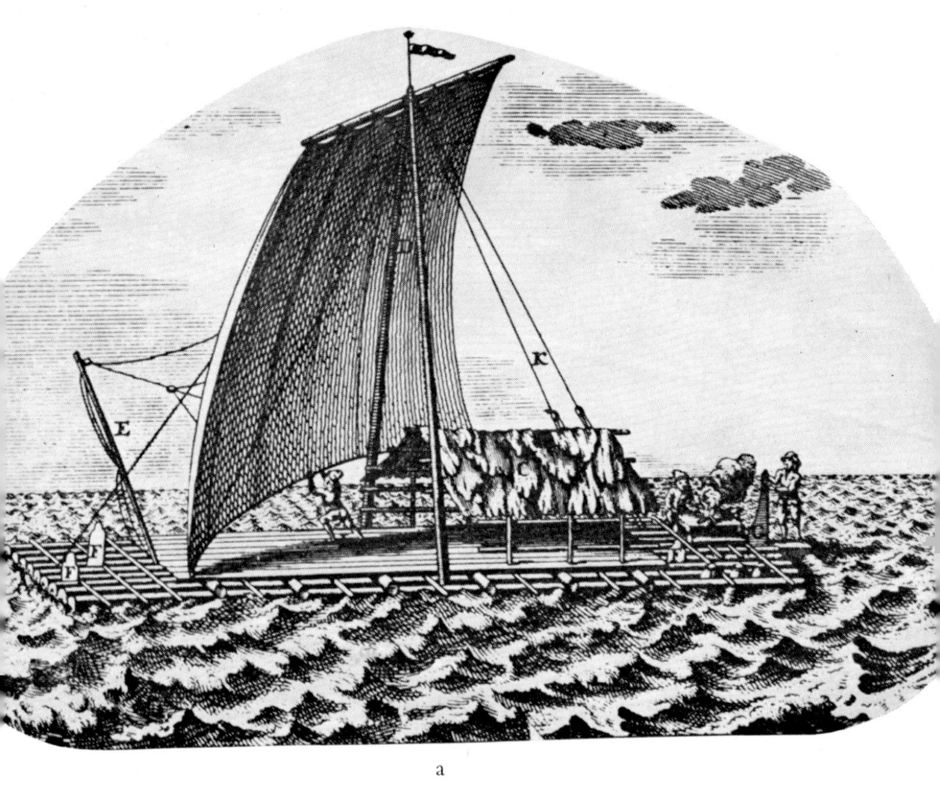

a

a. Old drawing of a balsa raft, Guayaquil, 1748;
b. Balsa raft at anchor in the harbour of Guayaquil, 1843.

b

a

6a. The *Kon-Tiki* was a medium sized balsa raft, 45 feet long and 18 feet wide;
b. Side view of the *Kon-Tiki*.

b

a

. W. Willis's raft, *Age Unlimited*, in New York harbour;
b. De Bisschop's raft at Tahiti.

b

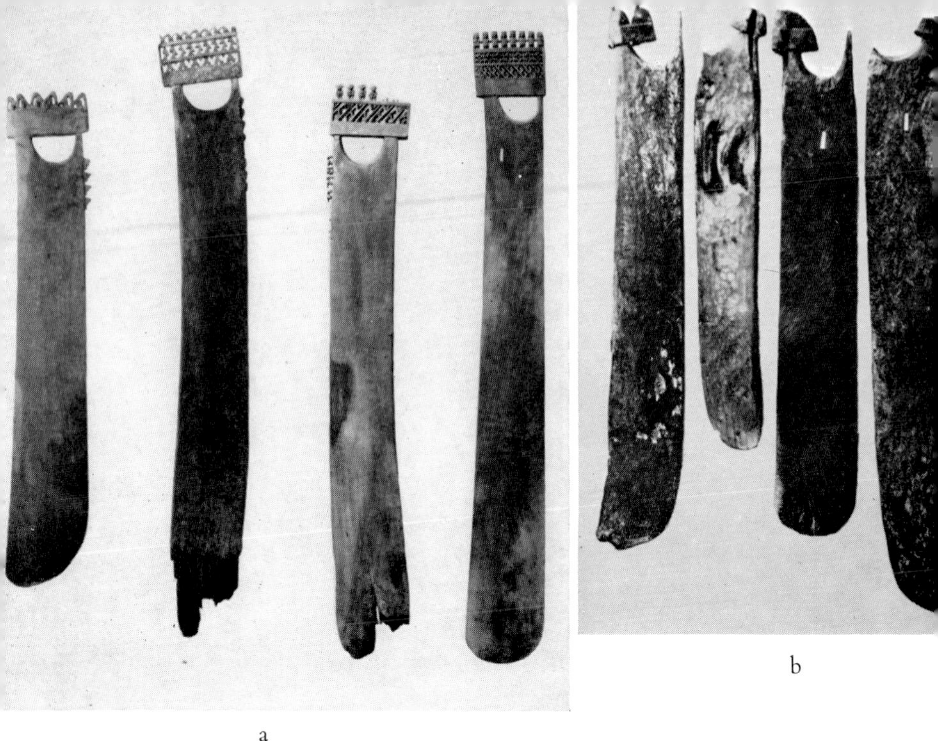

a

b

8a. Centreboards (*guara*) from prehistoric graves in Ica on the coast of South Peru; **b.** prehistoric centre-boards of purely functional design from the coast of South Peru; **c.** richly ornamented handle of a paddle from the coast of South Peru; **d.** ceremonial paddle from Polynesia with traditional ornamentation. These articles reveal a similarity of design and workmanship.

c

d

a

a. Miniature double-bladed paddle found with pre-Inca model raft (viewed from above and from the side) in desert grave on the Pacific coast below Tiahuanaco; **b. & c.** Miniature sails (spirit sails?) made from reeds and cotton. Many such sails have been found in prehistoric graves near Ancón in Peru.

b

c

10. The small ceramic figure of a frog held up in the foreground was found on the Galapagos Islands and evidently once formed part of a larger piece of pottery. The richly decorated vessel next to it, which shows similar figures of frogs, comes from Peru.

1. Vessel from the Peruvian coast. The pottery fragments being held against it, which bear the same plastic decoration, come from the Galapagos Islands.

a

12a. The Rano-Raraku crater on Easter Island. Blocks of stone and statues can be seen in the background, whilst in the foreground lies the crater lake with its totora reeds and a reed boat;

b. Giant heads of tall statues half buried in silt from the slopes of the Rano-Raraku crater.

b

3. Stone statue on Easter Island. The kneeling man belongs to the oldest cultural period.

a

14a. Wall built from great blocks of stone in Peru. Note the careful interlocking; **b.** The same technique may be observed on Easter Island in the walls of the *ahus* built in the oldest period.

b

15. Excavation of a giant statue on Easter Island 1955–56.

16. Statues on a terraced *ahu* still erect and still with their stone wigs balanced on top of their heads at the time of La Perouse's visit to the island in 1786.

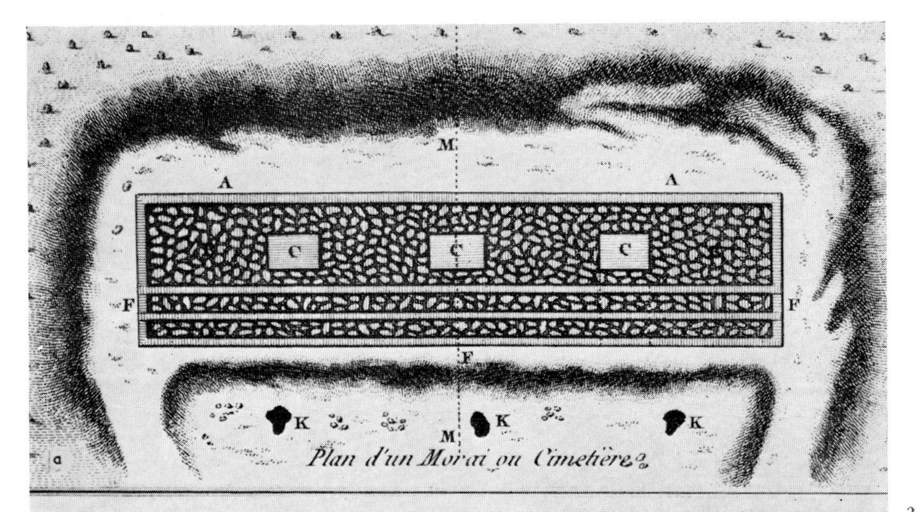

a

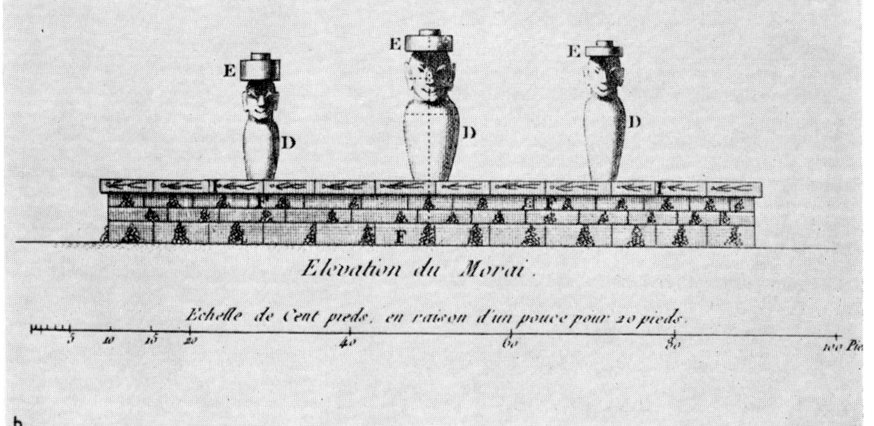

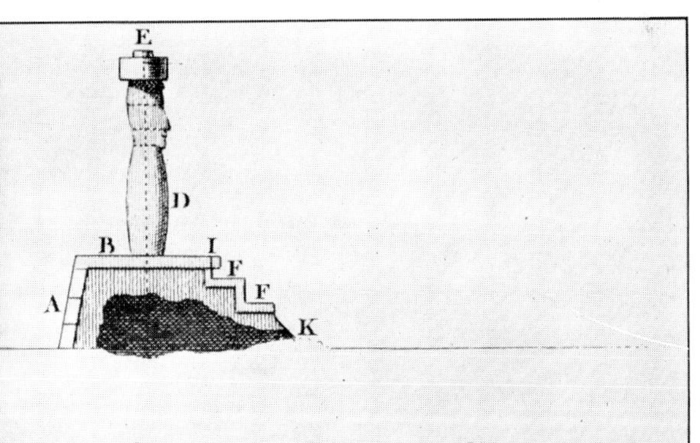

17a. & b. Ground plan, frontal elevation and transverse section of undamaged *ahu* in 1786.

b

a

18a. Orongo, carvings of birdmen; **b.** Orongo, carvings of birdmen and a makemake head.

b

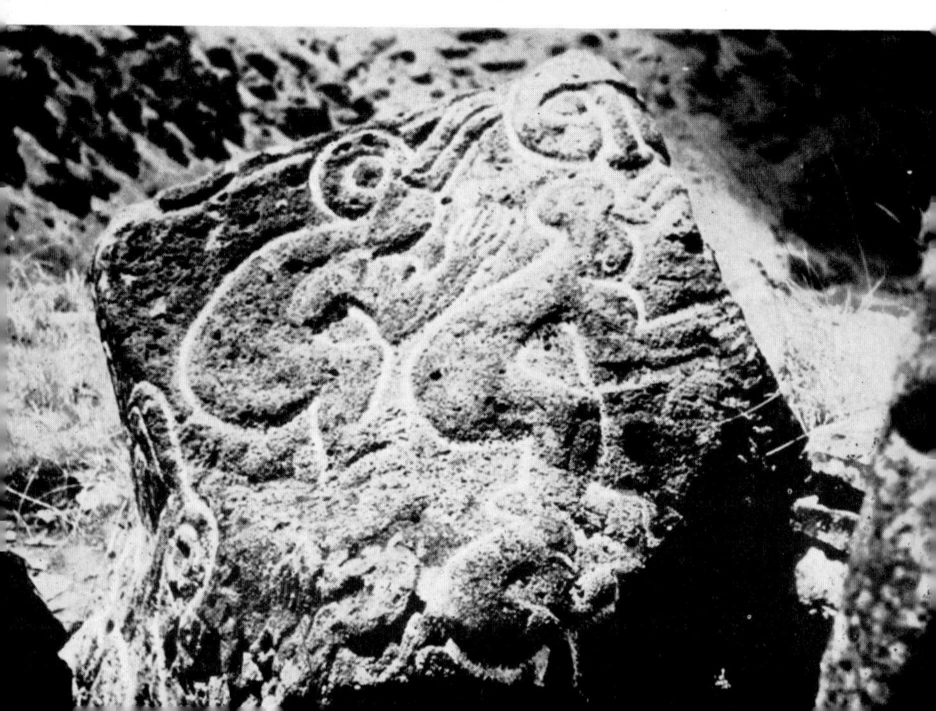

•. Stone head and stone bust with topknot from Easter Island. Note points of similarity between the stone bust and the stone statues on plates 20a & b.

a

b

20a. Red sandstone figure, Incatunuhuiri, Peru; **b.** Stone statue, Tiahuanaco.

21. Head and body of human statues, Pucara, Peru.

22. Stone statue from the Marquesas Group, Polynesia

a

23a. Easter Islanders' reed boat;
b. Reed boat from Lake Titicaca, Peru.

b

24. Father Sebastian Englert, the leading authority on the present-day population of Easter Island, wearing the order of St Olav awarded to him for his great assistance to the Norwegian archaeological expedition in 1955–56.

BIBLIOGRAPHY

Acosta, J. de: *Historia Natural y moral de las Indias, en que se tratan las cosas* . . . Sevilla 1590 (Eng. trans., London, 1604).

Agüera y Infanzon, F. A. de: *Journal of the principal occurrences during the Voyage of the Frigate 'Santa Rosalia' in the year 1770*. Hakluyt Soc., Ser. 2, No. 13, 1908.

Alazard, I.: Introduction to Roussel. In: Roussel, pp. 1–9, 1908.

Alfaro, A.: Memoria de la Secretaría de Fomento, 24 de junio de 1898. In: Reproduciones Cientificas, una expedición y legislación de la Isla del Coco. Instituto Geográfico de Costa Rica. San José, 1963.

Amherst and Thomson, B.: Introduction and notes to *The Discovery of the Solomon Islands by Alvaro de Mendaña in 1468*. Hakluyt Soc., Ser. 2, No. 7, London, 1901.

Andagoya, P. de: *Narrative of the Proceedings of Pedrarias Davila* . . . 1541–46. Hakluyt Soc., Vol. 34, 1865.

Anell, B.: Contribution to the History of Fishing in the Southern Seas. *Studia Ethnographica Upsaliensia*, 9, Uppsala, 1955.

Baker, J. G.: A synopsis of the genera and species of Museae. *Ann. of Bot.*, VII, London, 1893.

Balboa, M. C. de: *Miscellanea antarctica*. MS. in the New York Public Library, originally written between 1576 and 1586. Copied between 1700 and 1725 from the original which has been lost.

— *Histoire du Perou*. 1586. In: Ternaux-Compans: *Voyages, Relations et Mémoires originaux pour servir à l'histoire de la découverte de l'Amérique* Paris, 1840.

Balfour, H.: Some Ethnological Suggestions in Regard to Easter Island, or Rapanui. *Folk-Lore*, Vol. 28, pp. 356–81. London, 1917.

Bandelier, A. F.: *The Islands of Titicaca and Koati*. New York, 1910.

Barrau, J.: Introduction to Symposium on Plants and the Migrations of Pacific Peoples. *Bishop Museum Press*, pp. 1–6. Honolulu, 1963.

Barthel, T. S.: Die Entzifferung der Osterinselschrift. *Die Umschau*, H. 12, pp. 360–2, Frankfurt/Main, 1955.

— The 'Talking Boards' of Easter Island. *Scientific American*, Vol. 198, No. 6, pp. 61–8, New York, 1958a.

— Grundlagen zur Entzifferung der Osterinselschrift. Hamburg, 1958b.

—Wer waren die ersten Siedler auf der Osterinsel? *Ethnologica*, N.F., Vol. 2. Köln, 1960.

BARTHEL, T. S.: Native Documents from Easter Island. Appendix A to Report 16 in: Heyerdahl and Ferdon, 1965.

BASTIAN, A.: Bemerkungen zu den Holztafeln von Rapa-nui. *Zeits. Ges. f. Erdkunde*, Bd. 7, pp. 81–9. Berlin, 1872a.

— Über die auf der Osterinsel aufgefundenen Zeichentafeln. *Verhandlungen d. Berliner Ges. f. Anthropologie* . . . Bd. 4, p. 44. Berlin, 1872b.

BEECHEY, F. W.: *Narrative of a Voyage to the Pacific and Bering's Strait . . . in the Years 1824–28*. 2 Vols. London, 1831.

BEHRENS, C. F.: *Der wohlversuchte Süd-Länder, das ist: ausführliche Reise-Beschreibung um die Welt. 1722*. Translated into English: Hakluyt Society, Ser. 2, No. 13. Cambridge, 1908.

BENNETT, W. C.: Mnemonic and recording devices. *Handbook of South American Indians*, Vol. 5. Smithsonian Inst. Bur. of American Ethnology, Bull. 143. Washington D.C., 1949.

— Excavations at Tiahuanaco, Antrop. Papers. Amer. Mus. Nat. Hist., Vol. 34, pt. 3. New York, 1934.

— *Ancient Arts of the Andes*. New York, 1954.

BENZONI, G.: *La Historia del Mundo Nuevo*. Venice, 1565 (Translated into English by W. H. Smyth: History of the New World). Hakluyt Soc., No. 21. London, 1857.

BERGSLAND, K., and VOGT, H.: On the validity of glottochronology, *Current Anthropology*, Vol. 3, No. 2, pp. 115–53. Chicago, 1962.

BERRY, E. W.: *Cocos* and *Phymatocaryon* in the Pliocene of New Zealand. *Am. Jour. Science*, Vol. 5, No. 12. New Haven, Conn., 1926.

BERTONI, M. S.: Essai d'une monographie du genre *Ananas*. *Anal. Ci. Paraquaoys*, II, No. 4. Asunción, 1919.

BETANZOS, J. DE: *Suma y narración de los Incas*. 1551. Madrid, 1880.

BISSCHOP, E. DE: *Kaimiloa. D'Honolulu à Cannes par l'Australie et le Cap à bord d'une double pirogue polynesienne*. Paris, 1939.

BLAXLAND, G.: Treatise on the Aboriginal Inhabitants of Polynesia with evidence of their origin and antiquity. MS. loc. No. B 760, Mitchell Library, Sydney.

BROWN, F. B. H.: Flora of Southeastern Polynesia. I: Monocotyledons, 1931. III: Dicotyledons, 1935. *B. P. Bishop Mus. Bull.* 130. Honolulu, 1935.

BRUAYN, E. DE: Informe sobre el descubrimiento de un área arqueológica. Museo Nacional de Historia Natural, Publicación Ocasional, No. 2, pp. 1–16. Santiago de Chile, 1963.

BRYAN, E. H. JR.: *Hawaiian Nature Notes*. Honolulu 1935.

BUCK, P. (=Te Rangi Hiroa): *Vikings of the Sunrise*. New York, 1938a.

— Ethnology of Mangareva. *B.P. Bishop Mus. Bull.* 157. Honolulu, 1938b.

— An Introduction to Polynesian Anthropology, *B.P. Bishop Mus. Bull.* 187. Honolulu, 1945.

Butinov, N. A., and Knorozov, J. V.: Novye Materialy ob ostrove Paschi. *Sovetskaja Etnografija*, No. 6, pp. 38–42. Moscow, 1957.

Byam, G.: *Wanderings in some of the western republics of America*... London, 1850.

Campbell, J.: The Origin of the Haidahs of the Queen Charlotte Islands. *Trans. Roy. Soc. Canada*, Ser. 2, Vol. 3, Sec. II, 1897–98.

Candolle, A. de: *Origin of Cultivated Plants*. London, 1884.

Carroll, A.: The Easter Island Inscriptions, and the Translation and Interpretation of them. *Jour. Polynesian Soc.*, Vol. I, No. 4, pp. 103–6, 233–53. London, 1892.

Carter, G. F.: Plant Evidence for Early Contacts with America. *Southwestern Jour. Anthrop.*, VI, No. 2. Albuquerque, N.M., 1950.

Charnock, J.: *A History of Marine Architecture*. Vol. 1. London, 1801.

Christian, F. W.: Early Maori Migration as Evidenced by Physical Geography and Language. Report Sixteenth Meeting Australas. Ass. Adv. Sci., Wellington, N.Z., 1924.

Chubb, L. J.: Geology of Galápagos, Cocos, and Easter Island. *B.P. Bishop Mus. Bull.* 110, Honolulu, 1933.

Churchill, W.: Easter Island. The Rapanui Speech and the Peopling of Southeast Polynesia. Carnegie Inst. Wash. Publ. No. 174. Washington, 1912.

Clausen, R. T.: A Botanical Study of the Yam Beans (*Pachyrrhizus*). Cornell Univ. Mem. 264. Ithaca, N.Y., 1944.

Cobo, B.: *Historia del Nuevo Mundo*..., 1653. Ed. Marcos Jiménez de la Espada Sevilla, 1890–95.

Coe, M. D.: Archaeological Linkages with North and South America at la Victoria, Guatemala. *Am. Anthropologist*, Vol. 62, No. 3, 1960.

Colnett, J.: *A Voyage to the South Atlantic and round Cape Horn into the Pacific... in the Ship Rattler*. London 1798.

Cook, J.: *Second Voyage Towards the South Pole and Round the World, Performed in the 'Resolution' and 'Adventure'*. 1772–75. London, 1777.

Cook, O. F.: Food Plants of Ancient America. Ann. Rept. Smiths. Inst., Washington, D.C., 1903.

— History of the Coconut Palm in America. *Contr. U.S. Nat. Herb.*, Vol. 14. Washington, 1910–12.

Cook, O. F. and Cook, R. C.: The Maho, or Mahagua, as a Trans-Pacific Plant. *Jour. Wash. Acad. Sci.*, VIII, 1918.

Corney, B. G.: Editorial annotations to: Gonzalez (1770), 1908.

Cowley, W. A.: Manuscript in the British Museum, B. M. Sloane MS. 54, 1684.

Croft, T.: Letter of April 30, 1874 from Thomas Croft, Papeete, Tahiti, to the President of California Academy of Sciences. *California Acad. Sci., Proc.*, Vol. 5, pp. 318–23. San Francisco, 1875.

Dampier, W.: *Captain William Dampier's Voyage round the Terrestrial Globe, A Collection of Voyages*. 4 Vols. London, 1729.

DEGENER, O.: *Ferns and Flowering Plants of Hawaii National Park.* Honolulu, 1930.

DENIKER, J.: *The Races of Man.* London, 1900.

DIXON, R. B.: The Problem of the Sweet Potato in Polynesia. *Am. Anthropologist*, Vol. 34, 1932.

— Contacts with America across the Southern Pacific. In: *The American Aborigines, Their Origin and Antiquity.* A Collection of Papers, by Ten Authors, Assembled by D. Jenness. Univ. of Toronto Press, Toronto, 1933.

— The Long Voyages of the Polynesians. *Proceedings, Am. Philos. Soc.*, Vol. 74, No. 3, 1934.

EAMES, A. J., and ST. JOHN, H.: The Botanical Identity of the Hawaiian Ipu Nui or Large Gourd. *Am. Jour. Bot.*, XXX, No. 3, 1943.

EDMONDSON, C. H.: Viability of Coconut Seeds after Floating in Sea. *B.P. Bishop Mus., Occ. Papers*, Vol. 16, No. 12. Honolulu, 1941.

EISLEB, D.: Beitrag zur Systematik der altperuanischen 'Ruder' aus der Gegend von Ica. *Baessler-Archiv, N.F.*, Bd. 10, pp. 105–28. Berlin, 1963.

EMORY, K. P.: Stone Remains in the Society Islands. *B.P. Bishop Museum Bull.* No. 116. Honolulu, 1933.

— Oceanian Influence of American Indian Culture: Nordenskiöld's View. *Jour. Polynes. Soc.*, Vol. 51, 1942.

— Review of Archaeology of Easter Island (Heyerdahl and Ferdon 1961). *Am. Antiquity*, Vol. 28, No. 4, pp. 565–7, 1963.

ENGLERT, P. S.: *La Tierra de Hotu Matu'a. Historia, Etnologia y Lengua de Isle de Pascua.* Imprenta y edit. 'San Francisco' Padre las Casas, Chile, 1948.

— Outlines of Easter Island's ancient history. Lecture given before the Medical Expedition to Easter Island. MS. Hangaroa, 17.1.1965.

EYRAUD, E.: Lettre au T.R.P. Supérieur général de la Congrégation des Sacrés-Cœurs de Jésus et de Marie. Valparaiso, Décembre 1864. *Ann. Assoc. Propagation de la Foi*, Vol. 38, pp. 52–71, 124–38. Lyon, 1866.

FEDDE, F.: Papaveraceae-Hypercoideae et Papaveraceae-Papaveroideae. *Das Pflanzenreich*, H. 49, Leipzig, 1909.

FEDOROVA, I. K.: *On kohau rongo-rongo legends.* Nauka Publishing House. Moscow, 1964.

— Versions of myths and legends in manuscripts from Easter Island. Appendix C to Report 16 in: Heyerdahl and Ferdon, 1965.

FERDON, E. N., JR.: Easter Island Exchange Systems. *Southwestern Journal of Anthropology*, Vol. 14, pp. 136–51. Albuquerque, 1958.

— The ceremonial site of Orongo.—Sites E-4 and E-5.—Stone houses in the terraces of Site E-21.—Easter Island house types.—An Easter Island Hare Moa.—A Summary of the Excavated Record of Easter Island Prehistory. 6 Articles in: Heyerdahl and Ferdon 1961, pp. 221–55, 305–11, 313–21, 329–38, 381–3, 527–35.

FERDON, E. N., JR.: The Marquesas Islands. Surface architecture of the site of Paeke, Taipi Valley, Nukuhiva. Report 9 in Heyerdahl and Ferdon, 1965.

FORSTER, G.: *A voyage round the world, in His Britannic Majesty's Sloop, 'Resolution'* . . . 2 Vols. London, 1777.

FORSTER, J. R.: *Observations made during a voyage round the world.* London, 1778.

GARCILASSO DE LA VEGA, *Inca:* First Part of the Royal Commentaries of the Yncas. 1609. Hakluyt Soc., Vols. 41–5. London, 1869–71.

GEISELER, Kapitänlieutenant: *Die Oster-Insel. Eine Stätte prähistorischer Kultur in der Südsee.* Berlin, 1883.

GONZALEZ, F.: *The Voyage of Captain Don Felipe Gonzalez in the Ship of the San Lorenzo, with the Frigate Santa Rosalia in Company, to Easter Island in 1770–1771.* Hakluyt Soc., 2. Ser., Vol. 13, Cambridge, 1908.

GRAYDON, J. J.: Blood Groups and the Polynesians. *Mankind,* Vol. 4, pp. 329–39. Sydney, 1952.

GREENMAN, E. F.: The Upper Palaeolithic and the New World. *Current Anthropology,* Vol. 4. No. 1, pp. 41–91. Chicago, 1963.

GRETZER, W.: Die Schiffahrt im alten Peru vor der Entdeckung . . . Mitteil, Roemer-Museum Hildesheim, No. 24. Hannover, 1914.

GRISEBACH, A.: *Die Vegetation der Erde nach ihrer klimatischen Anordnung.* 2 Vols. Leipzig, 1872.

GUPPY, H. B.: *Observations of a Naturalist in the Pacific Between 1896 and 1899.* Vol. II. London, 1906.

HADDON, A. C.: Melanesian Influence in Easter Island. *Folk-Lore,* Vol. 29, No. 1, pp. 161–2. London, 1918.

HAGEN, V. W. VON: *Ecuador and the Galápagos Islands.* University of Oklahoma Press IX, 290 pp., 1949.

HARLEZ, C. DE: *L'Ile de Pâques et ses monuments graphiques.* Löwen, 1896.

HEINE-GELDERN, R. VON: Die Osterinselschrift. *Anthropos.* Vol. 33, 1938.

— Cultural Connections between Asia and pre-Columbian America. *Anthropos,* Vol. 45, Nos. 1–3, 1950.

HEYERDAHL, T.: *På Jakt efter Paradiset.* Oslo, 1938.

— Marquesas Islands. Report of the Standing Committee for the Protection of Nature in and around the Pacific for the years 1933–1938. *Proceedings Sixth Pacific Science Congress.* Berkeley and Los Angeles, 1940.

— Did Polynesian culture originate in America? *International Science,* Vol. 1, pp. 15–26. New York, 1941a.

— Turning Back Time in the South Seas. *National Geographical Magazine.* Vol. 79, No. 1. Washington, January 1941b.

— *The Kon-Tiki Expedition.* Oslo, 1948 (Translated into 57 languages).

— The Voyage of the Raft Kon-Tiki. An Argument for American Polynesian Diffusion. *Geographical Journal,* Vol. 115, Nos. 1–3. London, 1950.

HEYERDAHL, T.: *American Indians in the Pacific. The Theory behind the Kon-Tiki Expedition*. Stockholm, London, Chicago, 1952a.

— Objects and Results of the Kon-Tiki Expedition. *Proceedings* Thirtieth International Congress of Americanists. Cambridge, 1952b.

— Some Basic Problems in Polynesian Anthropology. *Proceedings* Thirtieth International Congress of Americanists, Cambridge, 1952c.

— En Gjenoppdaget Inka-kunst. Guara-metoden som lar flåter krysse og jibbe uten ror eller styreåre. *Teknisk Ukeblad*, Vol. 48. Oslo, 1954.

— The balsa raft in aboriginal navigation off Peru and Ecuador. *Southwestern Journal of Anthropology*, Vol. 11, No. 3, pp. 251–64. University of New Mexico, Albuquerque, 1955.

— *Aku-Aku. The Secret of Easter Island*. Oslo, 1957 (Translated into 27 languages).

— Guara navigation: Indigenous sailing off the Andean coast. *Southwestern Journal of Anthropology*, Vol. 13, No. 2, pp. 134–43. Albuquerque, 1957b.

— Guara sailing technique indigenous to South America. Actas del XXXIII Congreso de Americanistas. San José, Costa Rica, 1958.

— Merrill's reappraisal of ethnobotanical evidence for prehistoric contact between South America and Polynesia. Proc. of the 34th International Congress of Americanists. Vienna, 1960.

— An Introduction to Easter Island.—Surface Artifacts.—General discussion. 3 Articles in: Heyerdahl and Ferdon 1961. pp. 21–90, 397–489, 493–526.

— Archaeology in the Galápagos Islands. Papers in the Tenth Pacific Science Congress. University of Hawaii. Honolulu, 1961a.

— Prehistoric Voyages as Agencies for Melanesian and South American Plant and Animal Dispersals to Polynesia. In: *Plants and the Migrations of Pacific Peoples*. Tenth Pacific Science Congress. Honolulu, 1961b.

— Sea routes to Polynesia. '*Expedition*', *The Bulletin of the University Museum of the University of Pennsylvania*, Vol. 4, No. 1, pp. 22–9, 1961c.

— Statuene på Påsköen. Problem og Resultat. Lecture before the Swedish Society for Anthropology and Geography, 24. V. 1962. Part 2. Stockholm, 1962.

— Navel of the World. In: *Vanished Civilizations*. London, 1963.

— Feasible Ocean Routes to and from the Americas in pre-Columbian Times. Actas y Memorias del XXXV Congreso Internacional de Americanistas, Mexico, 1962. Mecixo, 1964a.

— Plant evidence for contacts with America before Columbus. *Antiquity*, Vol. XXXVIII, No. 150, pp. 120–33. Cambridge, 1964b.

— The Inca inspiration behind the Spanish discoveries of Polynesia and Melanesia. Lecture given at the 26th International Congress of Americanists, Barcelona, 1964c.

HEYERDAHL, T.: How far is Easter Island culture Polynesian? Lecture given at the 7th International Congress for Anthropology and Ethnology, Moscow, 1964d. MS.

— The statues of the Oipona me'ae, with a comparative analysis of possibly related stone monuments. Report 10 in: Heyerdahl and Ferdon, 1965.

— The concept of rongo-rongo among the historic population of Easter Island. Report 16 in: Heyerdahl and Ferdon, 1965.

— Notes on the pre-European Coconut Groves on Cocos Island. Report 17 in: Heyerdahl and Ferdon, 1965.

HEYERDAHL, T., and FERDON, E. N., JR., ed.: *Reports of the Norwegian Archaeological Expedition to Easter Island and the East Pacific*. Vol. I. Archaeology of Easter Island. Monographs of the School of American Research and the Museum of New Mexico, No. 24, Part 1, 1961. Vol. II. Miscellaneous Reports. Monographs of the School of American Research and the Kon-Tiki Museum, No. 24, Part 2, 1965. Santa Fe, New Mexico.

HEYERDAHL, T., and SKJÖLSVOLD, A.: Archaeological Evidence of pre-Spanish visits to the Galápagos Islands. Memoirs of the Society for American Archaeology, No. 12. Salt Lake City, 1956.

HILL, A. W.: The original home and mode of dispersal of the coconut. *Nature*, Vol. 124. London, 1929.

HILLEBRAND, W.: *Flora of the Hawaiian Islands*. Heidelberg, 1888.

HILL-TOUT, C.: Oceanic Origin of the Kwakiutl-Nootka and Salish Stocks of British Columbia and Fundamental Unity of Same with Additional Notes on the Déné. *Proc. Trans. Roy. Soc. Canada*, 2. Ser., Vol. 4, 1898.

HORNBOSTEL, E. VON: Chinesische Ideogramme in Amerika. *Anthropos*, Vol. 25, 1930.

HORNELL, J.: Was there a pre-Columbian Contact between the Peoples of Oceania and South America? *Journ. Polynesian Soc.*, Vol. 54, pp. 167–91, 1945.

— How did the sweet potato reach Oceania? *Journ. of Linnaean Society of London*, Vol. 53, No. 348, pp. 41–62. London, 1946.

HUMBOLDT, A. VON: *Vues des Cordillères, et monuments des peuples indigènes de l'Amerique*. Paris, 1810.

HUTCHINSON, J. B., SILOW, R. A., and STEPHENS, S. G.: *The Evolution of Gossypium and the Differentiation of the Cultivated Cottons*. London, New York and Toronto, 1947.

HUTCHINSON, T. J.: Anthropology of Prehistoric Peru. *Journ. of the Royal Anthropological Institute*, Vol. 4. London, 1875.

IBARRA GRASSO, D. E.: La escritura indígena Andina. *Ann. Lateranensi*, 12. Vatican City, 1948.

IZUMI, S., and SONO, T.: *Andes 2, Excavations at Kotosh, Peru 1960*. Tokyo 1963.

JACOBY, A.: *Señor Kon-Tiki*. Oslo, 1965.

JAKEMAN, M. W.: The XXIX International Congress of Americanists. Bull. Brigham Young Univ., March, 1950.

JAUSSEN, T.: *L'Ile de Pâques. Historique—Écriture et Répertoire des signes des tablettes ou bois d'Hibiscus Intelligents.* Paris, 1893.

— L'Ile de Pâques. Histoire et Ecriture. *Bulletin Géogr. Hist. et Descriptive,* No. 2, pp. 240–70. Paris, 1894.

— (s.a.): L'Empire des Maoris. Ile de Pâques ou Rapa-nui. *Ecriture de l'Ile de Pâques.* MS., 299 pp. 19 × 29, 3 cm, Congrégation des Sacrés Cœurs, 412 Vie Aurelia Antica, Rome.

JUAN, G., and ULLOA, A. DE: *Relación histórica del viaje à la América Meridional* . . . Vol. 1. Madrid, 1748.

KERCHOVE DE DENERGHEM, O. DE: *Les Palmiers; histoire iconographique, géographie, paléontologie, botanique, description, culture, emploi, etc.* Paris, 1878.

KNOCHE, W.: Vorläufige Bemerkung über die Entstehung der Standbilder auf der Osterinsel. *Zeitschrift f. Ethnologie,* Bd. 44, pp. 873–7. Berlin, 1912.

— *Die Osterinsel. Eine Zusammenfassung der chilenischen Osterinselexpedition des Jahres 1911.* Concepción, 1925.

KNOROZOV, J. V.: V poiskach ključa. *Nedelja,* 2–8 Aug. 1964. Moscow, 1964a.

— Recorded statements at Izvestija's Round Table Conference, August 10, 1964. In: 'Kon-Tiki' plyl ne zrja. *Izvestija,* 12 August 1964, p. 4. Moscow, 1964b.

— Manuscripts from Easter Island. Appendix B to Report 16 in: Heyerdahl and Ferdon, 1965.

KÖNIGSWALD, G. H. R. VON: Über sumatranische Schiffstücher und ihre Beziehungen zur Kunst Ozeaniens. In: *Südseestudien, Gedenkschrift zur Erinnerung an Felix Speiser,* pp. 27–50. Basel, 1951.

KÖRNICKE, F.: Über die Heimat unserer Gartenbohne *Phaseolus vulgaris. Verh. Naturhist.* Ver. Preuss. Rheinlande etc. Bonn, 1885.

KONDRATOV, A. M.: The hieroglyphic signs and different lists in the manuscripts from Easter Island. In: Heyerdahl and Ferdon 1965, Appendix D to Report 16 in: Heyerdahl and Ferdon, 1965.

KOTZEBUE, O. E. (KOCEBU, O.): Putešestvie v Južnyj okean i v Beringov proliv dlja *otyskanija Severo-vostočnogo morskogo prochoda, predprinjatoe v 1815, 1816, 1817, i 1818 godach.* 3 Vols. St. Petersburg 1821 (Eng. trans. London, 1821).

LAS CASAS, B. DE: *Historia de las Indias.* 1559. Colección de Documentos Inéditos para la Historia de España. Madrid, 1876.

LAVACHERY, H.: Les bois employés dans l'Ile de Pâques. Bull. Soc. des Américanistes de Belgique. March 1934, pp. 67–71, 1934.

— La Mission Franco-Belge dans l'Ile de Pâques. *Bulletin Société Royale de Géographie d'Anvers,* Vol. 55, pp. 313–61. Antwerp, 1935.

LAVACHERY, H. Easter Island, Polynesia. Annual Report of the Board of Regents of the Smithsonian Institution, pp. 391–6. Washington, 1936.

— *Les pétroglyphes de l'Ile de Pâques*. 2 Vols. Antwerp, 1939.

LESCALLIER, M.: *Traité pratique du gréement des vaisseaux et autres bâtiements de mer*. Vol. 1. Paris, 1741.

LINNÉ, S.: Zapotecan Antiquities and the Paulson Collection in the Ethnographical Museum of Sweden. Publications of the Ethnographic Museum of Sweden, N.S., 4. Stockholm, 1938.

LISJANSKIJ, JU. F.: Putesestvie vokrug sveta na korable i Nevai v 1803–1806 gg. St. Petersburg 1812. Eng. Trans. Lisiansky, London, 1814.

LIZARRAGA, R. DE: Descripción de las Indias. Crónica sobre el Antiguo Perú . . . 1560–1602. *Los Pequeños Grandes Libros de Historia Americana*. Ser. 1. Vol. 12. Lima, 1946.

LOTHROP, S. K.: Aboriginal navigation off the West Coast of South America. *Jour. Royal Anthropological Institute*. Vol. 62, pp. 229–56. London, 1932.

MARKHAM, C. R.: *Proceedings Royal Geographical Society*, Vol. 14, pp. 116–19, London, 1870.

MARTIUS, C. F. P. DE: *Historia Naturalis Palmarum*. 3 Vols. Monachii (München) 1823-1850.

MEANS, P. A.: Pre-Spanish Navigation Off the Andean Coast. *American Neptune*, Vol. 2, No. 2, 1942.

MEINICKE, C.: Die Holztafeln Von Rapanui. *Zeits. Ges. f. Erdkunde*, Bd. 6, pp. 548–51. Berlin, 1871.

MERRILL, E. D.: Comments on Cook's Theory as to the American Origin and prehistoric Polynesian Distribution of certain economic Plants, especially *Hibiscus tiliaceus Linnaeus*. *Philippine Jour. Sci.*, XVII. Manila, 1920.

— The improbability of pre-Columbian Eurasian-American contacts in the light of the origin and distribution of cultivated plants. *Journ. of the New York Botanical Garden*, Vol. 31, pp. 209–12. New York, 1930.

— The Phytogeography of Cultivated Plants in relation to Assumed pre-Columbian Eurasian-American Contacts. *American Anthropologist*, Vol. 33, No. 3, pp. 375-82. Menasha 1931.

— Domesticated plants in relation to the diffusion of culture. *Early Man*. Philadelphia 1937

— Merrilleana. A selection from the general writings of Elder Drew Merrill, ed. by Frans Verdoorn. *Chronica Botanica*, Vol. 10. Nos. 3–4. Waltham 1946.

— Observations on Cultivated Plants with Reference to Certain American Problems. *Ceiba*, Vol. 1, No. 1, pp. 2–36. Tegucigalpa, Honduras, 1950.

— The Botany of Cook's Voyages and Its Unexpected Significance in Relation to Anthropology, Biogeography and History. Chronica Botanica, Vol. 14, Nos. 5–6. Waltham, 1954.

MÉTRAUX, A.: The proto-Indian script and the Easter Island tablets. *Anthropos*, Vol. 33, 1938.

— Ethnology of Easter Island. *B.P. Bishop Museum Bulletin* 160. Honolulu, 1940.

— *Easter Island. A Stone Age Civilization of the Pacific*. New York, 1957.

MONTESINOS, F.: *Memorias antiguas historiales del Perú*. 1642. Translated into English by P. A. Means. London, 1920.

MORGAN, A. E.: *Nowhere Was Somewhere*. New York, 1946.

MORRELL, B., JR.: *A Narrative of Four Voyages to the South Sea*, . . . New York, 1832.

MOURANT, A. E.: *The distribution of human blood groups*. Springfield, Ill., 1954.

MULLOY, W.: The Ceremonial Center of Vinapu. In: Heyerdahl and Ferdon 1961, pp. 93–180—Report 9 in Heyerdahl and Ferdon, 1965.

MURPHY, R. C.: The earliest Spanish advances southward from Panama along the West Coast of South America. *Hispanic Amer. Hist. Rev.*, Vol. 21, Durham, N. Carolina, 1941.

NORDENSKIÖLD, E.: Picture-writings and other Documents by Néle and Ruben Perez Kantule. *Comparative Ethnographical Studies*, Vol. 7. Gothenburg, 1928.

— Origin of the Indian Civilizations in South America. *Comp. Ethnogr. Stud.* Vol. 9. Gothenburg 1931.

OLIVA, A.: Histoire de Pérou, 1631. Trans. by Bandelier, Paris 1857. Publ. Paris 1910

OVIEDO Y VALDÉS G. F. DE: *Historia general y natural de las Indias, islas y tierra-firme del mar océano* (1535-48). 4 Vols. Madrid 1855.

PACHACUTI-YAMQUI SALCAMAYHUA, J. DE STA CRUZ: *Relación de antigüedades deste reyno del Pirú*. 1620, Ed. M. J. de la Espada, Madrid, 1879.

PALMER, J. L.: A Visit to Easter Island, or Rapa Nui. *Royal Geogr. Soc. Proceedings*, Vol. 14, pp. 108–19. London, 1870.

— Davis or Easter Island. *Lit. and Phil. Soc. of Liverpool Proc.*, No. 29, pp. 275–97. London, 1875.

PARIS, F. E.: *Essai sur la construction navale des peuples extra-européens*. Paris, 1841–43.

LA PÉROUSE, J. F. G. DE: *A Voyage round the World Performed in the Years 1785, 1786, 1787, and 1788* . . . 2 Vols. and an Atlas (Orig. ed. Paris 1797). London, 1798.

PETIT-THOUARS, A. DU: *Voyage autour du monde sur la frégate La Vénus, pendant les années 1836–1839* . . . 2 Vols. and an Atlas. Paris, 1841.

PINART, A.: Voyage à l'Ile de Pâques. *Le Tour du Monde*, Vol. 36, pp. 225–40. Paris, 1878a.

— Exploration de l'Ile de Pâques. *Bull. Soc. Géogr.*, Ser. 6, Vol. 16, pp. 193–213. Paris, 1878b.

PIZARRO, PEDRO: *Relación del Descubrimiento y Conquista de los Reinos del Peru.* 1571. Colección de Documentos ineditos para la Historia de España, Vol. 5. Madrid, 1844. Translated into English and an American version by P. A. Means: *Relation of Discovery and Conquest of the Kingdoms of Peru.* 2 Vols. New York, 1921.

PORTER, D.: *Journal of a Cruise made to the Pacific Ocean.* Philadelphia, 1815.

PRAIN, D.: An account of the genus *Argemone. Jour. Bot.*, XXXIII, 1895.

RIVET, P.: *Relations commerciales précolombiennes entre l'Océanie et l'Amérique.* Festschrift P. W. Schmidt. Vienna, 1928.

— *Les origines de l'homme américain.* Montreal, 1943.

ROCHEBRUNE, A.-T. DE: Récherches d'ethnographie botanique sur la flore des sépultures péruviennes d'Ancon. *Actes Soc. Linn. Bordeaux*, Ser. 4. Vol. 3. Bordeaux, 1879.

ROGGEVEEN, J.: Extract from the official log of the voyage of Mynheer Jacob Roggeveen, in the Ships Den Arend, Thienhoven and De Afrikaanische Galey, in 1721–22, in so far as it relates to the discovery of Easter Island 1722. Hakluyt Soc., Ser. 2, No. 13. Cambridge, 1908.

ROSS, A. S. C.: Preliminary notice of some late eighteenth century numerals from Easter Island. *Man.* Vol. 36, No. 120, 1936.

ROUSSEL, H.: Vocabulaire de la Langue de d'Ile de Pâques ou Rape nui. *Le Muséon*, Nos. 2–3, pp. 159–254. Löwen, 1908.

— Ile de Pâques. Notice par le R. P. Hippolyte Roussel, SS. CC. Apôtre de l'île de Pâques. 1869. *Annales de la Congrégation des Sacrés-Cœurs de Jésus et de Marie*, No. 305, pp. 355–60, No. 307, pp. 423–30, No. 308, pp. 462–6, No. 309, pp. 495–9. Paris, 1926.

ROUTLEDGE, K.: *The Mystery of Easter Island. The Story of an Expedition.* London, 1919.

SÁAMANOS, J. DE: Relación de los primeros descubrimientos de Francisco Pizarro y Diego de Almagro: Sacada del códice número CXX de la Biblioteca Imperial de Viena. 1526. Colección de Documentos Inéditos para la Historia de España, Vol. 4. Madrid, 1844.

SARMIENTO DE GAMBOA, P. DE: *History of the Incas*, 1572. Hakluyt Soc., 2 Ser., Vol. 22. Cambridge, 1907.

SAUER, C. O.: Cultivated Plants of South and Central America. *Handbook of South American Indians*, Vol. VI. Smithsonian Inst. Bur. Amer. Ethn. Bull. 143. Washington, D.C., 1950.

SHAPIRO, H. L.: The physical relationship of the Easter Islanders. In: Métraux, 1940.

SHARP, B.: *The dangerous Voyage, and bold Attempts of Capt. Bartholomew Sharp . . ., The History of the Buccaneers of America*, Vol. 2, T.4. London, 1704.

SIMMONS, R. T., GRAYDON, J. J., SEMPLE, N. M., and FRY, E. I.: A blood group Genetical Survey in Cook Islanders, Polynesia, and Comparisons with

American Indians. *Amer. Jour. Physical Anthrop.*, Vol. 13, pp. 667–90. Philadelphia, 1955.

SKJÖLSVOLD, A.: House Foundations (Hare Paenga) in Rano Raraku.—Site E-2, a circular stone dwelling, Anakena.—The Stone Statues and Quarries of Rano Raraku. 3 Articles in: Heyerdahl and Ferdon, 1961, pp. 291–3, 295–303, 339–79.

SKOGMAN, C.: *Fregatten Eugenies resa omkring jorden åren 1851–53.* Vol. 1. Stockholm, 1854.

SKOTTSBERG, C.: *The Natural History of Juan Fernandez and Easter Island.* Uppsala, 1920.

— Le peuplement des îles pacifiques du Chili. Soc. de Biogéograph., Vol. 4. Paris, 1934.

— Derivation of the Flora and Fauna of Juan Fernandez and Easter Island. *The Natural History of Juan Fernandez and Easter Island*, Vol. 1, pp. 193–438. Uppsala, 1920–1956.

— *Påskön.* Göteborgs Handels- och Sjöfarts-Tidning, 7 Oct. 1957. Gothenburg.

SMITH, C. S.: A Temporal Sequence Derived from Certain Ahu.—Two Habitation Caves.—Tuu-ko-ihu Village.—The Poike Ditch. 4 Articles in: Heyerdahl and Ferdon 1961, pp. 181–219, 257–71, 287–9, 385–91.

SPILBERGEN, JORIS VAN: *Speculum Orientalis Occidentalisque Indiae navigationis, 1614–18.* Leiden, 1619.

STEVENSON, W. B.: *A Historical and Descriptive Narrative of Twenty Years' Residence in South America*, 3 Vols. London, 1825.

STEWARD, J. H.: The Comparative Ethnology of South American Indians. *Handbook of South American Indians*, Vol. 5. Washington, D.C., 1949.

STEWART, C. S.: *A visit to the South Seas in the U.S. ship 'Vincennes' during the years 1829 and 1830.* London, 1832.

STOKES, J. F. G.: Spaniards and the sweet potato in Hawaii and Hawaiian-American contacts. *Amer. Anthrop.*, Vol. 34, No. 4, 1932.

STONOR, C. R., and ANDERSON, E.: Maize among the Hill Peoples of Assam. *Ann. Missouri Bot. Gard.*, Vol. 36, No. 3, 1949.

SULLIVAN, L. R.: Marquesan Somatology with Comparative Notes on Samoa and Tonga. *B.P. Bishop Mus. Mem.*, Vol. 9, No. 2. Honolulu, 1923.

THOMSON, W. J.: Te Pito te Henua, or Easter Island. Rept. U.S. National Museum for the year ending June 30, 1889. Washington, D.C., 1889.

UHLE, M.: *Fundamentos Etnicos y Arqueologia de Arica y Tacna.* Universidad Central. Quito, 1922.

VALVERDE, V.: Relación del sitio del Cuzco y principio de la guerras civiles del Perú . . . 1535 a 1539. Colección de Libros Españoles Raros o Curiosos, Vol. 13. Madrid, 1879.

WAFER, L.: A New Voyage and Description of the Isthmus of America. 1699. In: Dampier, 1729, Vol. 3.

WALLACE, A. R.: Discussion of paper read by Prof. T. H. Huxley. In: Huxley, T.: On the Geographical Distribution of the Chief Modifications of Mankind. *Jour. Ethn. Soc. London, N.S.*, Vol. 2. London, 1870.

WECKLER, J. E.: Polynesian Explorers of the Pacific. Smithsonian Institution War Background Studies, No. 6. Washington, 1943.

WHITAKER, T. W., and BIRD, J. B.: Identification and Significance of the Cucurbit Materials from Huaca Prieta, Peru. Amer. Mus. Novitates, No. 1426. New York, 1949.

WILLIAMSON, R. W.: *Essays in Polynesian Ethnology*. Ed. by R. Piddington (Cambridge Univ. Press). Cambridge, 1939.

WITTMACK, L.: Über Bohnen aus altperuanischen Gräbern. *Sitzber. bot. Ver. d. Prov., Brandenburg*, Vol. 21. Brandenburg, 1880.

— Unsere jetzige Kenntnis vorgeschichtlicher Samen. *Ber. Deutsche Bot. Ges.* Vol. 4. Berlin, 1886.

— Die Heimat der Bohnen und der Kürbisse, *Ber. Deutsche Bot. Ges.*, Vol. 6, No. 8. Berlin, 1888.

YACOVLEFF, E., and HERRERA, F. L.: El mundo vegetal de los antiguos peruanos. *Rev. Mus. Nac.*, Vol. 3, No. 3, Lima 1934, and Vol. 4, No. 1, Lima, 1935.

ZÁRATE, A. DE: *Histoire de la Decouverte et de la Conquete du Perou.* (Orig. ed. Antwerp 1555.) Amsterdam, 1700.

ZUMBOHM, G.: Lettres du R. P. Gaspard Zumbohm au directeur des Annales sur la mission de l'Ile de Pâques. *Annales de la Congregation des Sacrés-Cœurs de Jésus et de Marie*, Vol. 5, No. 46, pp. 660–7. Oct. 1879. Vol. 6, No. 50, pp. 117–31. No. 52, pp. 231–42. No. 54, pp. 377–85, Feb.–June 1880. Paris, 1879–1880.

INDEX

Authors whose names appear in the Bibliography as entries, or in the Notes, do not feature also in the Index. Roman numerals refer to maps. Numbers in bold type refer to plates. Other illustrations are referred to by the pages on which they appear. 'I'. = Island. 'E.I'. = Easter Island.

INDEX

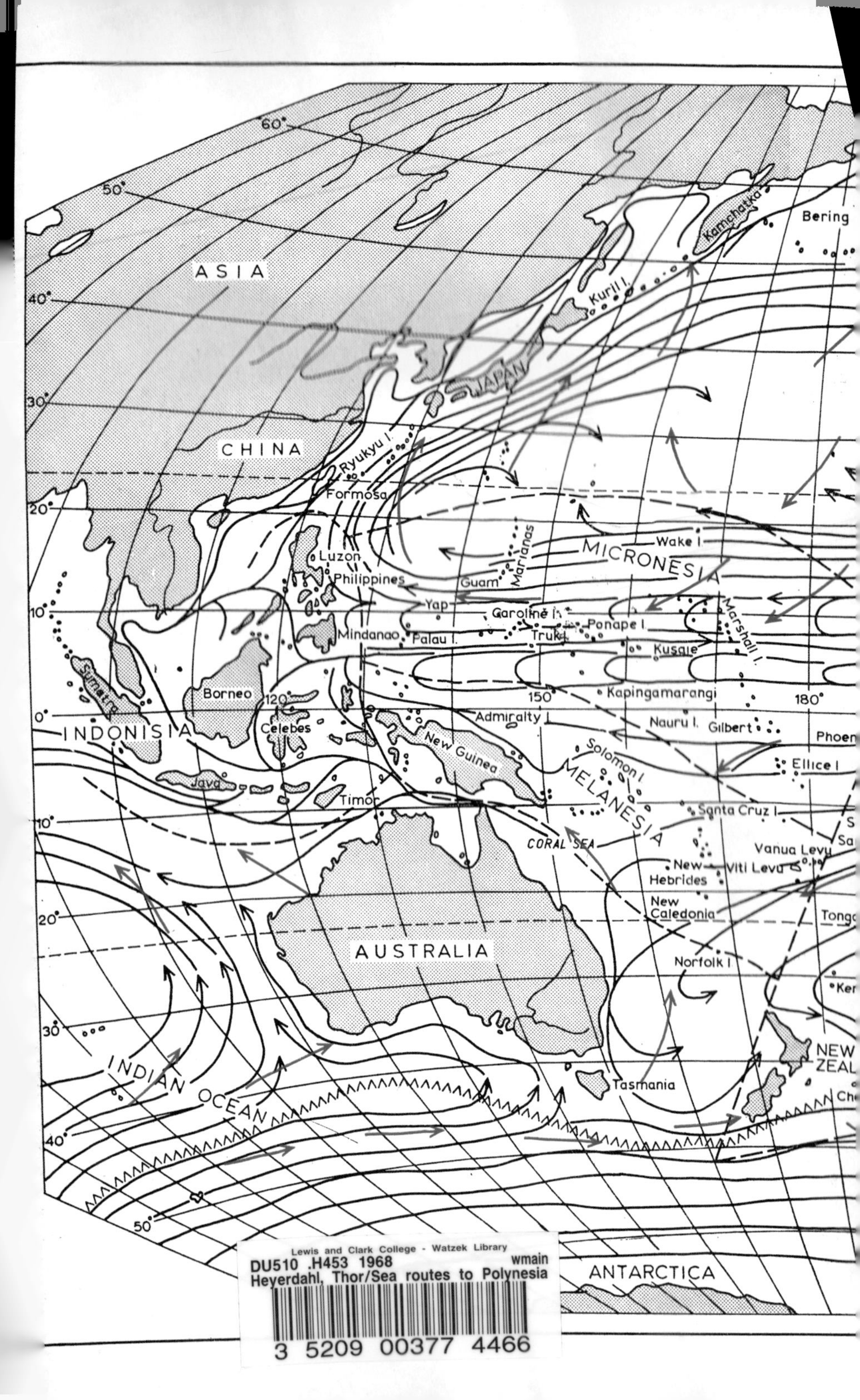

ASIA
CHINA
Kamchatka
Bering
Kuril I.
JAPAN
Ryukyu I.
Formosa
Luzon
Philippines
Mindanao
Guam
Marianas
Wake I.
MICRONESIA
Yap
Caroline I.
Ponape I.
Truk I.
Palau I.
Kusaie
Marshall I.
Kapingamarangi
Sumatra
Borneo
Celebes
INDONISIA
Java
Timor
New Guinea
Admiralty I.
Nauru I.
Gilbert
Phoen
Solomon I.
MELANESIA
Ellice I
Santa Cruz I.
CORAL SEA
Vanua Levu
Viti Levu
New Hebrides
New Caledonia
Tonga
AUSTRALIA
Norfolk I.
Ker
INDIAN OCEAN
Tasmania
NEW ZEAL
Ch
ANTARCTICA
60°
50°
40°
30°
20°
10°
0°
120°
150°
180°